C-3526　　CAREER EXAMINATION SERIES

This is your
PASSBOOK for...

Police Communications Technician

Test Preparation Study Guide
Questions & Answers

NATIONAL LEARNING CORPORATION®

COPYRIGHT NOTICE

This book is SOLELY intended for, is sold ONLY to, and its use is RESTRICTED to individual, bona fide applicants or candidates who qualify by virtue of having seriously filed applications for appropriate license, certificate, professional and/or promotional advancement, higher school matriculation, scholarship, or other legitimate requirements of education and/or governmental authorities.

This book is NOT intended for use, class instruction, tutoring, training, duplication, copying, reprinting, excerption, or adaptation, etc., by:

1) Other publishers
2) Proprietors and/or Instructors of "Coaching" and/or Preparatory Courses
3) Personnel and/or Training Divisions of commercial, industrial, and governmental organizations
4) Schools, colleges, or universities and/or their departments and staffs, including teachers and other personnel
5) Testing Agencies or Bureaus
6) Study groups which seek by the purchase of a single volume to copy and/or duplicate and/or adapt this material for use by the group as a whole without having purchased individual volumes for each of the members of the group
7) Et al.

Such persons would be in violation of appropriate Federal and State statutes.

PROVISION OF LICENSING AGREEMENTS – Recognized educational, commercial, industrial, and governmental institutions and organizations, and others legitimately engaged in educational pursuits, including training, testing, and measurement activities, may address request for a licensing agreement to the copyright owners, who will determine whether, and under what conditions, including fees and charges, the materials in this book may be used them. In other words, a licensing facility exists for the legitimate use of the material in this book on other than an individual basis. However, it is asseverated and affirmed here that the material in this book CANNOT be used without the receipt of the express permission of such a licensing agreement from the Publishers. Inquiries re licensing should be addressed to the company, attention rights and permissions department.

All rights reserved, including the right of reproduction in whole or in part, in any form or by any means, electronic or mechanical, including photocopying, recording, or by any information storage and retrieval system, without permission in writing from the Publisher.

Copyright © 2024 by
National Learning Corporation

212 Michael Drive, Syosset, NY 11791
(516) 921-8888 • www.passbooks.com
E-mail: info@passbooks.com

PUBLISHED IN THE UNITED STATES OF AMERICA

PASSBOOK® SERIES

THE *PASSBOOK® SERIES* has been created to prepare applicants and candidates for the ultimate academic battlefield – the examination room.

At some time in our lives, each and every one of us may be required to take an examination – for validation, matriculation, admission, qualification, registration, certification, or licensure.

Based on the assumption that every applicant or candidate has met the basic formal educational standards, has taken the required number of courses, and read the necessary texts, the *PASSBOOK® SERIES* furnishes the one special preparation which may assure passing with confidence, instead of failing with insecurity. Examination questions – together with answers – are furnished as the basic vehicle for study so that the mysteries of the examination and its compounding difficulties may be eliminated or diminished by a sure method.

This book is meant to help you pass your examination provided that you qualify and are serious in your objective.

The entire field is reviewed through the huge store of content information which is succinctly presented through a provocative and challenging approach – the question-and-answer method.

A climate of success is established by furnishing the correct answers at the end of each test.

You soon learn to recognize types of questions, forms of questions, and patterns of questioning. You may even begin to anticipate expected outcomes.

You perceive that many questions are repeated or adapted so that you can gain acute insights, which may enable you to score many sure points.

You learn how to confront new questions, or types of questions, and to attack them confidently and work out the correct answers.

You note objectives and emphases, and recognize pitfalls and dangers, so that you may make positive educational adjustments.

Moreover, you are kept fully informed in relation to new concepts, methods, practices, and directions in the field.

You discover that you are actually taking the examination all the time: you are preparing for the examination by "taking" an examination, not by reading extraneous and/or supererogatory textbooks.

In short, this PASSBOOK®, used directedly, should be an important factor in helping you to pass your test.

POLICE COMMUNICATIONS TECHNICIAN

DUTIES:

In the Police Department Communications Division, under direct supervision serves as a 911 emergency operator; obtains necessary information from callers in order to initiate emergency assistance; performs clerical, administrative and other duties related to the provision of emergency service; serves as a radio dispatcher of police resources; performs related work.

EXAMPLES OF TYPICAL TASKS

As a 911 emergency operator: answers telephone calls for assistance coming in via the 911 emergency number; determines nature and priority-code of emergency; inputs information into computer terminal; revises information already inputted in the computer; transmits information to radio dispatcher, emergency medical services or other response unit; refers callers to appropriate city agencies for non-emergency assistance; and other related tasks.

As a radio dispatcher: analyzes information on incidents received via computer from the 911 operator to determine order, means and extent of response; dispatches police units via radio/telephone; maintains control of units via radio/telephone; coordinates chases and close pursuits; types interim and final disposition codes into computer; performs vehicle license and registration checks; and other related tasks.

SCOPE OF THE EXAMINATION

The multiple-choice test may include questions on understanding written information; communicating written information to another person; remembering new information; recognizing the existence of a problem; combining separate pieces of information to form a general conclusion; applying general rules to a specific situation; understanding the order in which things should be done; combining information into a meaningful pattern quickly; identifying an object in its surroundings; recognizing where you are in relation to the space you are in; using a map or diagram to get from one position to another; knowledge of the basic geography of the city, including major roadways and landmarks, bridges, tunnels, parks, etc.; and other related areas.

HOW TO TAKE A TEST

I. YOU MUST PASS AN EXAMINATION

A. WHAT EVERY CANDIDATE SHOULD KNOW

Examination applicants often ask us for help in preparing for the written test. What can I study in advance? What kinds of questions will be asked? How will the test be given? How will the papers be graded?

As an applicant for a civil service examination, you may be wondering about some of these things. Our purpose here is to suggest effective methods of advance study and to describe civil service examinations.

Your chances for success on this examination can be increased if you know how to prepare. Those "pre-examination jitters" can be reduced if you know what to expect. You can even experience an adventure in good citizenship if you know why civil service exams are given.

B. WHY ARE CIVIL SERVICE EXAMINATIONS GIVEN?

Civil service examinations are important to you in two ways. As a citizen, you want public jobs filled by employees who know how to do their work. As a job seeker, you want a fair chance to compete for that job on an equal footing with other candidates. The best-known means of accomplishing this two-fold goal is the competitive examination.

Exams are widely publicized throughout the nation. They may be administered for jobs in federal, state, city, municipal, town or village governments or agencies.

Any citizen may apply, with some limitations, such as the age or residence of applicants. Your experience and education may be reviewed to see whether you meet the requirements for the particular examination. When these requirements exist, they are reasonable and applied consistently to all applicants. Thus, a competitive examination may cause you some uneasiness now, but it is your privilege and safeguard.

C. HOW ARE CIVIL SERVICE EXAMS DEVELOPED?

Examinations are carefully written by trained technicians who are specialists in the field known as "psychological measurement," in consultation with recognized authorities in the field of work that the test will cover. These experts recommend the subject matter areas or skills to be tested; only those knowledges or skills important to your success on the job are included. The most reliable books and source materials available are used as references. Together, the experts and technicians judge the difficulty level of the questions.

Test technicians know how to phrase questions so that the problem is clearly stated. Their ethics do not permit "trick" or "catch" questions. Questions may have been tried out on sample groups, or subjected to statistical analysis, to determine their usefulness.

Written tests are often used in combination with performance tests, ratings of training and experience, and oral interviews. All of these measures combine to form the best-known means of finding the right person for the right job.

II. HOW TO PASS THE WRITTEN TEST

A. NATURE OF THE EXAMINATION

To prepare intelligently for civil service examinations, you should know how they differ from school examinations you have taken. In school you were assigned certain definite pages to read or subjects to cover. The examination questions were quite detailed and usually emphasized memory. Civil service exams, on the other hand, try to discover your present ability to perform the duties of a position, plus your potentiality to learn these duties. In other words, a civil service exam attempts to predict how successful you will be. Questions cover such a broad area that they cannot be as minute and detailed as school exam questions.

In the public service similar kinds of work, or positions, are grouped together in one "class." This process is known as *position-classification*. All the positions in a class are paid according to the salary range for that class. One class title covers all of these positions, and they are all tested by the same examination.

B. FOUR BASIC STEPS

1) Study the announcement

How, then, can you know what subjects to study? Our best answer is: "Learn as much as possible about the class of positions for which you've applied." The exam will test the knowledge, skills and abilities needed to do the work.

Your most valuable source of information about the position you want is the official exam announcement. This announcement lists the training and experience qualifications. Check these standards and apply only if you come reasonably close to meeting them.

The brief description of the position in the examination announcement offers some clues to the subjects which will be tested. Think about the job itself. Review the duties in your mind. Can you perform them, or are there some in which you are rusty? Fill in the blank spots in your preparation.

Many jurisdictions preview the written test in the exam announcement by including a section called "Knowledge and Abilities Required," "Scope of the Examination," or some similar heading. Here you will find out specifically what fields will be tested.

2) Review your own background

Once you learn in general what the position is all about, and what you need to know to do the work, ask yourself which subjects you already know fairly well and which need improvement. You may wonder whether to concentrate on improving your strong areas or on building some background in your fields of weakness. When the announcement has specified "some knowledge" or "considerable knowledge," or has used adjectives like "beginning principles of…" or "advanced … methods," you can get a clue as to the number and difficulty of questions to be asked in any given field. More questions, and hence broader coverage, would be included for those subjects which are more important in the work. Now weigh your strengths and weaknesses against the job requirements and prepare accordingly.

3) Determine the level of the position

Another way to tell how intensively you should prepare is to understand the level of the job for which you are applying. Is it the entering level? In other words, is this the position in which beginners in a field of work are hired? Or is it an intermediate or advanced level? Sometimes this is indicated by such words as "Junior" or "Senior" in the class title. Other jurisdictions use Roman numerals to designate the level – Clerk I, Clerk II, for example. The word "Supervisor" sometimes appears in the title. If the level is not indicated by the title, check the description of duties. Will you be working under very close supervision, or will you have responsibility for independent decisions in this work?

4) Choose appropriate study materials

Now that you know the subjects to be examined and the relative amount of each subject to be covered, you can choose suitable study materials. For beginning level jobs, or even advanced ones, if you have a pronounced weakness in some aspect of your training, read a modern, standard textbook in that field. Be sure it is up to date and has general coverage. Such books are normally available at your library, and the librarian will be glad to help you locate one. For entry-level positions, questions of appropriate difficulty are chosen -- neither highly advanced questions, nor those too simple. Such questions require careful thought but not advanced training.

If the position for which you are applying is technical or advanced, you will read more advanced, specialized material. If you are already familiar with the basic principles of your field, elementary textbooks would waste your time. Concentrate on advanced textbooks and technical periodicals. Think through the concepts and review difficult problems in your field.

These are all general sources. You can get more ideas on your own initiative, following these leads. For example, training manuals and publications of the government agency which employs workers in your field can be useful, particularly for technical and professional positions. A letter or visit to the government department involved may result in more specific study suggestions, and certainly will provide you with a more definite idea of the exact nature of the position you are seeking.

III. KINDS OF TESTS

Tests are used for purposes other than measuring knowledge and ability to perform specified duties. For some positions, it is equally important to test ability to make adjustments to new situations or to profit from training. In others, basic mental abilities not dependent on information are essential. Questions which test these things may not appear as pertinent to the duties of the position as those which test for knowledge and information. Yet they are often highly important parts of a fair examination. For very general questions, it is almost impossible to help you direct your study efforts. What we can do is to point out some of the more common of these general abilities needed in public service positions and describe some typical questions.

1) General information

Broad, general information has been found useful for predicting job success in some kinds of work. This is tested in a variety of ways, from vocabulary lists to questions about current events. Basic background in some field of work, such as sociology or economics, may be sampled in a group of questions. Often these are principles which have become familiar to most persons through exposure rather than through formal training. It is difficult to advise you how to study for these questions; being alert to the world around you is our best suggestion.

2) Verbal ability

An example of an ability needed in many positions is verbal or language ability. Verbal ability is, in brief, the ability to use and understand words. Vocabulary and grammar tests are typical measures of this ability. Reading comprehension or paragraph interpretation questions are common in many kinds of civil service tests. You are given a paragraph of written material and asked to find its central meaning.

3) Numerical ability

Number skills can be tested by the familiar arithmetic problem, by checking paired lists of numbers to see which are alike and which are different, or by interpreting charts and graphs. In the latter test, a graph may be printed in the test booklet which you are asked to use as the basis for answering questions.

4) Observation

A popular test for law-enforcement positions is the observation test. A picture is shown to you for several minutes, then taken away. Questions about the picture test your ability to observe both details and larger elements.

5) Following directions

In many positions in the public service, the employee must be able to carry out written instructions dependably and accurately. You may be given a chart with several columns, each column listing a variety of information. The questions require you to carry out directions involving the information given in the chart.

6) Skills and aptitudes

Performance tests effectively measure some manual skills and aptitudes. When the skill is one in which you are trained, such as typing or shorthand, you can practice. These tests are often very much like those given in business school or high school courses. For many of the other skills and aptitudes, however, no short-time preparation can be made. Skills and abilities natural to you or that you have developed throughout your lifetime are being tested.

Many of the general questions just described provide all the data needed to answer the questions and ask you to use your reasoning ability to find the answers. Your best preparation for these tests, as well as for tests of facts and ideas, is to be at your physical and mental best. You, no doubt, have your own methods of getting into an exam-taking mood and keeping "in shape." The next section lists some ideas on this subject.

IV. KINDS OF QUESTIONS

Only rarely is the "essay" question, which you answer in narrative form, used in civil service tests. Civil service tests are usually of the short-answer type. Full instructions for answering these questions will be given to you at the examination. But in case this is your first experience with short-answer questions and separate answer sheets, here is what you need to know:

1) Multiple-choice Questions

Most popular of the short-answer questions is the "multiple choice" or "best answer" question. It can be used, for example, to test for factual knowledge, ability to solve problems or judgment in meeting situations found at work.

A multiple-choice question is normally one of three types—

- It can begin with an incomplete statement followed by several possible endings. You are to find the one ending which *best* completes the statement, although some of the others may not be entirely wrong.
- It can also be a complete statement in the form of a question which is answered by choosing one of the statements listed.

- It can be in the form of a problem – again you select the best answer.

Here is an example of a multiple-choice question with a discussion which should give you some clues as to the method for choosing the right answer:

When an employee has a complaint about his assignment, the action which will *best* help him overcome his difficulty is to
    A. discuss his difficulty with his coworkers
    B. take the problem to the head of the organization
    C. take the problem to the person who gave him the assignment
    D. say nothing to anyone about his complaint

In answering this question, you should study each of the choices to find which is best. Consider choice "A" – Certainly an employee may discuss his complaint with fellow employees, but no change or improvement can result, and the complaint remains unresolved. Choice "B" is a poor choice since the head of the organization probably does not know what assignment you have been given, and taking your problem to him is known as "going over the head" of the supervisor. The supervisor, or person who made the assignment, is the person who can clarify it or correct any injustice. Choice "C" is, therefore, correct. To say nothing, as in choice "D," is unwise. Supervisors have and interest in knowing the problems employees are facing, and the employee is seeking a solution to his problem.

2) True/False Questions

The "true/false" or "right/wrong" form of question is sometimes used. Here a complete statement is given. Your job is to decide whether the statement is right or wrong.

SAMPLE: A roaming cell-phone call to a nearby city costs less than a non-roaming call to a distant city.

This statement is wrong, or false, since roaming calls are more expensive.

This is not a complete list of all possible question forms, although most of the others are variations of these common types. You will always get complete directions for answering questions. Be sure you understand *how* to mark your answers – ask questions until you do.

V. RECORDING YOUR ANSWERS

Computer terminals are used more and more today for many different kinds of exams.
For an examination with very few applicants, you may be told to record your answers in the test booklet itself. Separate answer sheets are much more common. If this separate answer sheet is to be scored by machine – and this is often the case – it is highly important that you mark your answers correctly in order to get credit.
An electronic scoring machine is often used in civil service offices because of the speed with which papers can be scored. Machine-scored answer sheets must be marked with a pencil, which will be given to you. This pencil has a high graphite content which responds to the electronic scoring machine. As a matter of fact, stray dots may register as answers, so do not let your pencil rest on the answer sheet while you are pondering the correct answer. Also, if your pencil lead breaks or is otherwise defective, ask for another.

Since the answer sheet will be dropped in a slot in the scoring machine, be careful not to bend the corners or get the paper crumpled.

The answer sheet normally has five vertical columns of numbers, with 30 numbers to a column. These numbers correspond to the question numbers in your test booklet. After each number, going across the page are four or five pairs of dotted lines. These short dotted lines have small letters or numbers above them. The first two pairs may also have a "T" or "F" above the letters. This indicates that the first two pairs only are to be used if the questions are of the true-false type. If the questions are multiple choice, disregard the "T" and "F" and pay attention only to the small letters or numbers.

Answer your questions in the manner of the sample that follows:

32. The largest city in the United States is
    A. Washington, D.C.
    B. New York City
    C. Chicago
    D. Detroit
    E. San Francisco

1) Choose the answer you think is best. (New York City is the largest, so "B" is correct.)
2) Find the row of dotted lines numbered the same as the question you are answering. (Find row number 32)
3) Find the pair of dotted lines corresponding to the answer. (Find the pair of lines under the mark "B.")
4) Make a solid black mark between the dotted lines.

VI. BEFORE THE TEST

Common sense will help you find procedures to follow to get ready for an examination. Too many of us, however, overlook these sensible measures. Indeed, nervousness and fatigue have been found to be the most serious reasons why applicants fail to do their best on civil service tests. Here is a list of reminders:

- Begin your preparation early – Don't wait until the last minute to go scurrying around for books and materials or to find out what the position is all about.
- Prepare continuously – An hour a night for a week is better than an all-night cram session. This has been definitely established. What is more, a night a week for a month will return better dividends than crowding your study into a shorter period of time.
- Locate the place of the exam – You have been sent a notice telling you when and where to report for the examination. If the location is in a different town or otherwise unfamiliar to you, it would be well to inquire the best route and learn something about the building.
- Relax the night before the test – Allow your mind to rest. Do not study at all that night. Plan some mild recreation or diversion; then go to bed early and get a good night's sleep.
- Get up early enough to make a leisurely trip to the place for the test – This way unforeseen events, traffic snarls, unfamiliar buildings, etc. will not upset you.
- Dress comfortably – A written test is not a fashion show. You will be known by number and not by name, so wear something comfortable.

- Leave excess paraphernalia at home – Shopping bags and odd bundles will get in your way. You need bring only the items mentioned in the official notice you received; usually everything you need is provided. Do not bring reference books to the exam. They will only confuse those last minutes and be taken away from you when in the test room.
- Arrive somewhat ahead of time – If because of transportation schedules you must get there very early, bring a newspaper or magazine to take your mind off yourself while waiting.
- Locate the examination room – When you have found the proper room, you will be directed to the seat or part of the room where you will sit. Sometimes you are given a sheet of instructions to read while you are waiting. Do not fill out any forms until you are told to do so; just read them and be prepared.
- Relax and prepare to listen to the instructions
- If you have any physical problem that may keep you from doing your best, be sure to tell the test administrator. If you are sick or in poor health, you really cannot do your best on the exam. You can come back and take the test some other time.

VII. AT THE TEST

The day of the test is here and you have the test booklet in your hand. The temptation to get going is very strong. Caution! There is more to success than knowing the right answers. You must know how to identify your papers and understand variations in the type of short-answer question used in this particular examination. Follow these suggestions for maximum results from your efforts:

1) Cooperate with the monitor

The test administrator has a duty to create a situation in which you can be as much at ease as possible. He will give instructions, tell you when to begin, check to see that you are marking your answer sheet correctly, and so on. He is not there to guard you, although he will see that your competitors do not take unfair advantage. He wants to help you do your best.

2) Listen to all instructions

Don't jump the gun! Wait until you understand all directions. In most civil service tests you get more time than you need to answer the questions. So don't be in a hurry. Read each word of instructions until you clearly understand the meaning. Study the examples, listen to all announcements and follow directions. Ask questions if you do not understand what to do.

3) Identify your papers

Civil service exams are usually identified by number only. You will be assigned a number; you must not put your name on your test papers. Be sure to copy your number correctly. Since more than one exam may be given, copy your exact examination title.

4) Plan your time

Unless you are told that a test is a "speed" or "rate of work" test, speed itself is usually not important. Time enough to answer all the questions will be provided, but this does not mean that you have all day. An overall time limit has been set. Divide the total time (in minutes) by the number of questions to determine the approximate time you have for each question.

5) Do not linger over difficult questions

If you come across a difficult question, mark it with a paper clip (useful to have along) and come back to it when you have been through the booklet. One caution if you do this – be sure to skip a number on your answer sheet as well. Check often to be sure that you have not lost your place and that you are marking in the row numbered the same as the question you are answering.

6) Read the questions

Be sure you know what the question asks! Many capable people are unsuccessful because they failed to *read* the questions correctly.

7) Answer all questions

Unless you have been instructed that a penalty will be deducted for incorrect answers, it is better to guess than to omit a question.

8) Speed tests

It is often better NOT to guess on speed tests. It has been found that on timed tests people are tempted to spend the last few seconds before time is called in marking answers at random – without even reading them – in the hope of picking up a few extra points. To discourage this practice, the instructions may warn you that your score will be "corrected" for guessing. That is, a penalty will be applied. The incorrect answers will be deducted from the correct ones, or some other penalty formula will be used.

9) Review your answers

If you finish before time is called, go back to the questions you guessed or omitted to give them further thought. Review other answers if you have time.

10) Return your test materials

If you are ready to leave before others have finished or time is called, take ALL your materials to the monitor and leave quietly. Never take any test material with you. The monitor can discover whose papers are not complete, and taking a test booklet may be grounds for disqualification.

VIII. EXAMINATION TECHNIQUES

1) Read the general instructions carefully. These are usually printed on the first page of the exam booklet. As a rule, these instructions refer to the timing of the examination; the fact that you should not start work until the signal and must stop work at a signal, etc. If there are any *special* instructions, such as a choice of questions to be answered, make sure that you note this instruction carefully.

2) When you are ready to start work on the examination, that is as soon as the signal has been given, read the instructions to each question booklet, underline any key words or phrases, such as *least, best, outline, describe* and the like. In this way you will tend to answer as requested rather than discover on reviewing your paper that you *listed without describing*, that you selected the *worst* choice rather than the *best* choice, etc.

3) If the examination is of the objective or multiple-choice type – that is, each question will also give a series of possible answers: A, B, C or D, and you are called upon to select the best answer and write the letter next to that answer on your answer paper – it is advisable to start answering each question in turn. There may be anywhere from 50 to 100 such questions in the three or four hours allotted and you can see how much time would be taken if you read through all the questions before beginning to answer any. Furthermore, if you come across a question or group of questions which you know would be difficult to answer, it would undoubtedly affect your handling of all the other questions.

4) If the examination is of the essay type and contains but a few questions, it is a moot point as to whether you should read all the questions before starting to answer any one. Of course, if you are given a choice – say five out of seven and the like – then it is essential to read all the questions so you can eliminate the two that are most difficult. If, however, you are asked to answer all the questions, there may be danger in trying to answer the easiest one first because you may find that you will spend too much time on it. The best technique is to answer the first question, then proceed to the second, etc.

5) Time your answers. Before the exam begins, write down the time it started, then add the time allowed for the examination and write down the time it must be completed, then divide the time available somewhat as follows:
    - If 3-1/2 hours are allowed, that would be 210 minutes. If you have 80 objective-type questions, that would be an average of 2-1/2 minutes per question. Allow yourself no more than 2 minutes per question, or a total of 160 minutes, which will permit about 50 minutes to review.
    - If for the time allotment of 210 minutes there are 7 essay questions to answer, that would average about 30 minutes a question. Give yourself only 25 minutes per question so that you have about 35 minutes to review.

6) The most important instruction is to *read each question* and make sure you know what is wanted. The second most important instruction is to *time yourself properly* so that you answer every question. The third most important instruction is to *answer every question*. Guess if you have to but include something for each question. Remember that you will receive no credit for a blank and will probably receive some credit if you write something in answer to an essay question. If you guess a letter – say "B" for a multiple-choice question – you may have guessed right. If you leave a blank as an answer to a multiple-choice question, the examiners may respect your feelings but it will not add a point to your score. Some exams may penalize you for wrong answers, so in such cases *only*, you may not want to guess unless you have some basis for your answer.

7) Suggestions
    a. Objective-type questions
        1. Examine the question booklet for proper sequence of pages and questions
        2. Read all instructions carefully
        3. Skip any question which seems too difficult; return to it after all other questions have been answered
        4. Apportion your time properly; do not spend too much time on any single question or group of questions

5. Note and underline key words – *all, most, fewest, least, best, worst, same, opposite*, etc.
6. Pay particular attention to negatives
7. Note unusual option, e.g., unduly long, short, complex, different or similar in content to the body of the question
8. Observe the use of "hedging" words – *probably, may, most likely,* etc.
9. Make sure that your answer is put next to the same number as the question
10. Do not second-guess unless you have good reason to believe the second answer is definitely more correct
11. Cross out original answer if you decide another answer is more accurate; do not erase until you are ready to hand your paper in
12. Answer all questions; guess unless instructed otherwise
13. Leave time for review

b. Essay questions
1. Read each question carefully
2. Determine exactly what is wanted. Underline key words or phrases.
3. Decide on outline or paragraph answer
4. Include many different points and elements unless asked to develop any one or two points or elements
5. Show impartiality by giving pros and cons unless directed to select one side only
6. Make and write down any assumptions you find necessary to answer the questions
7. Watch your English, grammar, punctuation and choice of words
8. Time your answers; don't crowd material

8) Answering the essay question

Most essay questions can be answered by framing the specific response around several key words or ideas. Here are a few such key words or ideas:

M's: manpower, materials, methods, money, management
P's: purpose, program, policy, plan, procedure, practice, problems, pitfalls, personnel, public relations

a. Six basic steps in handling problems:
1. Preliminary plan and background development
2. Collect information, data and facts
3. Analyze and interpret information, data and facts
4. Analyze and develop solutions as well as make recommendations
5. Prepare report and sell recommendations
6. Install recommendations and follow up effectiveness

b. Pitfalls to avoid
1. *Taking things for granted* – A statement of the situation does not necessarily imply that each of the elements is necessarily true; for example, a complaint may be invalid and biased so that all that can be taken for granted is that a complaint has been registered

2. *Considering only one side of a situation* – Wherever possible, indicate several alternatives and then point out the reasons you selected the best one
3. *Failing to indicate follow up* – Whenever your answer indicates action on your part, make certain that you will take proper follow-up action to see how successful your recommendations, procedures or actions turn out to be
4. *Taking too long in answering any single question* – Remember to time your answers properly

IX. AFTER THE TEST

Scoring procedures differ in detail among civil service jurisdictions although the general principles are the same. Whether the papers are hand-scored or graded by machine we have described, they are nearly always graded by number. That is, the person who marks the paper knows only the number – never the name – of the applicant. Not until all the papers have been graded will they be matched with names. If other tests, such as training and experience or oral interview ratings have been given, scores will be combined. Different parts of the examination usually have different weights. For example, the written test might count 60 percent of the final grade, and a rating of training and experience 40 percent. In many jurisdictions, veterans will have a certain number of points added to their grades.

After the final grade has been determined, the names are placed in grade order and an eligible list is established. There are various methods for resolving ties between those who get the same final grade – probably the most common is to place first the name of the person whose application was received first. Job offers are made from the eligible list in the order the names appear on it. You will be notified of your grade and your rank as soon as all these computations have been made. This will be done as rapidly as possible.

People who are found to meet the requirements in the announcement are called "eligibles." Their names are put on a list of eligible candidates. An eligible's chances of getting a job depend on how high he stands on this list and how fast agencies are filling jobs from the list.

When a job is to be filled from a list of eligibles, the agency asks for the names of people on the list of eligibles for that job. When the civil service commission receives this request, it sends to the agency the names of the three people highest on this list. Or, if the job to be filled has specialized requirements, the office sends the agency the names of the top three persons who meet these requirements from the general list.

The appointing officer makes a choice from among the three people whose names were sent to him. If the selected person accepts the appointment, the names of the others are put back on the list to be considered for future openings.

That is the rule in hiring from all kinds of eligible lists, whether they are for typist, carpenter, chemist, or something else. For every vacancy, the appointing officer has his choice of any one of the top three eligibles on the list. This explains why the person whose name is on top of the list sometimes does not get an appointment when some of the persons lower on the list do. If the appointing officer chooses the second or third eligible, the No. 1 eligible does not get a job at once, but stays on the list until he is appointed or the list is terminated.

X. HOW TO PASS THE INTERVIEW TEST

The examination for which you applied requires an oral interview test. You have already taken the written test and you are now being called for the interview test – the final part of the formal examination.

You may think that it is not possible to prepare for an interview test and that there are no procedures to follow during an interview. Our purpose is to point out some things you can do in advance that will help you and some good rules to follow and pitfalls to avoid while you are being interviewed.

What is an interview supposed to test?

The written examination is designed to test the technical knowledge and competence of the candidate; the oral is designed to evaluate intangible qualities, not readily measured otherwise, and to establish a list showing the relative fitness of each candidate – as measured against his competitors – for the position sought. Scoring is not on the basis of "right" and "wrong," but on a sliding scale of values ranging from "not passable" to "outstanding." As a matter of fact, it is possible to achieve a relatively low score without a single "incorrect" answer because of evident weakness in the qualities being measured.

Occasionally, an examination may consist entirely of an oral test – either an individual or a group oral. In such cases, information is sought concerning the technical knowledges and abilities of the candidate, since there has been no written examination for this purpose. More commonly, however, an oral test is used to supplement a written examination.

Who conducts interviews?

The composition of oral boards varies among different jurisdictions. In nearly all, a representative of the personnel department serves as chairman. One of the members of the board may be a representative of the department in which the candidate would work. In some cases, "outside experts" are used, and, frequently, a businessman or some other representative of the general public is asked to serve. Labor and management or other special groups may be represented. The aim is to secure the services of experts in the appropriate field.

However the board is composed, it is a good idea (and not at all improper or unethical) to ascertain in advance of the interview who the members are and what groups they represent. When you are introduced to them, you will have some idea of their backgrounds and interests, and at least you will not stutter and stammer over their names.

What should be done before the interview?

While knowledge about the board members is useful and takes some of the surprise element out of the interview, there is other preparation which is more substantive. It *is* possible to prepare for an oral interview – in several ways:

1) Keep a copy of your application and review it carefully before the interview

This may be the only document before the oral board, and the starting point of the interview. Know what education and experience you have listed there, and the sequence and dates of all of it. Sometimes the board will ask you to review the highlights of your experience for them; you should not have to hem and haw doing it.

2) Study the class specification and the examination announcement

Usually, the oral board has one or both of these to guide them. The qualities, characteristics or knowledges required by the position sought are stated in these documents. They offer valuable clues as to the nature of the oral interview. For example, if the job involves supervisory responsibilities, the announcement will usually indicate that knowledge of modern supervisory methods and the qualifications of the candidate as a supervisor will be tested. If so, you can expect such questions, frequently in the form of a hypothetical situation which you are expected to solve. NEVER go into an oral without knowledge of the duties and responsibilities of the job you seek.

3) Think through each qualification required

Try to visualize the kind of questions you would ask if you were a board member. How well could you answer them? Try especially to appraise your own knowledge and background in each area, *measured against the job sought*, and identify any areas in which you are weak. Be critical and realistic – do not flatter yourself.

4) Do some general reading in areas in which you feel you may be weak

For example, if the job involves supervision and your past experience has NOT, some general reading in supervisory methods and practices, particularly in the field of human relations, might be useful. Do NOT study agency procedures or detailed manuals. The oral board will be testing your understanding and capacity, not your memory.

5) Get a good night's sleep and watch your general health and mental attitude

You will want a clear head at the interview. Take care of a cold or any other minor ailment, and of course, no hangovers.

What should be done on the day of the interview?

Now comes the day of the interview itself. Give yourself plenty of time to get there. Plan to arrive somewhat ahead of the scheduled time, particularly if your appointment is in the fore part of the day. If a previous candidate fails to appear, the board might be ready for you a bit early. By early afternoon an oral board is almost invariably behind schedule if there are many candidates, and you may have to wait. Take along a book or magazine to read, or your application to review, but leave any extraneous material in the waiting room when you go in for your interview. In any event, relax and compose yourself.

The matter of dress is important. The board is forming impressions about you – from your experience, your manners, your attitude, and your appearance. Give your personal appearance careful attention. Dress your best, but not your flashiest. Choose conservative, appropriate clothing, and be sure it is immaculate. This is a business interview, and your appearance should indicate that you regard it as such. Besides, being well groomed and properly dressed will help boost your confidence.

Sooner or later, someone will call your name and escort you into the interview room. *This is it.* From here on you are on your own. It is too late for any more preparation. But remember, you asked for this opportunity to prove your fitness, and you are here because your request was granted.

What happens when you go in?

The usual sequence of events will be as follows: The clerk (who is often the board stenographer) will introduce you to the chairman of the oral board, who will introduce you to the other members of the board. Acknowledge the introductions before you sit down. Do not be surprised if you find a microphone facing you or a stenotypist sitting by. Oral interviews are usually recorded in the event of an appeal or other review.

Usually the chairman of the board will open the interview by reviewing the highlights of your education and work experience from your application – primarily for the benefit of the other members of the board, as well as to get the material into the record. Do not interrupt or comment unless there is an error or significant misinterpretation; if that is the case, do not hesitate. But do not quibble about insignificant matters. Also, he will usually ask you some question about your education, experience or your present job – partly to get you to start talking and to establish the interviewing "rapport." He may start the actual questioning, or turn it over to one of the other members. Frequently, each member undertakes the questioning on a particular area, one in which he is perhaps most competent, so you can expect each member to participate in the examination. Because time is limited, you may also expect some rather abrupt switches in the direction the questioning takes, so do not be upset by it. Normally, a board member will not pursue a single line of questioning unless he discovers a particular strength or weakness.

After each member has participated, the chairman will usually ask whether any member has any further questions, then will ask you if you have anything you wish to add. Unless you are expecting this question, it may floor you. Worse, it may start you off on an extended, extemporaneous speech. The board is not usually seeking more information. The question is principally to offer you a last opportunity to present further qualifications or to indicate that you have nothing to add. So, if you feel that a significant qualification or characteristic has been overlooked, it is proper to point it out in a sentence or so. Do not compliment the board on the thoroughness of their examination – they have been sketchy, and you know it. If you wish, merely say, "No thank you, I have nothing further to add." This is a point where you can "talk yourself out" of a good impression or fail to present an important bit of information. Remember, *you close the interview yourself.*

The chairman will then say, "That is all, Mr. _____, thank you." Do not be startled; the interview is over, and quicker than you think. Thank him, gather your belongings and take your leave. Save your sigh of relief for the other side of the door.

How to put your best foot forward

Throughout this entire process, you may feel that the board individually and collectively is trying to pierce your defenses, seek out your hidden weaknesses and embarrass and confuse you. Actually, this is not true. They are obliged to make an appraisal of your qualifications for the job you are seeking, and they want to see you in your best light. Remember, they must interview all candidates and a non-cooperative candidate may become a failure in spite of their best efforts to bring out his qualifications. Here are 15 suggestions that will help you:

1) Be natural – Keep your attitude confident, not cocky

If you are not confident that you can do the job, do not expect the board to be. Do not apologize for your weaknesses, try to bring out your strong points. The board is interested in a positive, not negative, presentation. Cockiness will antagonize any board member and make him wonder if you are covering up a weakness by a false show of strength.

2) Get comfortable, but don't lounge or sprawl

Sit erectly but not stiffly. A careless posture may lead the board to conclude that you are careless in other things, or at least that you are not impressed by the importance of the occasion. Either conclusion is natural, even if incorrect. Do not fuss with your clothing, a pencil or an ashtray. Your hands may occasionally be useful to emphasize a point; do not let them become a point of distraction.

3) Do not wisecrack or make small talk

This is a serious situation, and your attitude should show that you consider it as such. Further, the time of the board is limited – they do not want to waste it, and neither should you.

4) Do not exaggerate your experience or abilities

In the first place, from information in the application or other interviews and sources, the board may know more about you than you think. Secondly, you probably will not get away with it. An experienced board is rather adept at spotting such a situation, so do not take the chance.

5) If you know a board member, do not make a point of it, yet do not hide it

Certainly you are not fooling him, and probably not the other members of the board. Do not try to take advantage of your acquaintanceship – it will probably do you little good.

6) Do not dominate the interview

Let the board do that. They will give you the clues – do not assume that you have to do all the talking. Realize that the board has a number of questions to ask you, and do not try to take up all the interview time by showing off your extensive knowledge of the answer to the first one.

7) Be attentive

You only have 20 minutes or so, and you should keep your attention at its sharpest throughout. When a member is addressing a problem or question to you, give him your undivided attention. Address your reply principally to him, but do not exclude the other board members.

8) Do not interrupt

A board member may be stating a problem for you to analyze. He will ask you a question when the time comes. Let him state the problem, and wait for the question.

9) Make sure you understand the question

Do not try to answer until you are sure what the question is. If it is not clear, restate it in your own words or ask the board member to clarify it for you. However, do not haggle about minor elements.

10) Reply promptly but not hastily

A common entry on oral board rating sheets is "candidate responded readily," or "candidate hesitated in replies." Respond as promptly and quickly as you can, but do not jump to a hasty, ill-considered answer.

11) Do not be peremptory in your answers

A brief answer is proper – but do not fire your answer back. That is a losing game from your point of view. The board member can probably ask questions much faster than you can answer them.

12) Do not try to create the answer you think the board member wants

He is interested in what kind of mind you have and how it works – not in playing games. Furthermore, he can usually spot this practice and will actually grade you down on it.

13) Do not switch sides in your reply merely to agree with a board member

Frequently, a member will take a contrary position merely to draw you out and to see if you are willing and able to defend your point of view. Do not start a debate, yet do not surrender a good position. If a position is worth taking, it is worth defending.

14) Do not be afraid to admit an error in judgment if you are shown to be wrong

The board knows that you are forced to reply without any opportunity for careful consideration. Your answer may be demonstrably wrong. If so, admit it and get on with the interview.

15) Do not dwell at length on your present job

The opening question may relate to your present assignment. Answer the question but do not go into an extended discussion. You are being examined for a *new* job, not your present one. As a matter of fact, try to phrase ALL your answers in terms of the job for which you are being examined.

Basis of Rating

Probably you will forget most of these "do's" and "don'ts" when you walk into the oral interview room. Even remembering them all will not ensure you a passing grade. Perhaps you did not have the qualifications in the first place. But remembering them will help you to put your best foot forward, without treading on the toes of the board members.

Rumor and popular opinion to the contrary notwithstanding, an oral board wants you to make the best appearance possible. They know you are under pressure – but they also want to see how you respond to it as a guide to what your reaction would be under the pressures of the job you seek. They will be influenced by the degree of poise you display, the personal traits you show and the manner in which you respond.

ABOUT THIS BOOK

This book contains tests divided into Examination Sections. Go through each test, answering every question in the margin. We have also attached a sample answer sheet at the back of the book that can be removed and used. At the end of each test look at the answer key and check your answers. On the ones you got wrong, look at the right answer choice and learn. Do not fill in the answers first. Do not memorize the questions and answers, but understand the answer and principles involved. On your test, the questions will likely be different from the samples. Questions are changed and new ones added. If you understand these past questions you should have success with any changes that arise. Tests may consist of several types of questions. We have additional books on each subject should more study be advisable or necessary for you. Finally, the more you study, the better prepared you will be. This book is intended to be the last thing you study before you walk into the examination room. Prior study of relevant texts is also recommended. NLC publishes some of these in our Fundamental Series. Knowledge and good sense are important factors in passing your exam. Good luck also helps. So now study this Passbook, absorb the material contained within and take that knowledge into the examination. Then do your best to pass that exam.

EXAMINATION SECTION

EXAMINATION SECTION
TEST 1

DIRECTIONS: Each question or incomplete statement is followed by several suggested answers or completions. Select the one that BEST answers the question or completes the statement. *PRINT THE LETTER OF THE CORRECT ANSWER IN TEE SPACE AT THE RIGHT.*

1. Police Communications Technicians must connect the caller to Transit Police when an incident occurs on a subway train or in the subway station.
   Which one of the following calls should be reported to Transit Police?

   A. The newsstand outside the entrance to the 86th Street subway was just robbed, and the suspects fled down the street.
   B. Soon after James Pike left the Columbus Circle subway station, his chain was snatched on the street corner.
   C. While traveling to work on the *D* line subway train, John Smith was mugged.
   D. A noisy group of school children have just come out of the Times Square subway station and are now annoying passersby on the street.

1.____

Question 2.

DIRECTIONS: Question 2 is to be answered SOLELY on the basis of the following information.
When a Police Communications Technician is notified by patrol cars that they are in a vehicular pursuit, the dispatcher should obtain the following in the order given:
   I. Location of pursuit
   II. Type of vehicle, color of vehicle, and direction of travel
   III. Nature of offense
   IV. License plate number and state
   V. Number of occupant(s) in vehicle
   VI. Identity of the patrol car in pursuit

2. Police Communications Dispatcher Johnson is working the 26th Division when an unknown patrol car announces via car radio that he is in pursuit of a white 1986 Cadillac traveling north on Vanbrunt Street from Ainsley Place. Dispatcher Johnson then asks the pursuing patrol car, *What is the car wanted for?* The Officer replies, *The car is wanted for a hit and run.*
   What information should Dispatcher Johnson obtain NEXT?

   A. The number of occupant(s) in the vehicle
   B. Location of pursuit
   C. License plate number and state
   D. Identity of the patrol car in pursuit

2.____

Question 3.

DIRECTIONS: Question 3 is to be answered SOLELY on the basis of the following information.

Robbery - involves the unlawful taking of property from a person by force or attempted use of immediate force.

Robbery in Progress - crime is occurring at the time the call came into 911, 5 minutes in the past or when suspects are still in the area.

3. Which of the following situations would be considered a ROBBERY IN PROGRESS?   3._____

   A. Female calls 911 stating that she has just arrived home and found her apartment has been robbed.
   B. Male calls 911 stating that he just discovered that someone picked his pocket.
   C. Female calls 911 stating that she saw a man grab an elderly woman's purse.
   D. Child calls 911 stating that some man is beating up his mother and is trying to take her purse.

4. On June 20, 2007 at 6:30 P.M., Police Communications Technician White receives a call   4._____
   from an anonymous complainant stating the following facts:
   Incident: Male with a gun sitting in a blue car
   Location of Incident: In front of 185 Hall St.
   Description of Suspect: Male, Black, bald, approximately 25 years old, dressed in red

   Dispatcher White needs to be accurate and clear when transferring above information to the police dispatcher. Which one of the following expresses the above information MOST clearly and accurately?

   A. On June 20, 2007 at 6:30 P.M., a call was received stating that a bald man, dressed in red, was in front of 185 Hall St. A black male, approximately 25 years old, is sitting in a blue car holding a gun.
   B. A call was received on June 20, 2007. at 6:30 P.M. stating that a bald black male, approximately 25 years old, who is dressed in red, is armed with a gun sitting in a blue car in front of 185 Hall St.
   C. A call was received on June 20, 2007 at 6:30 P.M. Sitting in a blue car in front of 185 Hall St. is a Black male, approximately 25 years old. Dressed in red with a bald head, a man is armed with a gun.
   D. A call was received stating that in front of 185 Hall St., a bald male, approximately 25 years old, dressed in red, is sitting in a blue car. A Black male is armed with a gun at 6:30 P.M. on June 20, 2007.

5. Police Communications Technician Dozier receives a call from a female who has just wit-   5._____
   nessed the following:
   Incident: White female police officer being assaulted
   Location of Incident: Surf Avenue and West 30th Street, in front of a candy store
   Description of Suspectp; Hispanic female wearing a green dress, possibly armed with a gun

   Dispatcher Dozier is about to relay the information to the dispatcher.
   Which one of the following expresses the above information MOST clearly and accurately?

   A. A call was received from a female on Surf Avenue and West 30th Street stating that a white female police officer is being assaulted by a Hispanic female wearing a green dress. She is possibly armed with a gun in front of a candy store.
   B. In front of a candy store at Surf Avenue and West 30th Street, a call was received from a female stating that a white female police officer is being assaulted by a Hispanic female wearing a green dress. She is possibly armed with a gun.

C. A call was received from a female stating that at the corner of Surf Avenue and West 30th Street in front of a candy store, there is a white female police officer being assaulted. The suspect is a Hispanic female wearing a green dress, who is possibly armed with a gun.
D. A call was received from a female stating that at the corner of West 30th Street and Surf Avenue, there is a white female police officer in front of a candy store being assaulted. She is wearing a green dress. The Hispanic female is possibly armed with a gun.

Questions 6-8.

DIRECTIONS: Questions 6 through 8 are to be answered SOLELY on the basis of the following passage.

At 10:35 A.M., Police Communications Technician Ross receives a second call from Mrs. Smith who is very upset because she has been waiting for the police and an ambulance since her first call, one hour ago. Mrs. Smith was mugged, and in resisting the attack, her nose was broken. The location of the incident is the uptown side of the subway station for the IND #2 train located at Jay Street and Borough Hall. Operator Ross advises Mrs. Smith to hold on and that she will check the status of her complaint. Operator Ross calls the Emergency Medical Service (EMS) and connects Mrs. Smith to the EMS operator. The EMS operator informs Mrs. Smith that an ambulance is coming from a far distance away and will be at the location at approximately 11:03 A.M. Operator Ross then calls the Transit Authority Police Department (TAPD). The TAPD received Mrs. Smith's first call at 9:37 A.M., and police arrived at location at 9:46 M. However, the police arrived at the downtown side of the subway station for the IND #3 train. TAPD informs Operator Ross that a police car will arrive at the correct location as soon as possible.

6. What is the CLOSEST approximate time that Mrs. Smith made her first call for help? _____ A.M.

   A. 9:35
   B. 9:46
   C. 10:35
   D. 11:03.

7. The ambulance was delayed because

   A. the ambulance responded to the downtown side of the subway station for the IND #2 train
   B. EMS never received Mrs. Smith's request for an ambulance
   C. a broken nose is not a priority request for an ambulance
   D. the ambulance was coming from a far distance

8. There was a delay in TAPD response to the crime scene because TAPD

   A. was coming from a far distance
   B. responded on the uptown side of the subway station for the IND #2 train
   C. was waiting for the -Police Department to respond first
   D. responded on the downtown side of the subway station for the IND #3 train

9. Extreme care must be taken when assigning solo cars (one police officer in a vehicle) to incidents. If anything in the job indicates that the job may be a potentially violent situation, a solo car should not be assigned.
In which one of the following incidents should a Police Communications Technician assign a solo car?
A

   A. disorderly male carrying a knife
   B. house that was broken into two days ago
   C. suspiciously occupied auto
   D. group of rowdy teenagers throwing beer bottles at passersbys

Question 10.

DIRECTIONS: Question 10 is to be answered SOLELY on the basis of the following information.

On the Police Communications Technician's screen, the following incidents appear which were called in at the same time:
   I. Caller states that she is looking out her 10th floor window and sees a man sleeping on the street in front of her home at Crescent Street and 4th Avenue.
   II. Caller states that he was driving down the block of Crescent Street between 3rd and 4th Avenues and just witnessed a man being beaten and mugged. The caller thinks that the victim is unconscious.
   III. Caller states there is a car accident at Crescent Street and 3rd Avenue, and one of the passengers suffered a broken arm.

10. Which of the above should the operator MOST likely consider as the same incident?

   A. I and II   B. II and III
   C. I and III   D. I, II, and III

11. Police Communications Operator Raymond receives a call regarding a rape and obtains the following information:
   Time of Rape: 10:35 P.M.
   Place of Rape: Sam's Laundromat, 200 Melrose Avenue
   Victim: Joan McGraw
   Crime: Rape
   Suspect: Male, Hispanic, carrying a gun
Operator Raymond is about to enter the incident into the computer.
Which one of the following expresses the above information MOST clearly and accurately?

   A. At 10:35 P.M., Joan McGraw was raped in Sam's Laundromat, located at 200 Melrose Avenue, by a Hispanic male carrying a gun.
   B. A Hispanic male was carrying a gun at 10:35 P.M. Joan McGraw was raped in Sam's Laundromat located at 200 Melrose Avenue.
   C. Carrying a gun, Joan McGraw was raped by a Hispanic male. This occurred in Sam's Laundromat located at 200 Melrose Avenue at 10:35 P.M.
   D. At 10:35 P.M., Joan McGraw was raped by a Hispanic male carrying a gun. Sam's Laundromat is located at 200 Melrose Avenue.

12. Police Communications Dispatcher Gold receives a call concerning a disorderly male in a local drug store. He obtains the following information:
   Place of Occurrence: Rapid-Serve Drug Store
   Complainant: George Meyer
   Crime: Threatening gestures and abusive language
   Suspect: Male, white
   Action Taken: The suspect was removed from premises by the police.
   Dispatcher Gold is about to enter the incident into the computer.
   Which one of the following expresses the above information MOST clearly and accurately?

   A. George Meyer called the police because a white male was removed from the Rapid-Serve Drug Store. He was making threatening gestures and using abusive language.
   B. George Meyer called the police and was removed from the Rapid-Serve Drug Store. A white male was making threatening gestures and using abusive language.
   C. At the Rapid-Serve Drug Store, a white male was making threatening gestures and using abusive language. George Meyer called the police and removed the suspect from the drug store.
   D. George Meyer called the police because a white male was making threatening gestures and using abusive language in the Rapid-Serve Drug Store. The suspect was removed from the drug store by the police.

Question 13.

DIRECTIONS: Question 13 is to be answered SOLELY on the basis of the following information.

When dispatching an incident involving a suspicious package, a Police Communications Technician should do the following in the order given:

   I. Assign a patrol car and Patrol Sergeant.
   II. Enter into the computer additional information received from assigned cars.
   III. Notify appropriate Emergency Assistance.
   IV. Notify the Bomb Squad.
   V. Notify the Duty Captain.

13. Police Communications Technician Berlin receives a call involving a suspicious package located on the corner of Gates Avenue and Blake Street. Dispatcher Berlin promptly assigns a patrol car and a Patrol Sergeant to the incident. Upon arrival, the Sergeant determines that there is a ticking sound coming from the box. The Sergeant immediately advises Dispatcher Berlin of the situation and tells Dispatcher Berlin to call the Fire Department and have them respond.
   What should Dispatcher Berlin to NEXT?

   A. Call the Fire Department.
   B. Notify the Bomb Squad.
   C. Enter additional information received from assigned cars into the computer.
   D. Notify the Duty Captain.

Questions 14-16.

DIRECTIONS: Questions 14 through 16 are to be answered SOLELY on the basis of the following passage.

Police Communications Technician Robbins receives a call at 5:15 P.M. from Mr. Adams reporting he witnessed a shooting in front of 230 Eagle Road. Mr. Adams, who lives at 234 Eagle Road, states he overheard two white males arguing with a Black man. He describes one white male as having blonde hair and wearing a black jacket with blue jeans, and the other white male as having brown hair and wearing a white jacket and blue jeans.

Mr. Adams recognized the Black man as John Rivers, the son of Mrs. Mary Rivers, who lives at 232 Eagle Road. At 5:10 P.M., the blonde male took a gun, shot John in the stomach, and dragged his body into the alleyway. The two males ran into the backyard of 240 Eagle Road and headed west on Randall Boulevard. Dispatcher Robbins connects Mr. Adams to the Emergency Medical Service. The Ambulance Receiving Operator processes the call at 5:25 P.M. and advises Mr. Adams that the next available ambulance will be sent.

14. Who was the eyewitness to the shooting?
    A. Dispatcher Robbins
    B. Mr. Adams
    C. Mrs. Rivers
    D. John Rivers

15. In front of what address was John Rivers shot?
    _____ Eagle Road.
    A. 230   B. 232   C. 234   D. 240

16. What is the description of the male who fired the gun? A male wearing a _____ jacket and blue jeans.
    A. white blonde-haired; white
    B. white brown-haired; black
    C. white blonde-haired; black
    D. Black brown-haired; white

17. A Police Communications Technician can have several calls for police response on their computer screen at one time. A dispatcher may have to determine which of the calls is the most serious and assign that one to the police first.
    Which one of the following situations should a dispatcher assign to the police FIRST?

    A. A robbery which occurred two hours ago, and the suspects have fled the scene
    B. A suspicious man offering a child candy to get the child into his van at the time of the call
    C. A woman returns to her car and finds her left fender dented
    D. A group of youths playing cards in the hallway

18. The following information was obtained by Police Communications Technician Fried regarding a call of an auto accident with injuries:
    Date of Accident: March 7, 2007
    Place of Accident: 50 West 96th Street
    Time of Accident: 3:15 P.M.
    Drivers: Susan Green and Nancy White

Injured: Nancy White
Action Taken: Emergency Medical Services (EMS) Operator 600 was notified
Dispatcher Fried is about to enter the above information into the computer.
Which one of the following expresses the above information MOST clearly and accurately?

- A. At 50 West 96th Street, Susan Green and Nancy White had an auto accident resulting in an injury to Nancy White. EMS Operator 600 was notifed to send an ambulance at 3:15 P.M. on March 7, 2007.
- B. EMS Operator 600 was notified to send an ambulance to 50 West 96th Street due to an auto accident between Nancy White and Susan Green, who was injured on March 7, 2007 at 3:15 P.M.
- C. Susan Green and Nancy White were involved in an auto accident at 50 West 96th Street on March 7, 2007. At 3:15 P.M., EMS Operator 600 was notified to send an ambulance for Nancy White.
- D. On March 7, 2007 at 3:15 P.M., Susan Green and Nancy White were involved in an auto accident at 50 West 96th Street. EMS Operator 600 was notified to send an ambulance for Nancy White who was injured in the accident.

Questions 19-20.

DIRECTIONS: Questions 19 and 20 are to be answered SOLELY on the basis of the following information.

At the beginning of their tours, Police Communications Technicians need to call the precinct to find out what patrol cars are covering which sections of the precinct and which special assignment cars are being used. Special assignment cars are used instead of regular patrol cars when certain situations arise. Special assignment cars should be assigned before a patrol car when a call comes in that is related to the car's special assignment, regardless of what section the incident is occurring in. Otherwise, a regular patrol car should be assigned.

Police Communications Technician Tanner is assigned to the 83rd Precinct. He calls the precinct and determines the following patrol cars and special assignment cars are being used:

Patrol cars are assigned as follows:
    Patrol Car 83A - Covers Sections A, B, C
    Patrol Car 83D - Covers Sections D, E, F
    Patrol Car 83G - Covers Sections G, H, I

Special assignment cars are assigned as follows:
    83SP1 - Burglary Car
    83SP2 - Religious Establishment
    83SP8 - Anti-Crime (plainclothes officers)

19. Dispatcher Tanner receives a call located in the 83rd Precinct in *E* Section. Which car should be assigned?

    A. 83D   B. 83A   C. 83SP8   D. 83SP2

20. Dispatcher Tanner receives a call concerning a burglary in *B* Section. Which is the CORRECT car to be assigned?

    A. 83A   B. 83G   C. 83SP1   D. 83SP2

KEY (CORRECT ANSWERS)

1.	C	11.	A
2.	C	12.	D
3.	D	13.	C
4.	B	14.	B
5.	C	15.	A
6.	A	16.	C
7.	D	17.	B
8.	D	18.	D
9.	B	19.	A
10.	A	20.	C

TEST 2

DIRECTIONS: Each question or incomplete statement is followed by several suggested answers or completions. Select the one that BEST answers the question or completes the statement. *PRINT THE LETTER OF THE CORRECT ANSWER IN THE SPACE AT THE RIGHT.*

1. Police Communications Technician Daniel receives a call stating the following: 1.____
    Date and Time of Call: June 21, 2007 at 12:30 P.M.
    Incident: Shots being fired
    Location: The roof of a building, located between Moore Street and Bushwick Avenue, exact address unknown
    Suspect: Male
    Complainant: Mr. Bernard
    Comments: Mr. Bernard will be wearing a brown coat and will direct officers to location of the incident.

    Dispatcher Daniel is about to enter the information into the computer.
    Which one of the following expresses the above information MOST clearly and accurately?
    On June 21, 2007,

    A. at 12:30 P.M., Dispatcher Daniel receives a call from a complainant stating that a male is on a roof of a building with an unknown address firing a gun, and he is wearing a brown coat. The complainant, Mr. Bernard, will be in front of the building to direct the police to the exact location of the incident.
    B. a male is firing a gun from a roof, stated complainant Mr. Bernard to Dispatcher Daniel. This is at Moore Street and Bushwick Avenue. At 12:30 P.M., the caller will be at the location to direct the police to the building where the male is firing the gun. He is wearing a brown coat.
    C. at 12:30 P.M., Dispatcher Daniel receives a call from a complainant, Mr. Bernard, who states that at a building with an unknown address, located between Moore Street and Bushwick Avenue, a male is firing a gun from a roof. Mr. Bernard will be at the location wearing a brown coat to direct the police to the exact building.
    D. Dispatcher Daniel receives a call from a complainant, Mr. Bernard, who is calling from a building with an unknown address. He informs Dispatcher Daniel that a male is firing a gun from a roof of a building between Moore Street and Bushwick Avenue. At 12:30 P.M., Mr. Bernard will be wearing a brown coat to direct the police to the incident.

Questions 2-4.

DIRECTIONS: Questions 2 through 4 are to be answered SOLELY on the basis of the following passage.

Mrs. Arroyo returns from work one evening to find her door open and loud noise coming from her apartment. She peeks through the crack of the door and sees a white male moving rapidly through her apartment wearing blue jeans and a pink T-shirt. She runs to the nearest public telephone and dials 911. Police Communications Technician Ms. Lopez takes the call. Mrs. Arroyo informs Operator Lopez that there is a strange man in her apartment. The operator asks the caller for her address, apartment number, name, and telephone number, and then puts Mrs. Arroyo on hold. Operator Lopez enters the address in the computer and, realizing it is a high priority call, tries to notify the Radio Dispatcher directly by depressing the *hotline* button.

The Radio Dispatcher does not respond, and Operator Lopez realizes the *hotline* button is not working. The operator then continues to enter the rest of the information into the computer and notifies the caller that the police will respond. Operator Lopez then walks into the dispatcher's room to make sure the dispatcher received the information entered into the computer, and then notifies the supervisor of her malfunctioning equipment.

2. The operator notified her supervisor because

   A. the suspect was still in the apartment
   B. the *hotline* button was not working
   C. she could not enter the address in the computer
   D. it was a high priority call

3. What was the FIRST action the operator took after putting the complainant on hold?

   A. Entered the caller's telephone number and name in the computer.
   B. Walked into the dispatcher's room.
   C. Entered the caller's address into the computer.
   D. Tried to notify the Radio Dispatcher by depressing the *hotline* button.

4. Operator Lopez depressed the *hotline* button

   A. to check if the *hotline* button was working properly
   B. because it was a high priority call
   C. to make sure the dispatcher received the information entered into the computer
   D. because the computer was not working properly

Question 5.

DIRECTIONS: Question 5 is to be answered SOLELY on the basis of the following information.

A Police Communications Technician occasionally receives calls from persons making threats against public officials, visiting dignitaries, or members of the Police Department. When this occurs, the Dispatcher should do the following in the order given:
   I. Obtain details of the threat
      (A) Who is being threatened and how
      (B) When it is going to happen
   II. Attempt to determine the sex and ethnicity of the caller
   III. Try to obtain the identity, address, and telephone number of the caller
   IV. Notify the supervisor

5. Police Communications Operator Frye receives a call and obtains from the caller that he is going to shoot the mayor on Election Day. Operator Frye determine the caller to be a male with a heavy Hispanic accent. Operator Frye asks the male for his name, address, and phone number. The caller does not respond and hangs up.
   What should Operator Frye do NEXT?

   A. Obtain details of the threats.
   B. Determine the sex and ethnicity of the caller.
   C. Obtain the identity, address, and phone number of the caller.
   D. Notify the supervisor.

Question 6.

DIRECTIONS: Question 6 is to be answered SOLELY on the basis of the following information.

A Police Communications Technician will call back complainants only under the following conditions:
1. Dispatcher needs clarification of information previously received from the complainant and/or
2. To notify the complainant that police need to gain entry to the location of the incident.

6. In which one of the following situations should a Police Communications Technician call back the complainant?

   A. While responding to an assigned incident, Patrol Car 79A gets a flat tire. Patrol Car 79A radios the dispatcher and advises the dispatcher to call the complainant and notify the complainant that there will be a delay in police response.
   B. Patrol Car 83B is assigned to an incident that occurred approximately 30 minutes ago. Patrol Car 83B advises the dispatcher that he is coming from a far distance and the dispatcher should call the complainant to find out which is the best way to get to the incident location.
   C. Patrol Car 66B is on the scene of an incident and is having a problem gaining entry into the building. Patrol Car 66B asks the dispatcher to call the complainant and ask him to meet the police officers from the patrol car outside the building.
   D. Patrol Car 90B is assigned to a burglary that occurred in the complainant's private home. It is raining heavily outside, so Patrol Car 90B asks the dispatcher to call and request the complainant to meet the police by the patrol car.

7. Police Communications Dispatcher Blake receives a call reporting a bank robbery and obtains the following information:

Time of Robbery:	11:30 A.M.
Place of Robbery:	Fidelity Bank
Crime:	Bank Robbery
Suspect:	Male, white, wearing blue jeans, blue jacket, carrying a brown bag
Witness:	Susan Lane of 731 Madison Avenue

   Dispatcher Blake is about to inform his supervisor of the facts concerning the bank robbery.
   Which one of the following expresses the above information MOST clearly and accurately?

   A. At 11:30 A.M., the Fidelity Bank was robbed. Susan Lane lives at 731 Madison Avenue. The witness saw a white male wearing blue jeans, a blue jacket, and carrying a brown bag.
   B. Susan Lane of 731 Madison Avenue witnessed the robbery of Fidelity Bank at 11:30 A.M. The suspect is a white male and was wearing blue jeans, a blue jacket, and carrying a brown bag.
   C. Wearing blue jeans, a blue jacket, and carrying a brown bag, Susan Lane of 731 Madison Avenue saw a white male robbing the Fidelity Bank. The robbery was witnessed at 11:30 A.M.

D. At 11:30 A.M., Susan Lane of 731 Madison Avenue witnessed the robbery of the Fidelity Bank. A white male wore blue jeans, a blue jacket, and carried a brown bag.

8. Police Communications Technician Levine receives an incident for dispatch containing the following information:

   Incident: A female being beaten
   Location: In front of 385 Wall Street
   Victim: White female
   Suspect: White, male, wearing a grey shirt, possibly concealing a gun underneath his shirt

   Dispatcher Levine is about to relay this information to the patrol car.
   Which one of the following expresses the above information MOST clearly and accurately?

   A. A white female is being beaten by a white male wearing a grey shirt, who is possibly concealing a gun underneath his shirt. This is occurring in front of 385 Wall Street.
   B. A white male is beating a white female wearing a grey shirt. He is possibly concealing a gun underneath his shirt in front of 385 Wall Street.
   C. A female is being beaten in front of 385 Wall Street. A white male is possibly concealing a gun underneath his shirt. She is white, and the suspect is wearing a grey shirt.
   D. In front of 385 Wall Street, a white female is being beaten by a suspect, possibly concealing a gun underneath his shirt. A white male is wearing a grey shirt.

Questions 9-11.

DIRECTIONS: Questions 9 through 11 are to be answered SOLELY on the basis of the following passage.

Police Communications Technician John Clove receives a call from a Social Worker, Mrs. Norma Harris of Presbyterian Hospital, who states there is a 16-year-old teenager on the other line, speaking to Dr. Samuel Johnson, a psychologist at the hospital. The teenager is threatening suicide and claims that she is an out-patient, but refuses to give her name, address, or telephone number. She further states that the teenager took 100 pills of valium and is experiencing dizziness, numbness of the lips, and heart palpitations. The teenager tells Dr. Johnson that she wants to die because her boyfriend left her because she is pregnant.

Dr. Johnson is keeping her on the line persuading her to give her name, telephone number, and address. The Social Worker asks the dispatcher to trace the call. The dispatcher puts the caller on hold and informs his supervisor, Mrs. Ross, of the incident. The supervisor contacts Telephone Technician Mr. Ralph Taylor. Mr. Taylor contacts the telephone company and speaks to Supervisor Wallace, asking him to trace the call between Dr. Johnson and the teenager. After approximately 10 minutes, the dispatcher gets back to the Social Worker and informs her that the call is being traced.

9. Why did the Social Worker call Dispatcher Clove?

   A. A teenager is threatening suicide.
   B. Mrs. Ross took 100 pills of valium.

C. Dr. Johnson felt dizzy, numbness of the lips, and heart palpitations.
D. An unmarried teenager is pregnant.

10. Who did Mr. Clove notify FIRST? 10._____

    A. Mrs. Norma Harris   B. Dr. Samuel Johnson
    C. Mr. Wallace   D. Mrs. Ross

11. The conversation between which two individuals is being traced? 11._____

    A. Mrs. Norma Harris and the 16-year-old teenager
    B. The Telephone Technician and Telephone Company Supervisor
    C. Dr. Johnson and the 16-year-old teenager
    D. The dispatcher and the Hospital Social Worker

Question 12.

DIRECTIONS: Question 12 is to be answered SOLELY on the basis of the following information.

On the Police Communications Technician's screen, the following incidents appear which were called in at the same time by three different callers:

    I. A fight is occurring at 265 Hall Street between Myrtle and Willoughby Ave. The fight started in Apartment 3C, and the two men are now fighting in the street.
    II. A fight took place between a security guard and a suspected shoplifter in a store at Hall St. and Willoughby Ave. The security guard is holding the suspect in the security office.
    III. A fight is occurring between two white males on the street near the corner of Hall Street and Myrtle Ave. One of the males has a baseball bat.

12. Which of the above should a Police Communications Technician MOST likely consider as the same incident? 12._____

    A. I and II   B. II and III
    C. I and III   D. I, II, and III

Questions 13-15.

DIRECTIONS: Questions 13 through 15 are to be answered SOLELY on the basis of the following passage.

Police Communications Technician Flood receives a call from Mr. Michael Watkins, Program Director for *Meals on Wheels,* a program that delivers food to elderly people who cannot leave their home. Mr. Watkins states he received a call from Rochelle Berger, whose elderly aunt, Estelle Sims, is a client of his. Rochelle Berger informed Mr. Watkins that she has just received a call from her aunt's neighbor, Sally Bowles, who told her that her aunt has not eaten in several days and is in need of medical attention.

After questioning Mr. Watkins, Dispatcher Flood is informed that Estelle Sims lives at 300 79th Street in Apartment 6K, and her telephone number is 686-4527; Sally Bowles lives in Apartment 6H, and her telephone number is 678-2456. Mr. Watkins further advises that if there is difficulty getting into Estelle Sims' apartment, to ring Sally Bowies' bell and she will let you in. Mr. Watkins gives his phone number as 776-0451, and Rochelle Berger's phone number is 291-7287. Dispatcher Flood advises Mr. Watkins that the appropriate medical assistance will be sent.

13. Who did Sally Bowles notify that her neighbor needed medical attention?   13.___

   A. Dispatcher Flood   B. Michael Watkins
   C. Rochelle Berger   D. Estelle Sims

14. If the responding medical personnel are unable to get into Apartment 6K, they should speak to   14.___

   A. Rochelle Berger   B. Sally Bowles
   C. Dispatcher Flood   D. Michael Watkins

15. Whose telephone number is 686-4527?   15.___

   A. Michael Watkins   B. Estelle Sims
   C. Sally Bowles   D. Rochelle Berger

16. Police Communications Technicians often receive calls regarding incidents where a response from the Fire Department may be necessary.   16.___
    In which one of the following situations would a request from the dispatcher for the Fire Department to respond be MOST critical?
    A(n)

   A. fire hydrant has been opened by children on a hot August afternoon
   B. abandoned auto is parked in front of a fire hydrant
   C. neighbor's cat has climbed up a tree and is stuck
   D. excited woman smells smoke coming from the floor below

Question 17.

DIRECTIONS: Question 17 is to be answered SOLELY on the basis of the following information.

When a patrol car confirms that a murder has taken place, the Police Communications Technician should notify the following people in the order given:
   I. Patrol Sergeant
   II. Dispatching Supervisor
   III. Operations Unit
   IV. Crime Scene Unit
   V. Precinct Detective Unit
   VI. Duty Captain

17. Police Communications Technician Rodger assigns a patrol car to investigate a man who was shot and killed. The patrol car arrives on the scene and confirms that a murder has taken place. The Patrol Sergeant hears what has happened on his police radio and informs Dispatcher Rodger that he is going to respond to the scene. The Dispatching Supervisor walks over to Dispatcher Rodger and is informed of the situation.   17.___
    Who should Dispatcher Rodger notify NEXT?

   A. Operations Unit   B. Patrol Sergeant
   C. Precinct Detective Unit   D. Crime Scene Unit

18. Police Communications Technician Peterson receives a call from a woman inside the subway station reporting that her purse has just been snatched. Dispatcher Peterson obtained the following information relating to the crime:
    Place of Occurrence: E. 42nd Street and Times Square
    Time of Occurrence: 5:00 P.M.
    Crime: Purse Snatched
    Victim: Thelma Johnson
    Description of Suspect: Black, female, brown hair, blue jeans, red T-shirt
    Dispatcher Peterson is about to relay the information to the Transit Authority Police Dispatcher.
    Which one of the following expresses the above information MOST clearly and accurately?

    A. At 5:00 P.M., a brown-haired Black woman snatched a purse inside the subway station at E. 42nd Street and Times Square belonging to Thelma Johnson. She was wearing blue jeans and a red T-shirt.
    B. A purse was snatched from Thelma Johnson by a woman with brown hair in the subway station at 5:00 P.M. A Black female was wearing blue jeans and a red T-shirt at E. 42nd Street and Times Square.
    C. At 5:00 P.M., Thelma Johnson's purse was snatched inside the subway station at E. 42nd Street and Times Square. The suspect is a Black female with brown hair who is wearing blue jeans and a red T-shirt.
    D. Thelma Johnson reported at 5:00 P.M. her purse was snatched. In the subway station at E. 42nd Street and Times Square, a Black female with brown hair was wearing blue jeans and a red T-shirt.

19. Police Communications Technician Hopkins receives a call of an assault and obtains the following information concerning the incident:
    Place of Occurrence: Times Square
    Time of Occurrence: 3:15 A.M.
    Victim: Peter Polk
    Victim's Address: 50 E. 60 Street
    Suspect: Male, Hispanic, 5'6", 140 lbs., dressed in black
    Injury: Broken nose
    Action Taken: Victim transported to St. Luke's Hospital
    Dispatcher Hopkins is about to enter the job into the computer system.
    Which one of the following expresses the above information MOST clearly and accurately?

    A. At 3:15 A.M., Peter Polk was assaulted in Times Square by a Hispanic male, 5'6", 140 lbs., dressed in black, suffering a broken nose. Mr. Polk lives at 50 E. 69 Street and was transported to St. Luke's Hospital.
    B. At 3:15 A.M., Peter Polk was assaulted in Times Square by a Hispanic male, 5'6", 140 lbs., dressed in black, who lives at 50 E. 69 Street. Mr. Polk suffered a broken nose and was transported to St. Luke's Hospital.
    C. Peter Polk, who lives at 50 E. 69 Street, was assaulted at 3:15 A.M. in Times Square by a Hispanic male, 5'6", 140 lbs., dressed in black. Mr. Polk suffered a broken nose and was transported to St. Luke's Hospital.
    D. Living at 50 E. 69 Street, Mr. Polk suffered a broken nose and was transported to St. Luke's Hospital. At 3:15 A.M., Mr. Polk was assaulted by a Hispanic male, 5'6", 140 lbs., who was dressed in black.

20. A Police Communications Technician is required to determine which situations called in to 911 require police assistance and which calls require non-emergency assistance. Which one of the following calls should a dispatcher MOST likely refer to non-emergency assistance?

    A. Mr. Moss threatens the owner of Deluxe Deli with bodily harm for giving him incorrect change of twenty dollars.
    B. The manager refuses to take back Mrs. Thompson's defective toaster because she doesn't have a receipt. Mrs. Thompson leaves the store.
    C. Mrs. Frank is having a violent argument with the manager of Donna's Dress Shop because he is refusing to exchange a dress she recently purchased.
    D. The manager of Metro Supermarket refuses to take back a stale loaf of bread, so the consumer punches him in the face.

KEY (CORRECT ANSWERS)

1.	C	11.	C
2.	B	12.	C
3.	C	13.	C
4.	B	14.	B
5.	D	15.	B
6.	C	16.	D
7.	B	17.	A
8.	A	18.	C
9.	A	19.	C
10.	D	20.	B

EXAMINATION SECTION
TEST 1

DIRECTIONS: Each question or incomplete statement is followed by several suggested answers or completions. Select the one that BEST answers the question or completes the statement. *PRINT THE LETTER OF THE CORRECT ANSWER IN THE SPACE AT THE RIGHT.*

Questions 1-3.

DIRECTIONS: Questions 1 through 3 are to be answered SOLELY on the basis of the following passage.

    On May 15 at 10:15 A.M., Mr. Price was returning to his home at 220 Kings Walk when he discovered two of his neighbor's apartment doors slightly opened. One neighbor, Mrs. Kagan, who lives alone in Apartment 1C, was away on vacation. The other apartment, IB, is occupied by Martin and Ruth Stone, an elderly couple, who usually take a walk everyday at 10:00 A.M. Fearing a robbery might be taking place, Mr. Price runs downstairs to Mr. White in Apartment BI to call the police. Police Communications Technician Johnson received the call at 10:20 A.M. Mr. Price gave his address and stated that two apartments were possibly being burglarized. Communications Technician Johnson verified the address in the computer and then asked Mr. Price for descriptions of the suspects. He explained that he had not seen anyone, but he believed that they were still inside the building. Communications Technician Johnson immediately notified the dispatcher who assigned two patrol cars at 10:25 A.M., while Mr. Price was still on the phone. Communications Technician Johnson told Mr. Price that the police were responding to the location.

1. Who called Communications Technician Johnson?
   A. Mrs. Kagan   B. Mr. White
   C. Mrs. Stone   D. Mr. Price

2. What time did Communications Technician Johnson receive the call? _____ A.M.
   A. 10:00   B. 10:15   C. 10:20   D. 10:25

3. Which tenant was away on vacation?
   The tenant in Apartment
   A. 1C   B. IB   C. BI   D. ID

4. Dispatcher Watkins receives the following information regarding a complaint.
   Place of occurrence: St. James Park
   Complaint: Large group of intoxicated males throwing beer bottles and playing loud music
   Complainant: Oscar Aker
   Complainant's Address: 13 St. James Square, Apt. 2B
   Dispatcher Watkins is not certain if this incident should be reported to 911 or Mr. Aker's local precinct. Dispatcher Watkins is about to notify his supervisor of the call. Which one of the following expresses the above information MOST clearly and accurately?

A. Mr. Aker, who lives at 13 St. James Square, Apt. 2B, called to make a complaint of a large group of intoxicated males who are throwing beer bottles and playing loud music in St. James Park.
B. Mr. Aker, who lives at 13 St. James Square, called to complain about a large group of intoxicated males, in Apt. 2B. They are throwing beer bottles and playing loud music in St. James Park.
C. Mr. Aker of 13 St. James Square, Apt. 2B, called to complain about loud music. There were a large group of intoxicated males throwing beer bottles in St. James Park.
D. As a result of intoxicated males throwing beer bottles Mr. Aker of 13 St. James Square, Apt. 2B, called to complain. A large group was playing loud music in St. James Park.

5. Communications Operator Davis recorded the following information from a caller:

Crime:	Rape
Time of Rape:	11:30 A.M.
Place of Rape:	Ralph's Dress Shop, 200 Lexington
Avenue Victim:	Linda Castro - employee at Ralph's Dress Shop
Description of Suspect:	Male, white
Weapon:	Knife

Communications Operator Davis needs to be clear and accurate when relaying information to the patrol car. Which one of the following expresses the above information MOST clearly and accurately?

A. Linda Castro was at 200 Lexington Avenue when she was raped at knife point by a white male. At 11:30 A.M., she is an employee of Ralph's Dress Shop.
B. At 11:30 A.M., Linda Castro reported that she was working in Ralph's Dress Shop located at 200 Lexington Avenue. A white male raped her while she was working at knife point.
C. Linda Castro, an employee of Ralph's Dress Shop, located at 200 Lexington Avenue, reported that at 11:30 A.M. a white male raped her at knife point in the dress shop.
D. At 11:30 A.M., a white male pointed a knife at Linda Castro. He raped an employee of Ralph's Dress Shop, which is located at 200 Lexington Avenue.

Question 6.

DIRECTIONS: Question 6 is to be answered SOLELY on the basis of the following information.

Police Communications Technicians frequently receive low priority calls, which are calls that do not require an immediate police response. When a low priority call is received, the Police Communications Technician should transfer the caller to a tape-recorded message which states *there will be a delay in police response.*

6. Police Communications Technicians should transfer to the low priority taped message a call reporting a

A. hubcap missing from an auto
B. child has just swallowed poison

C. group of youths fighting with knives
D. woman being assaulted

Questions 7-9.

DIRECTIONS: Questions 7 through 9 are to be answered SOLELY on the basis of the following passage.

On Tuesday, March 20 at 11:55 P.M., Dispatcher Uzel receives a call from a female stating that she immediately needs the police. The dispatcher asks the caller for her address. The excited female answers, *I can not think of it right now.* The dispatcher tries to calm down the caller. At this point, the female caller tells the dispatcher that her address is 1934 Bedford Avenue. The caller then realizes that 1934 Bedford Avenue is her mother's address and gives her address as 3455 Bedford Avenue. Dispatcher Uzel enters the address into the computer and tells the caller that the cross streets are Myrtle and Willoughby Avenues. The caller answers, *I don't live near Willoughby Avenue.* The dispatcher repeats her address at 3455 Bedford Avenue. Then the female states that her name is Linda Harris and her correct address is 5534 Bedford Avenue. Dispatcher Uzel enters the new address into the computer and determines the cross streets to be Utica Avenue and Kings Highway. The caller agrees that these are the cross streets where she lives.

7. What is the caller's CORRECT address?

   A. Unknown
   B. 1934 Bedford Avenue
   C. 3455 Bedford Avenue
   D. 5534 Bedford Avenue

8. What are the cross streets of the correct address?

   A. Myrtle Avenue and Willoughby Avenue
   B. Utica Avenue and Kings Highway
   C. Bedford Avenue and Myrtle Avenue
   D. Utica Avenue and Willoughby Avenue

9. Why did the female caller telephone Dispatcher Uzel?

   A. She needed the cross streets for her address.
   B. Her mother needed assistance.
   C. The purpose of the call was not mentioned.
   D. She did not know where she lived.

Question 10.

DIRECTIONS: Question 10 is to be answered SOLELY on the basis of the following information.

When performing vehicle license plate checks, Operators should do the following in the order given:
   I. Request the license plate in question.
   II. Repeat the license plate back to the patrol car officers.
   III. Check the license plate locally in the computer.
   IV. Advise the patrol car officers of the results of the local check.
   V. Check the license plate nationally in the computer.
   VI. Advise the patrol car officers of the results of the nationwide check.

10. Operator Johnson gets a request from a patrol car officer for a license plate check on a suspicious car. The patrol car officer tells Operator Johnson that the license plate number is XYZ-843, which Operator Johnson repeats back to the patrol car officer. Operator Johnson checks the license plate locally and determines that the car was stolen in the New York City area.
What should Operator Johnson do NEXT?

   A. Repeat the license plate back to patrol car officers.
   B. Check the license plate nationally.
   C. Advise the patrol car officers of the results of the local check.
   D. Advise the patrol ear officers of the results of the nationwide check.

11. Police Communications Technician Hughes receives a call from the owner of The Diamond Dome Jewelry Store, reporting a robbery. He obtains the following information from the caller:

Place of Occurrence:	The Diamond Dome Jewelry Store, 10 Exchange Place
Time of Occurrence:	10:00 A.M.
Crime:	Robbery of a $50,000 diamond ring
Victim:	Clayton Pelt, owner of The Diamond Dome Jewelry Store
Description of Suspect:	Male, white, black hair, blue suit and gray shirt
Weapon:	Gun

   Communications Technician Hughes is about to relay the information to the dispatcher. Which one of the following expresses the above information MOST clearly and accurately?

   A. Clayton Pelt reported that at 10:00 A.M. his store, The Diamond Dome Jewelry Store, was robbed at gunpoint. At 10 Exchange Place, a white male with black hair took a $50,000 diamond ring. He was wearing a blue suit and gray shirt.
   B. At 10:00 A.M., a black-haired male robbed a $50,000 diamond ring from The Diamond Dome Jewelry Store, which is owned by Clayton Pelt. A white male was wearing a blue suit and gray shirt and had a gun at 10 Exchange Place.
   C. At 10:00 A.M., Clayton Pelt, owner of The Diamond Dome Jewelry Store, which is located at 10 Exchange Place, was robbed of a $50,000 diamond ring at gunpoint. The suspect is a white male with black hair wearing a blue suit and gray shirt.
   D. In a robbery that occurred at gunpoint, a white male with black hair robbed The Diamond Dome Jewelry Store, which is located at 10 Exchange Place. Clayton Pelt, the owner who was robbed of a $50,000 diamond ring, said he was wearing a blue suit and a gray shirt at 10:00 A.M.

12. Dispatcher Sanders receives the following information from the computer:

Place of Occurrence:	Bushwick Housing Projects, rear of Building 12B
Time of Occurrence:	6:00 P.M.
Crime:	Mugging
Victim:	Hispanic female
Suspect:	Unknown

   Dispatcher sanders is about to relay the information to the patrol car.
   Which one of the following expresses the above information MOST clearly and accurately?

A. In the rear of Building 12B, a Hispanic female was mugged. An unknown suspect was in the Bushwick Housing Projects at 6:00 P.M.
B. At 6:00 P.M., a Hispanic female was mugged by an unknown suspect in the rear of Building 12B, in the Bushwick Housing Projects.
C. At 6:00 P.M., a female is in the rear of Building 12B in the Bushwick Housing Projects. An unknown suspect mugged a Hispanic female.
D. A suspect's identity is unknown in the rear of Building 12B in the Bushwick Housing Project at 6:00 P.M. A Hispanic female was mugged.

Questions 13-15.

DIRECTIONS: Questions 13 through 15 are to be answered SOLELY on the basis of the following passage.

Dispatcher Clark, who is performing a 7:30 A.M. to 3:30 P.M. tour of duty, receives a call from Mrs. Gold. Mrs. Gold states there are four people selling drugs in front of Joe's Cleaners, located at the intersection of Main Street and Broadway. After checking the location in the computer, Dispatcher Clark asks the caller to give a description of each person. She gives the following descriptions: one white male wearing a yellow shirt, green pants, and red sneakers; one Hispanic male wearing a red and white shirt, black pants, and white sneakers; one black female wearing a green and red striped dress and red sandals; and one black male wearing a green shirt, yellow pants, and green sneakers. She also states that the Hispanic male, who is standing near a blue van, has the drugs inside a small black shoulder bag. She further states that she saw the black female hide a gun inside a brown paper bag and place it under a black car parked in front of Joe's Cleaners. The drug selling goes on everyday at various times. During the week, it occurs from 7 A.M. to 1 P.M. and from 5 P.M. to 12 A.M., but on weekends it occurs from 3 P.M. until 7 A.M.

13. Which person was wearing red sneakers?

    A. Black male
    B. Hispanic male
    C. Black female
    D. White male

14. Mrs. Gold stated the drugs were located

    A. under the blue van
    B. inside the black shoulder bag
    C. under the black car
    D. inside the brown paper bag

15. At what time does Mrs. Gold state the drugs are sold on weekends?

    A. 7:30 A.M. - 3:30 P.M.
    B. 7:00 A.M. - 1:00 P.M.
    C. 5:00 P.M. - 12:00 A.M.
    D. 3:00 P.M. - 7:00 A.M.

16. Police Communications Technician Bentley receives a call of an auto being stripped. He obtains the following information from the caller:
    Place of Occurrence: Corner of West End Avenue and W. 72nd Street
    Time of Occurrence: 10:30 P.M.
    Witness: Mr. Simpson
    Suspects: Two white males
    Crime: Auto stripping
    Action Taken: Suspects fled before police arrived

Communications Technician Bentley is about to enter the incident into the computer and send the information to the dispatcher.
Which one of the following expresses the above information MOST clearly and accurately?

- A. At 10:30 P.M., Mr. Simpson witnessed two white males stripping an auto parked at the corner of West End Avenue and W. 72nd Street. The suspects fled before the police arrived.
- B. An auto was parked at the corner of West End Avenue and W. 72nd Street. Two white males who were stripping at 10:30 P.M. were witnessed by Mr. Simpson. Before the police arrived, the suspects fled.
- C. Mr. Simpson saw two white males at the corner of West End Avenue and W. 72nd Street. Fleeing the scene before the police arrived, the witness saw the suspects strip an auto.
- D. Before the police arrived at 10:30 P.M. on the corner of West End Avenue and W. 72nd Street, Mr. Simpson witnessed two white males. The suspects, who stripped an auto, fled the scene.

17. 911 Operator Washington receives a call of a robbery and obtains the following information regarding the incident:

Place of Occurrence: First National Bank, 45 West 96th Street
Time of Occurrence: 2:55 P.M.
Amount Taken: $10,000
Description of Suspect: Male, black, wearing a leather jacket, blue jeans, and white shirt
Weapon: Gun

911 Operator Washington is about to enter the call into the computer.
Which one of the following expresses the above information MOST clearly and accurately?

- A. At 2:55 P.M., the First National Bank, located at 45 West 96th Street, was robbed at gunpoint of $10,000. The suspect is a black male and is wearing a leather jacket, blue jeans, and a white shirt.
- B. Ten thousand dollars was robbed from the First National Bank at 2:55 P.M. A black male was wearing a leather jacket, blue jeans, and a white shirt at 45 West 96th Street. He also had a gun.
- C. At 2:55 P.M., a male was wearing a leather jacket, blue jeans, and a white shirt. The First National Bank located at 45 West 96th Street was robbed by a black male. Ten thousand dollars was taken at gunpoint.
- D. Robbing the First National Bank, a male wore a leather jacket, blue jeans, and a white shirt at gunpoint. A black male was at 45 W. 96th Street. At 2:55 P.M., $10,000 was taken.

Questions 18-20.

DIRECTIONS: Questions 18 through 20 are to be answered SOLELY on the basis of the following passage.

Police Communications Technician Gordon receives a call from a male stating there is a bomb set to explode in the gym of Public School 85 in two hours. Realizing the urgency of the call, the Communications Technician calls the radio dispatcher, who assigns Patrol Car 43A to the scene. Communications Technician Gordon then notifies her supervisor, Miss Smith, who first reviews the tape of the call, then calls the Operations Unit which is notified of all serious incidents, and she reports the facts. The Operations Unit notifies the Mayor's Information Agency and Borough Headquarters of the emergency situation.

18. Who did Communications Technician Gordon notify FIRST? 18.____

    A. Supervisor Smith
    B. Operations Unit
    C. Patrol Car 43A
    D. Radio dispatcher

19. The Operations Unit was notified 19.____

    A. to inform school personnel of the bomb
    B. so they can arrive at the scene before the bomb is scheduled to go off
    C. to evacuate the school
    D. due to the seriousness of the incident

20. Who did Miss Smith notify? 20.____

    A. Patrol Car 43A
    B. Operations Unit
    C. Mayor's Information Agency
    D. Borough Headquarters

KEY (CORRECT ANSWERS)

1.	D	11.	C
2.	C	12.	B
3.	A	13.	D
4.	A	14.	B
5.	C	15.	D
6.	A	16.	A
7.	D	17.	A
8.	B	18.	D
9.	C	19.	D
10.	C	20.	B

TEST 2

DIRECTIONS: Each question or incomplete statement is followed by several suggested answers or completions. Select the one that BEST answers the question or completes the statement. *PRINT THE LETTER OF THE CORRECT ANSWER IN THE SPACE AT THE RIGHT.*

1. A Police Communications Technician receives a call reporting a large gathering. She obtained the following information:

    Place of Occurrence: Cooper Square Park
    Time of Occurrence: 1:15 A.M.
    Occurrence: Youths drinking and playing loud music
    Complainant: Mrs. Tucker, 20 Cooper Square
    Action Taken: Police scattered the crowd

    Communications Technician Carter is about to relay the information to the dispatcher.
    Which one of the following expresses the above information MOST clearly and accurately?

    A. The police responded to Cooper Square Park because Mrs. Tucker, who called 911, lives at 20 Cooper Square. The group of youths was scattered due to drinking and playing loud music at 1:15 A.M.
    B. Mrs. Tucker, who lives at 20 Cooper Square, called 911 to make a complaint of a group of youths who were drinking and playing loud music in Cooper Square Park at 1:15 A.M. The police responded and scattered the crowd.
    C. Loud music and drinking in Cooper Square Park by a group of youths caused the police to respond and scatter the crowd. Mrs. Tucker called 911 and complained. At 1:15 A.M., she lives at 20 Cooper Square.
    D. Playing loud music and drinking, Mrs. Tucker called the police. The police scattered a group of youths in Cooper Square Park at 1:15 A.M. Mrs. Tucker lives at 20 Cooper Square.

1.____

2. Dispatcher Weston received a call from the owner of a gas station and obtained the following information:

    Place of Occurrence: Blin's Gas Station, 1800 White Plains Road
    Time of Occurrence: 10:30 A.M.
    Occurrence: Left station without paying
    Witness: David Perilli
    Description of Auto: A white Firebird, license plate GEB275
    Suspect: Male, white, wearing blue jeans and a black T-shirt

    Dispatcher Weston is about to enter the information into the computer.
    Which one of the following expresses the above information MOST clearly and accurately?

    A. At 10:30 A.M., David Perilli witnessed a white male wearing blue jeans and a black T-shirt leave Blin's Gas Station, located at 1800 White Plains Road, without paying. The suspect was driving a white Firebird with license plate GEB275.
    B. Wearing blue jeans and a black T-shirt, David Perilli witnessed a white male leave Blin's Gas Station without paying. He was driving a white Firebird with license plate GEB275. This occurred at 1800 White Plains Road at 10:30 A.M.
    C. David Perilli witnessed a male wearing blue jeans and a black T-shirt driving a white Firebird. At 10:30 A.M., a white male left Blin's Gas Station, located at 1800 White Plains Road, without paying. His license plate was GEB275.

2.____

24

D. At 10:30 A.M., David Perilli witnessed a white male leaving Blin's Gas Station without paying. The driver of a white Firebird, license plate GEB275, was wearing blue jeans and a black T-shirt at 1800 White Plains Road.

Questions 3-4.

DIRECTIONS: Questions 3 and 4 are to be answered SOLELY on the basis of the following information.

Police Communications Technicians are required to assist callers who need non-emergency assistance. The callers are referred to non-emergency agencies. Listed below are some non-emergency situations and the agencies to which they should be referred.

Agency
Local Precinct   Unoccupied suspicious car
Environmental Protection Agency   Open fire hydrant
Sanitation Department   Abandoned car
S.P.C.A.   Injured, stray or sick animal
Transit Authority   Transit Authority travel information

3. Communications Technician Carter received a call from Mr. Cane, who stated that a car without license plates had been parked in front of his house for five days. Mr. Crane should be referred to the

   A. A.S.P.C.A.
   B. Transit Authority
   C. Sanitation Department
   D. Environmental Protection Agency

4. Mrs. Dunbar calls to report that a dog has been hit by a car and is lying at the curb in front of her house. Mrs. Dunbar should be referred to the

   A. Sanitation Department
   B. Local Precinct
   C. Environmental Protection Agency
   D. A.S.P.C.A.

5. Operator Bryant received a call of a robbery and obtained the following information:
   Place of Occurrence: Deluxe Deli, 303 E. 30th Street
   Time of Occurrence: 5:00 P.M.
   Crime: Robbery of $300
   Victim: Bonnie Smith, cashier of Deluxe Deli
   Description of Suspect: White, female, blonde hair, wearing black slacks and a red shirt
   Weapon: Knife

   Operator Bryant is about to enter this information into the computer.
   Which one of the following expresses the above information MOST clearly and accurately?

A. Bonnie Smith, the cashier of the Deluxe Deli reported at 5:00 P.M. that she was robbed of $300 at knifepoint at 303 East 30th Street. A white female with blonde hair was wearing black slacks and a red shirt.
B. At 5:00 P.M., a blonde-haired female robbed the 303 East 30th Street store. At the Deluxe Deli, cashier Bonnie Smith was robbed of $300 by a white female at knifepoint. She was wearing black slacks and a red shirt.
C. In a robbery that occurred at knifepoint, a blonde-haired white female robbed $300 from the Deluxe Deli. Bonnie Smith, cashier of the 303 East 30th Street store, said she was wearing black slacks and a red shirt at 5:00 P.M.
D. At 5:00 P.M., Bonnie Smith, cashier of the Deluxe Deli, located at 303 East 30th Street, was robbed of $300 at knifepoint. The suspect is a white female with blonde hair wearing black slacks and a red shirt.

6. 911 Operator Landers receives a call reporting a burglary that happened in the past. He obtained the following information from the caller:

Place of Occurrence: 196 Simpson Street
Date of Occurrence: June 12
Time of Occurrence: Between 8:30 A.M. and 7:45 P.M.
Victim: Mr. Arnold Frank
Items Stolen: $300 cash, stereo, assorted jewelry, and a VCR

911 Operator Landers is about to enter the incident into the computer.
Which one of the following expresses the above information MOST clearly and accurately?

A. Mr. Arnold Frank stated that on June 12, between 8:30 A.M. and 7:45 P.M., someone broke into his home at 196 Simpson Street and took $300 in cash, a stereo, assorted jewelry, and a VCR.
B. Mr. Arnold Frank stated between 8:30 A.M. and 7:45 P.M., he lives at 196 Simpson Street. A stereo, VCR, $300 in cash, and assorted jewelry were taken on June 12.
C. Between 8:30 A.M. and 7:45 P.M. on June 12, Mr. Arnold Frank reported someone broke into his home. At 196 Simpson Street, a VCR, $300 in cash, a stereo, and assorted jewelry were taken.
D. A stereo, VCR, $300 in cash, and assorted jewelry were taken between 8:30 M. and 7:45 P.M. On June 12, Mr. Arnold Frank reported he lives at 196 Simpson Street.

Questions 7-9.

DIRECTIONS: Questions 7 through 9 are to be answered SOLELY on the basis of the following passage.

Communications Operator Harris receives a call from Mrs. Stein who reports that a car accident occurred in front of her home. She states that one of the cars belongs to her neighbor, Mrs. Brown, and the other car belongs to Mrs. Stein's son, Joseph Stein. Communications Operator Harris enters Mrs. Stein's address into the computer and receives information that no such address exists. She asks Mrs. Stein to repeat her address. Mrs. Stein repeats her address and states that gasoline is leaking from the cars and that smoke is coming from their engines. She further states that people are trapped in the cars and then hangs up.

Communications Operator Harris notifies her supervisor, Jones, that she received a call but was unable to verify the address and that the caller hung up. Mrs. Jones listens to the tape of the call and finds that the caller stated 450 Park Place not 415 Park Place. She advises Communications Operator Harris to enter the correct address, then notify Emergency Service Unit to respond to the individuals trapped in the cars, the Fire Department for the smoke condition, and Emergency Medical Service for any possible injuries.

7. Who did Communications Operator Harris notify concerning the problem with the caller's address?

   A. Mrs. Brown
   B. Joseph Stein
   C. Joseph Brown
   D. Mrs. Jones

8. Which agency was Communications Operator Harris advised to notify concerning individuals trapped in the cars?

   A. Emergency Medical Service
   B. Fire Department
   C. Emergency Service Unit
   D. NYC Police Department

9. Which agency did Supervisor Jones advise Communications Operator Harris to notify for the smoke condition?

   A. NYC Police Department
   B. Emergency Medical Service
   C. Fire Department
   D. Emergency Service Unit

Question 10.

DIRECTIONS: Question 10 is to be answered SOLELY on the basis of the following information.

When a Police Communications Technician receives a call concerning a bank robbery, a Communications Technician should do the following in the order given:

   I. Get address and name of the bank from the caller.
   II. Enter the address into the computer.
   III. Use the *Hotline* button to alert the dispatcher of the serious incident going into the computer.
   IV. Get back to the caller and get the description of the suspect and other pertinent information.
   V. Enter additional information into the computer and send it to the dispatcher.
   VI. Upgrade the seriousness of the incident so it appears first on dispatcher's screen.
   VII. Notify the Supervising Police Communications Technician of the bank robbery.

10. Police Communications Technician Brent receives a call from Mr. Ross stating that while he was on line at the Trust Bank, at West 34th Street and 9th Avenue, he witnessed a bank robbery. Communications Technician Brent enters the address into the computer, then presses the *Hotline* button and alerts the dispatcher that there was a bank robbery at the Trust Bank on West 34th Street and 9th Avenue. Mr. Ross continues to state that the robber is a white male in his 30's wearing a light blue shirt and blue jeans.
After obtaining other pertinent information, the NEXT step Communications Technician Brent should take is to

   A. enter additional information into the computer and send it to the dispatcher
   B. upgrade the seriousness of the incident so it appears first on the dispatcher's screen
   C. notify his supervisor of the bank robbery
   D. use the *Hotline* button to alert the dispatcher of a serious incident going into the computer

11. Dispatcher Wilson receives a call regarding drugs being sold in the lobby of an apartment building. He obtains the following information:
   Place of Occurrence: 305 Willis Avenue
   Time of Occurrence: 2:00 P.M.
   Witnesses: Roy Rodriguez and Harry Armstrong
   Suspect: Melvin Talbot, left the scene before the police arrived
   Crime: Drug sale
   Dispatcher Wilson is about to enter this incident into the computer.
   Which one of the following expresses the above information MOST clearly and accurately?

   A. Roy Rodriguez and Harry Armstrong reported that they witnessed Melvin Talbot selling drugs in the lobby of 305 Willis Avenue at 2:00 P.M. The suspect left the scene before the police arrived.
   B. In the lobby, Roy Rodriguez reported at 2:00 P.M. he saw Melvin Talbot selling drugs with Harry Armstrong. He left the lobby of 305 Willis Avenue before the police arrived.
   C. Roy Rodriguez and Harry Armstrong witnessed drugs being sold at 305 Willis Avenue. Before the police arrived at 2:00 P.M., Melvin Talbot left the lobby.
   D. Before the police arrived, witnesses stated that Melvin Talbot was selling drugs. At 305 Willis Avenue, in the lobby, Roy Rodriguez and Harry Armstrong said he left the scene at 2:00 P.M.

12. Operator Rogers receives a call of a car being stolen. He obtains the following information:
   Place of Occurrence: Parking lot at 1723 East 20th Street
   Time of Occurrence: 2:30 A.M.
   Vehicle Involved: 1988 Toyota Corolla
   Suspects: Male, Hispanic, wearing a red T-shirt
   Crime: Auto theft
   Witness: Janet Alonzo
   Operator Rogers is entering the information into the computer.
   Which one of the following expresses the above information MOST clearly and accurately?

A. At 2:30 A.M., wearing a red T-shirt, Janet Alonzo witnessed a 1988 Toyota Corolla being stolen by a male Hispanic in the parking lot at 1723 East 20th Street.
B. A male Hispanic, wearing a red T-shirt, was in the parking lot at 1723 East 20th Street." At 2:30 A.M., Janet Alonzo witnessed a 1988 Toyota Corolla being stolen.
C. At 2:30 A.M., Janet Alonzo witnessed a 1988 Toyota Corolla in the parking lot at 1723 East 20th Street being stolen by a male Hispanic who is wearing a red T-shirt.
D. Janet Alonzo witnessed a 1988 Toyota Corolla in the parking lot being stolen. At 2:30 A.M., a male Hispanic was wearing a red T-shirt at 1723 East 20th Street.

Question 13.

DIRECTIONS: Question 13 is to be answered SOLELY on the basis of the following information.

There are times when Police Communications Technicians have to reassign officers in a patrol car from a less serious incident which does not require immediate police response to an incident of a more serious nature which does require immediate police response. Police Communications Technicians must choose among the assigned patrol cars and determine which one is assigned to the least serious incident, then reassign that one to the situation which requires immediate police response.

Communications Technician Reese is working the 13th Division which covers the 79th Precinct. There are only four patrol cars working in the 79th Precinct. They are assigned as follows:

79A is assigned to a car accident with injuries involving an intoxicated driver.

79B is assigned to a group of teenagers playing loud music in a park.

79C is assigned to a group of teenagers trying to steal liquor in a liquor store, who are possibly armed with guns.

79D is assigned to a suspicious man in a bank, with possible intentions to rob the bank.

13. If Communications Technician Reese receives a call of an incident that requires immediate police response, which patrol car should be reassigned?

A. 79A   B. 79B   C. 79C   D. 79D

Questions 14-16.

DIRECTIONS: Questions 14 through 16 are to be answered SOLELY on the basis of the following information.

On May 12, at 3:35 P.M., Police Communications Technician Connor receives a call from a child caller requesting an ambulance for her mother, whom she cannot wake. The child did not know her address, but gave Communications Technician Connor her apartment number and telephone number. Communications Technician Connor's supervisor, Ms. Bendel, is advised of the situation and consult's Cole's Directory, a listing published by the Bell Telephone Company, to obtain an address when only the telephone number is known. The telephone number is unlisted. Ms. Bendel asks Communications Technician Taylor to call Telco Security to obtain an address from their telephone number listing. Communications Technician Taylor speaks to Ms. Morris of Telco Security and obtains the address. Communications Technician Connor, who is still talking with the child, is given the address by Communications Technician Taylor. She enters the information into the computer system and transfers the caller to the Emergency Medical Service.

14. What information did Communications Technician Connor obtain from the child caller? 14.___

    A. Telephone number and apartment number
    B. Name and address
    C. Address and telephone number
    D. Apartment number and address

15. Communications Technician Taylor obtained the address from 15.___

    A. Communications Technician Connor
    B. Ms. Morris
    C. Supervisor Bendel
    D. the child caller

16. The caller's address was obtained by calling 16.___

    A. Cole's Directory
    B. Telco Security
    C. Emergency Medical Service
    D. The Telephone Company

Question 17.

DIRECTIONS: Question 17 is to be answered SOLELY on the basis of the following information.

The following incidents appear on the Police Communications Technician's computer screen which were called in by three different callers at the same time:

   I. At 3040 Hill Avenue between Worth and Centre Streets, there are two people fighting in the third floor hallway. One of them has a shiny metal object.
   II. In a building located on Hill Avenue between Worth and Centre Streets, a man and a woman are having an argument on the third floor. The woman has a knife in her hand.
   III. In front of Apartment 3C on the third floor, a husband and wife are yelling at each other. The wife is pointing a metal letter opener at her husband. The building is located on the corner of Hill Avenue and Worth Street.

17. A Police Communications Technician may be required to combine into one incident many calls that appear on the computer screen if they seem to be reporting the same incident. Which of the above should a Police Communications Technician combine into one incident? 17.___

    A. I and II
    B. I and III
    C. II and III
    D. I, II, and III

Questions 18-19.

DIRECTIONS: Questions 18 and 19 are to be answered SOLELY on the basis of the following information.

Police Communications Technicians must be able to identify and assign codes to the crimes described in the calls they receive. All crimes are coded by number and by priority. The priority code number indicates the seriousness of the crime. The lower the priority number, the more serious the crime.

Listed below is a chart of several crimes and their definitions. The corresponding crime code and priority code number are given.

CRIME	DEFINITION	CRIME CODE	PRIORITY CODE
Criminal Mischief:	Occurs when a person intentionally damages another person's property	29	6
Harrassment:	Occurs when a person intentionally annoys another person by striking, shoving, or kicking them without causing injury	27	8
Aggravated Harrassment:	Occurs when a person intentionally annoys another person by using any form of communication	28	9
Theft of Service:	Occurs when a person intentionally avoids payment for services given	25	7

18. Communications Technician Rogers received a call from Mrs. Freeman, who stated that her next door neighbor, whom she had an argument with, has thrown a rock through her apartment window.
    Which one of the following is the CORRECT crime code?

    A. 29   B. 28   C. 27   D. 25

19. Communications Technician Tucker received a call from a man who stated that he is a waiter at the Frontier Diner. He states that one of his customers was refusing to pay for his meal.
    Which one of the following is the CORRECT priority code number for this crime?

    A. 6   B. 7   C. 8   D. 9

    Dispatcher Matthews received a call of a bomb threat. He obtained the following information;
    Address of Occurrence: 202 Church Avenue
    Location: 2nd floor men's room
    Time of Call: 12:00 P.M.
    Time of Occurrence: 2:00 P.M.
    Terrorist Organization: People *Against Government*

Caller: Anonymous male member of *People* Against Government
Action Taken: Supervisor Jones notified of the bomb threat

Dispatcher Matthews is about to enter the information into the computer.
Which one of the following expresses the above information MOST clearly and accurately?

- A. An anonymous male called Dispatcher Matthews and told him that a bomb is set to go off at 202 Church Avenue in the 2nd floor men's room at 2:00 P.M. Dispatcher Matthews notified Supervisor Jones that the caller is from *People Against Government* at 12:00 P.M.
- B. Dispatcher Matthews received a call in the 2nd floor men's room of a bomb threat from an anonymous male member of the *People Against Government* terrorist organization. He notified Supervisor Jones at 12:00 P.M. that a bomb is set to go off at 2:00 P.M. at 202 Church Avenue.
- C. Dispatcher Matthews received a call at 202 Church Avenue from the *People Against Government,* a terrorist organization. An anonymous male stated that a bomb is set to go off at 2:00 P.M. in the 2nd floor men's room. At 12:00 P.M., Dispatcher Matthews notified Supervisor Jones of the call.
- D. At 12:00 P.M., Dispatcher Matthews received a call from an anonymous male caller who states that he is from a terrorist organization known as *People Against Government*. He states that a bomb has been placed in the 2nd floor men's room of 202 Church Avenue and is set to go off at 2:00 P.M. Dispatcher Matthews notified Supervisor Jones of the bomb threat.

KEY (CORRECT ANSWERS)

1.	B	11.	A
2.	A	12.	C
3.	C	13.	B
4.	D	14.	A
5.	D	15.	B
6.	A	16.	B
7.	D	17.	D
8.	C	18.	A
9.	C	19.	B
10.	A	20.	D

EXAMINATION SECTION

TEST 1

DIRECTIONS: Each question or incomplete statement is followed by several suggested answers or completions. Select the one that BEST answers the question or completes the statement. *PRINT THE LETTER OF THE CORRECT ANSWER IN THE SPACE AT THE RIGHT.*

Questions 1-6.

DIRECTIONS: Questions 1 through 6 are to be answered SOLELY on the basis of the numbered boxes on the Arrest Report and paragraph below.

ARREST REPORT

1. Arrest Number	2. Precinct of Arrest		3. Date/Time of Arrest	4. Defendant's Name	5. Defendant's Address
6. Defendant's Date of Birth	7. Sex	8. Race	9. Height	10. Weight	11. Location of Arrest	12. Date and Time of Occurrence
13. Location of Occurrence	14. Complaint Number		15. Victim's Name	16. Victim's Address	17. Victim's Date of Birth
18. Precinct of Complaint	19. Arresting Officer's Name		20. Shield Number	21. Assigned Unit Precinct	2. Date of Complaint

On Friday, December 13 at 11:45 P.M., while leaving a store at 235 Spring Street, Grace O'Connell, a white female, 5'2" 130 lbs., was approached by a white male, 5'11", 200 lbs., who demanded her money and jewelry. As the man ran and turned down River Street, Police Officer William James, Shield Number 31724, assigned to the 14th Precinct, gave chase and apprehended him in front of 523 River Street. The prisoner, Gerald Grande, who resides at 17 Water Street, was arrested at 12:05 A.M., was charged with robbery, and taken to the 13th Precinct, where he was assigned Arrest Number 53048. Miss O'Connell, who resides at 275 Spring St., was given Complaint Number 822460.

1. On the basis of the Arrest Report and the above paragraph, the CORRECT entry for Box Number 3 should be
    A. 11:45 P.M., 12/13
    B. 11:45 P.M., 12/14
    C. 12:05 A.M., 12/13
    D. 12:05 A.M., 12/14

1.____

2. On the basis of the Arrest Report and the above paragraph, the CORRECT entry for Box Number 21 should be
    A. 12th Precinct
    B. 14th Precinct
    C. Mounted Unit
    D. 32nd Precinct

2.____

3. On the basis of the Arrest Report and the above paragraph, the CORRECT entry for Box Number 11 should be
   A. 235 Spring St.
   B. 523 River St.
   C. 275 Spring St.
   D. 17 Water St.

3._____

4. On the basis of the Arrest Report and the above paragraph, the CORRECT entry for Box Number 2 should be
   A. 13th Precinct
   B. 14th Precinct
   C. Mounted Unit
   D. 32nd Precinct

4._____

5. On the basis of the Arrest Report and the above paragraph, the CORRECT entry for Box Number 13 should be
   A. 523 River St.
   B. 17 Water St.
   C. 275 Spring St.
   D. 235 Spring St.

5._____

6. On the basis of the Arrest Report and the above paragraph, the CORRECT entry for Box Number 14 should be
   A. 53048   B. 31724   C. 12/13   D. 82460

6._____

Questions 7-10.

DIRECTIONS: Questions 7 through 10 are to be answered SOLELY on the basis of the following information.

You are required to file various documents in file drawers which are labeled according to the following pattern:

DOCUMENTS

MEMOS		LETTERS		REPORTS		INQUIRIES	
File	Subject	File	Subject	File	Subject	File	Subject
84PM1	(A-L)	84PC1	(A-L)	84PR1	(A-L)	84PQ1	(A-L)
84PM2	(M-Z)	84PC2	(M-Z)	84PR2	(M-Z)	84PQ2	(M-Z)

7. A letter dealing with a burglary should be filed in the drawer labeled
   A. 84PM1   B. 84PC1   C. 84PR1   D. 84PQ2

7._____

8. A report on *Statistics* should be found in the drawer labeled
   A. 84PM1   B. 84PC2   C. 84PR2   D. 84PQ2

8._____

9. An inquiry is received about parade permit procedures. It should be filed in the drawer labeled
   A. 84PM2   B. 84PC1   C. 84PR1   D. 84PQ2

9._____

10. A police officer has a question about a robbery report you filed. You should pull this file from the drawer labeled
    A. 84PM1   B. 84PM2   C. 84PR1   D. 84PR2

10._____

Questions 11-18.

DIRECTIONS: Questions 11 through 18 are to be answered SOLELY on the basis of the following information.

Below are listed the code number, name, and area of investigation of six detective units. Each question describes a crime.
For each question, choose the option (A, B, C, or D) which contains the code number for the detective unit responsible for handling that crime.

DETECTIVE UNITS

Unit Code No.	Unit Name	Unit's Area of Investigation
01	Senior Citizens Unit	All robberies of senior citizens 65 years or older
02	Major Case Unit	Any bank robbery; a commercial robbery where value of goods or money stolen is over $25,000
03	Robbery Unit	Any commercial, non-bank robbery where the value of the stolen goods or money is $25,000 or less; robberies of individuals under 65 years of age
04	Fraud and Larceny Unit	Confidence games and pickpockets
05	Special Investigations Unit	Burglaries of premises where the value of goods removed or monies taken is $15,000 or less
06	Burglary Unit	Burglaries of premises where the value of goods removed or monies taken is over $15,000

11. Mrs. Green calls the precinct and reports that her apartment was burglarized while she was on vacation and that precious jewelry and silverware, valued at $27,000, were taken.
    To which unit code number should her complaint be referred?
    A. 05   B. 02   C. 03   D. 06

12. Sylvia Bailey, Manager of the Building and Loan Savings Bank, reports that a man handed one of her tellers a note stating, *This is a robbery*. He had a gun and demanded money. The teller gave the man $500 in small bills, and the man then left.
    To which unit code should the complaint be referred?
    A. 02   B. 06   C. 03   D. 05

13. Mrs. Miniver, a 67-year-old widow, states that she was beaten and robbed by two men in the elevator of her apartment building.
    To which unit code number should the complaint be referred?
    A. 06   B. 01   C. 03   D. 02

14. Mr. Whipple, Manager of T.V.A. Supermarket, reports that during the night someone entered the store and removed merchandise valued at $12,500.
    To which unit code number should the complaint be referred?
    A. 05   B. 03   C. 06   D. 02

15. Mr. Gold, owner of Gold's Jewelry Exchange, reports that two men, armed with shotguns, robbed his store and removed money and jewelry valued at $28,000.
    To which unit code number should the complaint be referred?
    A. 05   B. 03   C. 06   D. 02

16. Mr. Watson, a 62-year-old man, was walking in Central Park when he was approached by a man with a knife and was robbed of $72.
    To which unit code number should the complaint be referred?
    A. 01   B. 06   C. 03   D. 02

17. The Ace Jewelry Manufacturing Company was broken into over the weekend when the building was closed. The owner stated that $35,000 in gold, silver, diamonds, and jewelry were taken.
    To which unit code number should the complaint be referred?
    A. 02   B. 03   C. 06   D. 05

18. Mrs. Vargas, 62, reports that she gave Mr. Greene of the Starlite Realty Corporation $1,000 to locate a new apartment for her family. A week went by, and she never heard from Mr. Greene. She called the Starlite Realty Corporation, and they informed her that Mr. Greene never worked for Starlite Realty Corporation and that they have no record of the $1,000 deposit of Mrs. Vargas.
    To which unit code number should the complaint be referred?
    A. 04   B. 03   C. 01   D. 05

Questions 19-24.

DIRECTIONS: Questions 19 through 24 consist of sentences which contain examples of correct or incorrect English usage. Examine each sentence with reference to grammar, spelling, punctuation, and capitalization. Choose one of the following options that would be BEST for correct English usage:
A. The sentence is correct.
B. There is one mistake.
C. There are two mistakes.
D. There are three mistakes.

19. Mrs. Fitzgerald came to the 59th Precinct to retreive her property which were stolen earlier in the week.

20. The two officer's responded to the call, only to find that the perpatrator and the 20.____
    victim have left the scene.

21. Mr. Coleman called the 61st Precinct to report that, upon arriving at his store, 21.____
    he discovered that there was a large hole in the wall and that three boxes of
    radios were missing

22. The Administrative Leiutenant of the 62nd Precinct held a meeting which was 22.____
    attended by all the civilians, assigned to the Precinct.

23. Three days after the robbery occured the detective apprahended two 23.____
    suspects and recovered the stolen items.

24. The Community Affairs Officer of the 64th Precinct is the liaison between 24.____
    the Precinct and the community; he works closely with various community
    organizations, and elected officials.

Questions 25-32.

DIRECTIONS: Questions 25 through 32 are to be answered on the basis of the following
paragraph, which contains some deliberate errors in spelling and/or grammar
and/or punctuation. Each line of the paragraph is preceded by a number.
There are 9 lines and 9 numbers.

Line No.	Paragraph Line
1	The protection of life and property are, one of
2	the oldest and most important functions of a city.
3	New York city has its own full-time police Agency.
4	The police Department has the power an it shall
5	be there duty to preserve the Public piece,
6	prevent crime detect and arrest offenders, suppress
7	riots, protect the rites of persons and property, etc.
8	The maintainance of sound relations with the community they
9	serve is an important function of law enforcement officers.

25. How many errors are contained in line one? 25.____
    A. One   B. Two   C. Three   D. None

26. How many errors are contained in line two? 26.____
    A. One   B. Two   C. Three   D. None

27. How many errors are contained in line three? 27.____
    A. One   B. Two   C. Three   D. None

28. How many errors are contained in line four? 28.____
    A. One   B. Two   C. Three   D. None

29. How many errors are contained in line five? 29.____
    A. One   B. Two   C. Three   D. None

30. How many errors are contained in line six? 30.____
    A. One   B. Two   C. Three   D. None

31. How many errors are contained in line seven? 31.____
    A. One   B. Two   C. Three   D. None

32. How many errors are contained in line eight? 32.____
    A. One   B. Two   C. Three   D. None

Questions 33-40.

DIRECTIONS: Questions 33 through 40 are to be answered on the basis of the material contained in the INDEX OF CRIME IN CENTRAL CITY, U.S.A. 2011-2020 appearing below. Certain information is various columns is deliberately left blank.
The correct answer (A, B, C, or D) to these questions requires you to make computations that will enable you to fill in the blanks correctly.

INDEX OF CRIME IN CENTRAL CITY, U.S.A., 2011-2020									
	Crime Index Total	Violent Crime[1]	Property Crime[2]	Murder	Forcible Rape	Robbery	Aggravated Assault	Burglary	Larceny Theft	Motor Vehicle Theft
2011	8,717	875		19	51	385	420	2,565	4,347	930
2012	10,252	974	9278	20	55	443	456		5,262	977
2013	11,256	1,026	10,230	20		465	485	3,253	5,977	1,000
2014	11,304	986		18	58	420	490	3,089	6,270	959
2015	10,935	1,009	9,926	19	63	405	522	3,053	5,605	968
2016	11,140	1,061	10,079	19	67	417	558	3,104	5,983	992
2017	12,152	1,178	10,974	23	75	466	614	3,299	6,578	1,097
2018	13,294	1,308	11,986	23	83		654	3,759	7,113	1,114
2019	13,289	1,321	11,968	22	82	574	643	3,740	7,154	1,074
2020	12,856	1,285	11,571	22	77	536	650	3,415	7,108	1,048

33. What was the TOTAL number of Property Crimes in 2011? 33.____
    A. 9,740   B. 10,252   C. 16,559   D. 7,842

34. What was the TOTAL number of Burglaries for 2012? 34.____
    A. 2,062   B. 3,039   C. 3,259   D. 4,001

35. In 2020, the total number of Aggravated Assaults was MOST NEARLY what percent of the total number of Violent Crimes for that year? 35.____
    A. 49.1   B. 46.3   C. 50.6   D. 41.7

36. In 2015, Property Crime was MOST NEARLY what percent of the Crime Index Total? 36.____
    A. 90.8   B. 9.3   C. 10.1   D. 89.9

37. What was the TOTAL number of Property Crimes for 2014? 37._____
    A. 10,318   B. 11,304   C. 98   D. 10,808

38. What was the TOTAL number of Robberies for 2018? 38._____
    A. 654   B. 571   C. 548   D. 1,202

39. Robbery made up what percent of the TOTAL number of Violent Crimes for 2020? 39._____
    A. 68.8%   B. 4.1%   C. 21.9%   D. 41.7%

40. What was the TOTAL number of Forcible Rapes for 2013? 40._____
    A. 47   B. 56   C. 55   D. 101

KEY (CORRECT ANSWERS)

1.	D	11.	D	21.	A	31.	A
2.	B	12.	A	22.	C	32.	A
3.	B	13.	B	23.	C	33.	D
4.	A	14.	A	24.	B	34.	B
5.	D	15.	D	25.	C	35.	C
6.	D	16.	C	26.	D	36.	A
7.	B	17.	C	27.	C	37.	A
8.	C	18.	A	28.	B	38.	C
9.	D	19.	C	29.	C	39.	D
10.	D	20.	D	30.	B	40.	B

TEST 2

DIRECTIONS: Each question or incomplete statement is followed by several suggested answers or completions. Select the one that BEST answers the question or completes the statement. *PRINT THE LETTER OF THE CORRECT ANSWER IN THE SPACE AT THE RIGHT.*

Questions 1-8.

DIRECTIONS: Each of Questions 1 through 8 consists of three lines of code letters and numbers. The numbers on each line should correspond to the code letters on the same line in accordance with the table below.

Code Letter	X	B	L	T	V	M	P	F	J	S
Corresponding Number	0	1	2	3	4	5	6	7	8	9

On some of the lines, an error exists in the coding. Compare the letters and numbers in each question carefully. If you find an error or errors on:
Only <u>one</u> of the lines in the question, mark your answer A;
Any <u>two</u> of the lines in the question, mark your answer B;
All <u>three</u> lines in the question, mark your answer C;
<u>None</u> of the lines in the question, mark your answer D.

SAMPLE QUESTION: MSXVLPT—5904263
SBFJLTP—9178246
XVMBTPF—8451367

In the above sample, the first line is correct since each code letter listed has the correct corresponding number. On the second line, an error exists because code letter T should have number 3 instead of number 4. On the third line, an error exists because the code letter X should have the number 0 instead of the number 8. Since there are errors on two of the three lines, the correct answer is B.

1. VFSTPLM—4793625
   SBXFLTP—9017236
   BT[JFSV—1358794   1.____

2. TSLFVPJ—3927468
   JLFTVXS—8273409
   MVSXBFL—5490172   2.____

3. XFTJSVT—0739843
   VFMTFLB—4753721
   LTFJSFM—2378985   3.____

4. SJMSJVL—9859742
   VFBXMPF—3710568
   PFPXLBS—7670219   4.____

5. MFPXVFP—5764076   5.____
    PTFJBLX—6378120
    VXSVSTB—4094931

6. BXFPVJT—1076483   6.____
    STFMVLT—9375423
    TXPBTTM—3061335

7. VLSBLVP—4290246   7.____
    FPSFBMV—7679154
    XTMXMLL—0730522

8. JFVPMTJ—8746538   8.____
    TFPMXBL—3765012
    TJSFMFX—4987570

Questions 9-18.

DIRECTIONS: Questions 9 through 18 each consists of two columns, each containing four lines of names, numbers and/or addresses. For each question, compare the lines in Column I with the lines in Column II to see if they match exactly, and mark your answer (A, B, C, or D) according to the following instructions:
- A. all four lines match exactly
- B. only three lines match exactly
- C. only two lines match exactly
- D. only one line matches exactly

9. (1) Earl Hodgson   Earl Hodgson   9.____
    (2) 1409870   1408970
    (3) Shore Ave.   Schore Ave.
    (4) Macon Rd.   Macon Rd.

10. (1) 9671485   9671485   10.____
    (2) 470 Astor Court   470 Astor Court
    (3) Halprin, Phillip   Halperin, Phillip
    (4) Frank D. Poliseo   Frank D. Poliseo

11. (1) Tandem Associates   Tandom Associates   11.____
    (2) 144-17 Northern Blvd. 144-17 Northern Blvd.
    (3) Alberta Forchi   Albert Forchi
    (4) Kings Park, NY 10751   Kings Point, NY 10751

12. (1) Bertha C. McCormack   Bertha C. McCormack   12.____
    (2) Clayton, MO   Clayton, MO
    (3) 976-4242   976-4242
    (4) New City, NY 10951   New City, NY 10951

13. (1) George C. Morill   George C. Morrill   13.____
    (2) Columbia, SC 29201   Columbia, SD 29201
    (3) Louis Ingham   Louis Ingham
    (4) 3406 Forest Ave.   3406 Forest Ave.

14. (1) 506 S. Elliott Pl.   506 S. Elliott Pl.   14.____
    (2) Herbert Hall   Hurbert Hall
    (3) 4712 Rockaway Pkway   4712 Rockaway Pkway
    (4) 169 E. 7 St.   169 E. 7 St.

15. (1) 345 Park Ave.   345 Park Pl.   15.____
    (2) Colman Oven Corp.   Coleman Oven Corp.
    (3) Robert Conte   Robert Conti
    (4) 6179846   6179846

16. (1) Grigori Schierber   Grigori Schierber   16.____
    (2) Des Moines, Iowa   Des Moines, Iowa
    (3) Gouverneur Hospital   Gouverneur Hospital
    (4) 91-35 Cresskill Pl.   91-35 Cresskill Pl.

17. (1) Jeffery Janssen   Jeffrey Janssen   17.____
    (2) 8041071   8041071
    (3) 40 Rockefeller Plaza 40 Rockafeller Plaza
    (4) 407 6 St.   406 7 St.

18. (1) 5971996   5871996   18.____
    (2) 3113 Knickerbocker Ave. 3113 Knickerbocker Ave.
    (3) 8434 Boston Post Rd. 8424 Boston Post Rd.
    (4) Penn Station   Penn Station

Questions 19-22.

DIRECTIONS: Questions 19 through 22 are to be answered by looking at the 4 groups of names and addresses listed below (I, II, III, and IV) and then finding out the number of groups that have their corresponding numbered lines exactly the same.

Group I
Line 1 Ingersoll Public Library
Line 2 Reference and Research Dept.
Line 3 95-12 238 St.
Line 4 East Elmhurst, N.Y. 11357

Group II
Ingersoil Public Library
Reference and Research Dept.
95-12 238 St.
East Elmhurst, N.Y. 11357

Group III
Line 1 Ingersoll Public Library
Line 2 Reference and Research Dept.
Line 3 92-15 283 St.
Line 4 East Elmhurst, N.Y. 11357

Group IV
Ingersoll Poblic Library
Referance and Research Dept.
95-12 283 St.
East Elmhurst, N.Y. 1357

19. In how many groups is line one exactly the same?   19._____
    A. Two   B. Three   C. Four   D. None

20. In how many groups is line two exactly the same?   20._____
    A. Two   B. Three   C. Four   D. None

21. In how many groups is line three exactly the same?   20._____
    A. Two   B. Three   C. Four   D. None

22. In how many groups is line four exactly the same?   22._____
    A. Two   B. Three   C. Four   E. None

Questions 23-26.

DIRECTIONS: Questions 23 through 26 are to be answered by looking at the 4 groups of names and addresses listed below (I, II, III, and IV) and then finding out the number of groups that have their corresponding numbered lines exactly the same.

Group I
Line 1 Richmond General Hospital
Line 2 Geriatric Clinic
Line 3 3975 Paerdegat St.
Line 4 Loudonville, New York 11538

Group II
Richman General Hospital
Geriatric Clinic
3975 Peardegat St.
Londonville, New York 11538

Group III
Line 1 Richmond General Hospital
Line 2 Geriatric Clinic
Line 3 3795 Paerdegat St.
Line 4 Loudonville, New York 11358

Group IV
Richmend General Hospital
Geriatric Clinic
3975 Paerdegat St.
Loudonville, New York 11538

23. In how many groups is line one exactly the same?   23._____
    A. Two   B. Three   C. Four   D. None

24. In how many groups is line two exactly the same?   24._____
    A. Two   B. Three   C. Four   D. None

25. In how many groups is line three exactly the same?   25._____
    A. Two   B. Three   C. Four   D. None

26. In how many groups is line four exactly the same?   26._____
    A. Two   B. Three   C. Four   D. None

Questions 27-34.

DIRECTIONS: Each of Questions 27 through 34 consists of four or six numbered names. For each question, choose the option (A, B, C, or D) which indicates the order in which the names should be filed in accordance with the following file instructions:

5 (#2)

- File alphabetically according to last name, then first name, then middle initial.
- File according to each successive letter within a name.
- When comparing two names where the letters in the longer name are identical with the corresponding letters in the shorter name, the shorter name is filed first.
- When the last names are the same, initials are always filed before names beginning with the same letter.

27. I. Ralph Robinson
     II. Alfred Ross
     III. Luis Robles
     IV. James Roberts
     The CORRECT filing sequence for the above names should be
        A. IV, II, I, III   B. I, IV, III, II   C. III, IV, I, II   D. IV, I, III, II

27.____

28. I. Irwin Goodwin
     II. Inez Gonzalez
     III. Irene Goodman
     IV. Ira S. Goodwin
     V. Ruth I. Goldstein
     VI. M.B. Goodman
     The CORRECT filing sequence for the above names should be
        A. V, II, I, IV, III, VI   B. V, II, VI, III, IV, I
        C. V, II, III, VI, IV, I   D. V, II, III, VI, I, IV

28.____

29. I. George Allan
     II. Gregory Allen
     III. Gary Allen
     IV. George Allen
     The CORRECT filing sequence for the above names should be
        A. IV, III, I, II   B. I, IV, II, III   C. III, IV, I, II   D. I, III, IV, II

29.____

30. I. Simon Kauffman
     II. Leo Kauffman
     III. Robert Kaufmann
     IV. Paul Kauffman
     The CORRECT filing sequence for the above names should be
        A. I, IV, II, III   B. II, IV, I, III   C. III, II, IV, I   D. I, II, III, IV

30.____

31. I. Roberta Williams
     II. Robin Wilson
     III. Roberta Wilson
     IV. Robin Williams
     The CORRECT filing sequence for the above names should be
        A. III, II, IV, I   B. I, IV, III, II   C. I, II, III, IV   D. III, I, II, IV

31.____

44

32.
   I. Lawrence Shultz
   II. Albert Schultz
   III. Theodore Schwartz
   IV. Thomas Schwarz
   V. Alvin Schultz
   VI. Leonard Shultz
   The CORRECT filing sequence for the above names should be
   A. II, V, III, IV, I, VI
   B. IV, III, V, I, II, VI
   C. II, V, I, VI, III, IV
   D. I, VI, II, V, III, IV

33.
   I. McArdle
   II. Mayer
   III. Maletz
   IV. McNiff
   V. Meyer
   VI. MacMahon
   The CORRECT filing sequence for the above names should be
   A. I, IV, VI, III, II, V
   B. II, I, IV, VI, III, V
   C. VI, III, II, I, IV, V
   D. VI, III, II, V, I, IV

34.
   I. Jack E. Johnson
   II. R.H. Jackson
   III. Bertha Jackson
   IV. J.T. Johnson
   V. Ann Johns
   VI. John Jacobs
   The CORRECT filing sequence for the above names should be
   A. II, III, VI, V, IV, I
   B. III, II, VI, V, IV, I
   C. VI, II, III, I, V, IV
   D. III, II, VI, IV, V, I

Questions 35-40.

DIRECTIONS: Questions 35 through 40 are to be answered SOLELY on the basis of the following passage.

An aide assigned to the Complaint Room must be familiar with the various forms used by that office. Some of these forms and their uses are:

Complaint Report:	Used to record information on or information about crimes reported to the Police Department.
Complaint Report Follow-Up:	Used to record additional information after the initial complaint report has been filed
Aided Card:	Used to record information pertaining to sick and injured persons aided by the police.
Accident Report:	Used to record information on or information about injuries and/or property damage involving motorized vehicles.
Property Vouch:	Used to record information on or information about property which comes into possession of the Police Department. (Motorized vehicles are not included.)

Auto Voucher: Used to record information on or information about a motorized vehicle which comes into possession of the Police Department.

35. Mr. Brown walks into the police precinct and informs the Administrative Aide that, while he was at work, someone broke into his apartment and removed property belonging to him. He does not know everything that was taken, but he wants to make a report now and will make a list of what was taken and bring it in later.
According to the above passage, the CORRECT form to use in this situation should be the
   A. Property Voucher   B. Complaint Report
   C. Complaint Report Follow-Up   D. Aided Card

36. Mrs. Wilson telephones the precinct and informs the Administrative Aide she wishes to report additional property which was taken from her apartment. The Administrative Aide finds a Complaint Report had been previously filed for Mrs. Wilson.
According to the above passage, the CORRECT form to use in this situation should be the
   A. Property Voucher   B. Complaint Report
   C. Complaint Report Follow-Up   D. Aided Card

37. Police Officer Jones walks into the Complaint Room and informs the Administrative Aide that, while he was on patrol, he observed a woman fall to the sidewalk and remain there, apparently hurt. He comforted the injured woman and called for an ambulance, which came and brought the woman to the hospital.
According to the above passage, the CORRECT form on which to record this information should be the
   A. Accident Report   B. Complaint Report
   C. Complaint Report Follow-Up   D. Aided Card

38. Police Officer Smith informed the Administrative Aide assigned to the Complaint Room that Mr. Green, while crossing the street, was struck by a motorcycle and had to be taken to the hospital.
According to the above passage, the facts regarding this incident should be recorded on which one of the following forms?
   A. Accident Report   B. Complaint Report
   C. Complaint Report Follow-Up   D. Aided Card

39. Police Officer Williams reports to the Administrative Aide assigned to the Complaint Room that he and his partner, Police Officer Murphy, found an auto which was reported stolen and had the auto towed into the police garage.
Of the following forms listed in the above passage, which is the CORRECT one to use to record this information?
   A. Property Voucher   B. Auto Voucher
   C. Complaint Report Follow-Up   D. Complaint Report

40. Administrative Aide Lopez has been assigned to the Complaint Room. During her tour of duty, a person who does not identify herself hands Ms. Lopez a purse. The person states that she found the purse on the street. She then leaves the station house.
   According to the information in the above passage, which is the CORRECT form to fill out to record the incident?
   A. Property Voucher
   B. Auto Voucher
   C. Complaint Report Follow-Up
   D. Complaint Report

40.____

KEY (CORRECT ANSWERS)

1.	B	11.	D	21.	A	31.	B
2.	D	12.	A	22.	C	32.	A
3.	B	13.	C	23.	A	33.	C
4.	C	14.	B	24.	C	34.	B
5.	A	15.	D	25.	A	35.	B
6.	D	16.	A	26.	A	36.	C
7.	C	17.	D	27.	D	37.	D
8.	A	18.	C	28.	C	38.	A
9.	C	19.	A	29.	D	39.	B
10.	B	20.	B	30.	B	40.	A

EXAMINATION SECTION
TEST 1

DIRECTIONS: Each question or incomplete statement is followed by several suggested answers or completions. Select the one that BEST answers the question or completes the statement. *PRINT THE LETTER OF THE CORRECT ANSWER IN THE SPACE AT THE RIGHT.*

1. You are operating the switchboard and you receive an outside call for an extension line which is busy.
   The one of the following which you should do FIRST is to
   A. ask the caller to try again later
   B. ask the caller to wait and inform him every thirty seconds about the status of the extension line
   C. tell the caller the line is busy and ask him if he wishes to wait
   D. tell the caller the line is busy and that you will connect him as soon as possible

   1.____

2. A person comes to your work area. He makes comments which make no sense, gives foolish opinions, and tells you that he has enemies who are after him. He appears to be mentally ill.
   Of the following, the FIRST action to take is to
   A. humor him by agreeing and sympathize with him
   B. try to reason with him and point out that his fears or opinions are unfounded
   C. have him arrested immediately
   D. tell him to leave at once

   2.____

3. You are speaking with someone on the telephone who asks you a question which you cannot answer. You estimate that you can probably obtain the requested information in about five minutes.
   Of the following, the MOST appropriate course of action would be to tell the caller that
   A. the information will take a short while to obtain, and then ask her for her name and number so that you can call her back when you have the information
   B. the information is available now, but she should call back later
   C. you do not know the answer and refer her to another division you think might be of service
   D. she is being placed on *hold* and that you will be with her in about five minutes

   3.____

4. A person with a very heavy foreign accent comes to your work area and starts talking to you. He is very excited and is speaking too rapidly for you to understand what he is saying.
   Of the following, the FIRST action for you to take is to

   4.____

49

A. refer the person to your supervisor
B. continue your work and ignore the person in the hope that he will be discouraged and leave the building
C. ask or motion to the person to speak more slowly and have him repeat what he is trying to communicate
D. assume that the person is making a complaint, tell him that his problem will be taken care of, and then go back to your work

5. Assume that you are responsible for handling supplies. You notice that you are running low on a particular type of manila file folder exceptionally fast. You believe that someone in the precinct is taking the folders for other than official use.
In this situation, the one of the following that you should do FIRST is to
A. put up a notice stating that supplies have been disappearing and ask for the staff's cooperation in eliminating the problem
B. speak to your supervisor about the matter and let him decide on a course of action
C. watch the supply cabinet to determine who is taking the folders
D. ignore the situation and put in a requisition for additional folders

6. One afternoon, several of the officers ask you to perform different tasks. Each task requires a half day of work. Each officer tells you that his assignment must be finished by 4 P.M. the next day.
Of the following, the BEST way to handle this situation is to
A. do the assignments as quickly as you can, in the order in which the officers handed them to you
B. do some work on each assignment in the order of the ranks of the assigning officers and hand in as much as you are able to finish
C. speak to your immediate supervisor in order to determine the priority of assignments
D. accept all four assignments but explain to the last officer that you may not be able to finish his job

7. Every morning, several officers congregate around your work station during their breaks. You find their conversations very distracting.
The one of the following which you should do FIRST is to
A. ask them to cooperate with you by taking their breaks somewhere else
B. concentrate as best you can because their breaks do not last very long
C. reschedule your break to coincide with theirs
D. tell your supervisor that the officers are very uncooperative

8. One evening when you are very busy, you answer the phone and find that you are speaking with one of the neighborhood cranks, an elderly man who constantly complains that his neighbors are noisy.
In this situation, the MOST appropriate action for you to take is to
A. hang up and go on with your work
B. note the complaint and process it in the usual way
C. tell the man that his complaint will be investigated and then forget about it
D. tell the man that you are very buy and ask him to call back later

9. One morning you answer a telephone call for Lieutenant Jones, who is busy on another line. You inform the caller that Lieutenant Jones is on another line and this party says he will hold. After two minutes, Lieutenant Jones is still speaking on the first call.
Of the following, the FIRST thing for you to do is to
   A. ask the second caller whether it is an emergency
   B. signal Lieutenant Jones to let him know there is another call waiting for him
   C. request that the second caller try again later
   D. inform the second caller that Lieutenant Jones' line is still busy

10. The files in your office have been overcrowded and difficult to work with since you started working there. One day your supervisor is transferred and another aide in your office decides to discard three drawers of the oldest materials.
For him to take this action is
   A. *desirable*; it will facilitate handling the more active materials
   B. *undesirable*; no file should be removed from its point of origin
   C. *desirable*; there is no need to burden a new supervisor with unnecessary information
   D. *undesirable*; no file should be discarded without first noting what material has been discarded

11. You have been criticized by the lieutenant-in-charge because of spelling errors in some of your typing. You have only copied the reports as written, and you realize that the errors occurred in work given to you by Sergeant X.
Of the following, the BEST way for you to handle this situation is to
   A. tell the lieutenant that the spelling errors are Sergeant X's, not yours, because they occur only when you type his reports
   B. tell the lieutenant that you only type the reports as given to you, without implicating anyone
   C. inform Sergeant X that you have been unjustly criticized because of his spelling errors and politely request that he be more careful in the future
   D. use a dictionary whenever you have doubt regarding spelling

12. You have recently found several items misfiled. You believe that this occurred because a new administrative aide in your section has been making mistakes.
The BEST course of action for you to take is to
   A. refile the material and say nothing about it
   B. send your supervisor an anonymous note of complaint about the filing errors
   C. show the errors to the new administrative aide and tell him why they are errors in filing
   D. tell your supervisor that the new administrative aide makes a lot of errors in filing

13. One of your duties is to record information on a standard printed form regarding missing cars. One call you receive concerns a custom-built auto which has apparently been stolen. There seems to be no place on the form for many of the details which the owner gives you.

Of the following, the BEST way for you to obtain an adequate description of this car would be to
- A. complete the form as best you can and attach another sheet containing the additional information the owner gives you
- B. complete the form as best you can and request that the owner submit a photograph of the missing car
- C. scrap the form since it is inadequate in this case and make out a report based on the information the owner gives you
- D. complete the form as best you can and ignore extraneous information that the form does not call for

14. One weekend, you develop a painful infection in one hand. You know that your typing speed will be much slower than normal, and the likelihood of your making mistakes will be increased.
    Of the following, the BEST course of action for you to take in this situation is to
    - A. report to work as scheduled and do your typing assignments as best you can without complaining
    - B. report to work as scheduled and ask your co-workers to divide your typing assignments until your hand heals
    - C. report to work as scheduled and ask your supervisor for non-typing assignments until your hand heals
    - D. call in sick and remain on medical leave until your hand is completely healed so that you can perform your normal duties

15. When filling out a departmental form during an interview concerning a citizen complaint, an administrative aide should know the purpose of each question that he asks the citizen.
    For such information to be supplied by the department is
    - A. *advisable*, because the aide may lose interest in the job if he is not fully informed about the questions he has to ask
    - B. *inadvisable*, because the aide may reveal the true purpose of the questions to the citizens
    - C. *advisable*, because the aide might otherwise record superficial or inadequate answers if he does not fully understand the questions
    - D. *inadvisable*, because the information obtained through the form may be of little importance to the aide

16. Which one of the following is NOT a general accepted rule of telephone etiquette for an administrative aide?
    - A. Answer the telephone as soon as possible after the first ring
    - B. Speak in a louder than normal tone of voice, on the assumption that the caller is hard-of-hearing
    - C. Have a pencil and paper ready at all times with which to make notes and take messages
    - D. Use the tone of your voice to give the caller the impression of cooperativeness and willingness to be of service

5 (#1)

17. The one of the following which is the BEST reason for placing the date and time of receipt of incoming mail is that this procedure
    A. aids the filing of correspondence in alphabetical order
    B. fixes responsibility for promptness in answering correspondence
    C. indicates that the mail has been checked for the presence of a return address
    D. makes it easier to distribute the mail in sequence

17.____

18. Which one of the following is the FIRST step that you should take when filing a document by subject?
    A. Arrange related documents by date with the latest date in front
    B. Check whether the document has been released for filing
    C. Cross-reference the document if necessary
    D. Determine the category under which the document will be filed

18.____

19. The one of the following which is NOT generally employed to keep tract of frequently used material requiring future attention is a
    A. card tickler file   B. dated follow-up folder
    C. periodic transferral of records   D. signal folder

19.____

20. Assume that a newly appointed administrative aide arrives 15 minutes late for the start of his tour of duty. One of his co-workers tells him not to worry because he has signed him in on time. The co-worker assures him that he would be willing to over for him anytime he is late and hopes the aide will do the same for him. The aide agrees to do so.
    This arrangement is
    A. *desirable*; it prevents both men from getting a record for tardiness
    B. *undesirable*; signing in for each other is dishonest
    C. *desirable*; cooperation among co-workers is an important factor in morale
    D. *undesirable*; they will get caught if one is held up in a lengthy delay

20.____

21. An administrative aide takes great pains to help a citizen who approaches him with a problem. The citizen thanks the aide curtly and without enthusiasm. Under these circumstances, it would be MOST courteous for the aide to
    A. tell the citizen he was glad to be of service
    B. ask the citizen to put the compliment into writing and send it to his supervisor
    C. tell the citizen just what pains he took to render this service so that the citizen will be fully aware of his efforts
    D. make no reply and ignore the citizen's remarks

21.____

22. Assume that your supervisor spends a week training you, a newly appointed administrative aide, to sort fingerprint for filing purposes. After doing this type of filing for several day, you get an idea which you believe would improve upon the method in use.
    Of the following, the BEST action for you to take in this situation is to
    A. wait to see whether your idea still look good after you have had more experience
    B. try your idea out before bringing it up with your supervisor

22.____

C. discuss your idea with your supervisor
D. forget about this idea since the fingerprint sorting system was devised by experts

23. Which one of the following is NOT a useful filing practice?
    A. Filing active records in the most accessible parts of the file cabinet
    B. Filling a file drawer to capacity in order to save space
    C. Gluing small documents to standard-size paper before filing
    D. Using different colored tab for various filing categories

24. A citizen comes in to make a complaint to an administrative aide.
    The one of the following action which would be the MOST serious example of discourtesy would be for the aide to
    A. refuse to look up from his desk even though he knows someone is waiting to speak to him
    B. not use the citizen's name when addressing him once his identity has been ascertained
    C. interrupt the citizen's story to ask questions
    D. listen to the complaint and refer the citizen to a special office

25. Suppose that one of your neighbors walks into the precinct where you are an administrative aide and asks you to make 100 copies of a letter on the office duplicating machine for his personal use.
    Of the following, what action should you take FIRST in this situation?
    A. Pretend that you do not know the person and order him to leave the building
    B. Call a police officer and report the person for attempting to make illegal use of police equipment
    C. Tell the person that you will copy the letter but only when you are off-duty
    D. Explain to the person that you cannot use police equipment for non-police work

KEY (CORRECT ANSWERS)

1. C
2. A
3. A
4. C
5. B

6. C
7. A
8. B
9. D
10. D

11. D
12. C
13. A
14. C
15. C

16. B
17. B
18. B
19. C
20. B

21. A
22. C
23. B
24. A
25. D

TEST 2

DIRECTIONS: Each question or incomplete statement is followed by several suggested answers or completions. Select the one that BEST answers the question or completes the statement. *PRINT THE LETTER OF THE CORRECT ANSWER IN THE SPACE AT THE RIGHT.*

Questions 1-6.

DIRECTIONS: Questions 1 through 6 are to be answered on the basis of the information supplied in the chart below.

LAW ENFORCEMENT OFFICERS KILLED
(By Type of Activity)
2012-2021

2012-2016 ☐
2017-2021 ▦

Activity	2012-2016	2017-2021
RESPONDING TO DISTURBANCE CALLS	48	50
BURGLARIES IN PROGRESS OR PURSUING BURGLARY SUSPECT	28	25
ROBBERIES IN PROGRESS OR PURSUING ROBBERY SUSPECT	48	74
ATTEMPTING OTHER ARRESTS	56	112
CIVIL DISORDERS	2	8
HANDLING, TRANSPORTING, CUSTODY OF PRISONERS	12	17
INVESTIGATING SUSPICIOUS PERSONS AND CIRCUMSTANCES	28	29
AMBUSH	13	29
UNPROVOKED MENTALLY DERANGED	5	20
TRAFFIC STOPS	10	19

1. According to the above chart, the percent of the total number of law enforcement officers killed from 2012-2021 in activities related to burglaries and robberies is MOST NEARLY _____ percent.   1._____
    A. 8.4   B. 19.3   C. 27.6   D. 36.2

2. According to the above chart, the two of the following categories which increased from 2012–16 to 2017–21 by the same percent are
   A. ambush and traffic stops
   B. attempting other arrests and ambush
   C. civil disorders and unprovoked mentally deranged
   D. response to disturbance calls and investigating suspicious persons and circumstances

3. According to the above chart, the percentage increase in law enforcement officers killed from the 2012-16 period to the 2017-21 period is MOST NEARLY _____ percent.
   A. 34   B. 53   C. 65   D. 100

4. According to the above chart, in which one of the following activities did the number of law enforcement officers killed increase by 100 percent?
   A. Ambush
   B. Attempting other arrests
   C. Robberies in progress or pursuing robbery suspect
   D. Traffic stops

5. According to the above chart, the two of the following activities during which the total number of law enforcement officers killed from 2012 to 2021 was the same are
   A. burglaries in progress or pursuing burglary suspect and investigating suspicious persons and circumstances
   B. handling, transporting, custody of prisoner and traffic stops
   C. investigating suspicious persons and circumstances and ambush
   D. responding to disturbance calls and robberies in progress or pursuing robbery suspect

6. According to the categories in the above chart, the one of the following statements which can be made about law enforcement officers killed from 2012 to 2016 is that
   A. the number of law enforcement officers killed during civil disorders equals one-sixth of the number killed responding to disturbance calls
   B. the number of law enforcement officers killed during robberies in progress or pursuing robbery suspect equals 25 percent of the number killed while handling or transporting prisoners
   C. the number of law enforcement officers killed during traffic stops equals one-half the number killed for unprovoked reasons or by the mentally deranged
   D. twice as many law enforcement officers were killed attempting other arrests as were killed during burglaries in progress or pursuing burglary suspect

Questions 7-10.

DIRECTIONS: Assume that all arrests fall into two mutually exclusive categories, felonies and misdemeanors. Last week 620 arrests were made in Precinct A, of which 403 were for felonies. Questions 7 through 10 are to be answered on the basis of this information.

7. The percent of all arrests made in Precinct A last week which were for felonies was _____ percent.
   A. 55   B. 60   C. 65   D. 70

8. If 3/5 of all persons arrested for felonies and 1/4 of all persons arrested for misdemeanors were carrying weapons, then the number of arrests involving persons carrying weapons in Precinct A last week was MOST NEARLY
   A. 135   B. 295   C. 415   D. 525

9. If five times as many men as women were arrested for felonies, and half as many women as men were arrested for misdemeanors, then the number of women arrested in Precinct A last week was APPROXIMATELY
   A. 90   B. 120   C. 175   D. 210

10. If the ratio of arrests made on weekends (Friday through Sunday) to arrests made on weekdays (Monday through Thursday) is 2:1, then the number of arrests made in Precinct A last weekend was
    A. 308   B. 340   C. 372   D. 413

11. The police precincts covering the county receive calls at the average rate of two per minute during the 8 A.M. to 4 P.M. tour, but this rate increases by 50 percent during the 4 P.M. to 12 A.M. tour. However, the initial rate decreases by 50 percent during the 12 A.M. to 8 A.M. tour.
    The number of calls received by the precincts covering the county on this basis is one 24-hour day is
    A. 960   B. 1,440   C. 2,880   D. 3,360

12. If an administrative aide is expected to handle 15 calls per hour and Precinct C averages 840 calls during the 4 P.M. to 12 A.M. tour, then the number of aides needed in Precinct C to handle calls during this tour is
    A. 4   B. 5   C. 6   D. 7

13. If in a group of ten administrative aides, four type 40 words per minute, one types 45, two type 50, two type 60, and one types 65, then the average speed in the group is
    A. 49   B. 50   C. 51   D. 52

14. An administrative aide works from midnight to 8 A.M. on a certain day and then is off for 64 hours.
    He is due back at work at
    A. 8 A.M.   B. 12 noon   C. 4 P.M.   D. 12 midnight

4 (#2)

15. If a certain aide take one hour to type 2 accident reports or 6 missing person reports, then the length of time he will require to finish 7 accident reports and 15 missing persons reports is _____ hours _____ minutes.
    A. 6; 0   B. 6; 30   C. 8; 0   D. 8; 40

    15._____

16. If one administrative aide can alphabetize 320 reports per hour and another can do 280 per hour, then the number of reports that both could alphabetize during an 8-hour tour is
    A. 4,800   B. 5,200   C. 5,400   D. 5,700

    16._____

17. If 1,000 candidates applied for administrative aide, and out of those applying 7/8 appear for the written test, and out of those who take the written test 66 2/4 percent pass it, and out of those who pass the written test 85 percent pass the medical exam, then the number of candidates still eligible to become administrative aides will be about
    A. 245   B. 495   C. 585   D. 745

    17._____

18. If the number of murders in the city in 2018 was 415, and the number of murders has increased by 8 percent each year since that year, then in 2021 we would expect the number of murders to be about
    A. 484   B. 523   C. 548   D. 565

    18._____

19. If a person reported missing on April 15 was found murdered on July 4, how many days was he missing? (Include April 15 but NOT July 4 in the total.)
    A. 76   B. 80   C. 82   D. 84

    19._____

20. Suppose that a pile of 96 file cards measures one inch in height and that it takes you ½ hour to file these cards away.
    If you are given three piles of cards which measure 2½ inches high, 1¾ inches high, and $3^3/_8$ inches high, respectfully, the time it would take to file the cards is MOST NEARLY _____ hours and _____ minutes.
    A. 2; 30   B. 3; 50   C. 6; 45   D. 8; 15

    20._____

Questions 21-30.

DIRECTIONS: Questions 21 through 30 test how good you are at catching mistakes in typing or printing. In each question, the name and addresses in Column II should be an exact copy of the name and address in Column I.
Mark your answer:
A. if there is no mistake in either name or address
B. if there is a mistake in both name and address
C. if there is a mistake only in the name
D. if there is a mistake only in the address

COLUMN I   COLUMN II

21. Milos Yanocek   Milos Yanocek   21._____
    33-60 14 Street   33-60 14 Street
    Long Island City, NY 11011   Long Island City, NY 11001

22. Alphonse Sabattelo	Alphonse Sabbattelo	22.____
24 Minnetta Lane	24 Minetta Lane
New York, NY 10006	New York, NY 10006

23. Helen Stearn	Helene Steam	23.____
5 Metroplitan Oval	5 Metropolitan Oval
Bronx, NY 10462	Bronx, NY 10462

24. Jacob Weisman	Jacob Weisman	24.____
231 Francis Lewis Boulevard	231 Francis Lewis Boulevard
Forest Hills, NY 11325	Forest Hill, NY 11325

25. Riccardo Fuente	Riccardo Fuentes	25.____
135 West 83 Street	134 West 88 Street
New York, NY 10024	New York, NY 10024

26. Dennis Lauber	Dennis Lauder	26.____
52 Avenue D	52 Avenue D
Brooklyn, NY 11216	Brooklyn, NY 11216

27. Paul Cutter	Paul Cutter	27.____
195 Galloway Avenue	175 Galloway Avenue
Staten Island, NY 10356	Staten Island, NY 10365

28. Sean Donnelly	Sean Donnelly	28.____
45-58 41 Avenue	45-58 41 Avenue
Woodside, NY 11168	Woodside, NY 11168

29. Clyde Willot	Clyde Willat	29.____
1483 Rockaway Avenue	1483 Rockaway Avenue
Brooklyn, NY 11238	Brooklyn, NY 11238

30. Michael Stanakis	Michael Stanakis	30.____
419 Sheriden Avenue	419 Sheraden Avenue
Staten Island, NY 10363	Staten Island, NY 10363

Questions 31-40.

DIRECTIONS: Questions 31 through 40 are to be answered SOLELY on the basis of the following information.

Column I consists of serial numbers of dollar bills. Column II shows different ways of arranging the corresponding serial numbers.

The serial numbers of dollar bills in Column I begin and end with a capital letter and have an eight-digit number in between. The serial numbers in Column I are to be arranged according to the following rules:

First: In alphabetical order according to the first letter.
Second: When two or more serial numbers have the same first letter, in alphabetical order according to the last letter.
Third: When two or more serial numbers have the same first and last letters, in numerical order, beginning with the lowest number.

The serial numbers in Column I are numbered (1) through (5) in the order in which they are listed. In Column II, the numbers (1) through (5) are arranged in four different ways to show different arrangements of the corresponding serial numbers. Choose the answer in Column II in which the serial numbers are arranged according to the above rules.

SAMPLE QUESTION:

	COLUMN I		COLUMN II
(1)	E75044127B	(A)	4, 1, 3, 2, 5
(2)	B96399104A	(B)	4, 1 2, 3, 5
(3)	B93939086A	(C)	4, 3, 2 5, 1
(4)	B47064465H	(D)	3, 2, 5, 4, 1
(5)	B99040922A		

In the sample question, the four serial numbers starting with B should be put before the serial numbers starting with E. The serial numbers starting with B and ending with A should be put before the serial number starting with B and ending with H. The three serial numbers starting with B and ending with A should be listed in numerical order, beginning with the lowest number. The correct way to arrange the serial numbers, therefore, is

(3) B93939086A
(2) B96399104A
(5) B99040922A
(4) B47064465H
(1) B75044127B

Since the order of arrangement is 3, 2, 5, 4, 1, the answer to the sample question is (D).

		COLUMN I		COLUMN II	
31.	(1)	P44343324Y	A.	2, 3, 1, 4, 5	31.____
	(2)	P44141341S	B.	1, 5, 3, 2, 4	
	(3)	P44141431L	C.	4, 2, 3, 5, 1	
	(4)	P41143413W	D.	5, 3, 2, 4, 1	
	(5)	P44313433H			
32.	(1)	D89077275M	A.	3, 2, 5, 3, 1	32.____
	(2)	D98073724N	B.	1, 4, 3, 2, 5	
	(3)	D90877274N	C.	4, 1, 5, 2, 3	
	(4)	D98877275M	D.	1, 3, 2, 5, 3	
	(5)	D98873725N			

33. (1) H32548137E A. 2, 4, 5, 1, 3   33.____
    (2) H35243178A B. 1, 5, 2, 3, 4
    (3) H35284378F C. 1, 5, 2, 4, 3
    (4) H35288337A D. 2, 1, 5, 3, 4
    (5) H32883173B

34. (1) K24165039H A. 4, 2, 5, 3, 1   34.____
    (2) F24106599A B. 2, 3, 4, 1, 5
    (3) L21406639G C. 4, 2, 5, 1, 3
    (4) C24156093A D. 1, 3, 4, 5, 2
    (5) K24165593D

35. (1) H79110642E A. 2, 1, 3, 5, 4   35.____
    (2) H79101928E B. 2, 1, 4, 5, 3
    (3) A79111567F C. 3, 5, 2, 1, 4
    (4) H79111796E D. 4, 3, 5, 1, 2
    (5) A79111618F

36. (1) P16388385W A. 3, 4, 5, 2, 1   36.____
    (2) R16388335V B. 2, 3, 4, 5, 1
    (3) P16383835W C. 2, 4, 3, 1, 5
    (4) R18386865V D. 3, 1, 5, 2, 4
    (5) P18686865W

37. (1) B42271749G A. 4, 1, 5, 2, 3   37.____
    (2) B42271779G B. 4, 1, 2, 5, 3
    (3) E43217779G C. 1, 2, 4, 5, 3
    (4) B42874119C D. 5, 3, 1, 2, 4
    (5) E42817749G

38. (1) M57906455S A. 4, 1, 5, 3, 2   38.____
    (2) N87077758S B. 3, 4, 1, 5, 2
    (3) N87707757B C. 4, 1, 5, 2, 3
    (4) M57877759B D. 1, 5, 3, 2, 4
    (5) M57906555S

39. (1) C69336894Y A. 2, 5, 3, 1, 4   39.____
    (2) C69336684V B. 3, 2, 5, 1, 4
    (3) C69366887W C. 3, 1, 4, 5, 2
    (4) C69366994Y D. 2, 5, 1, 3, 4
    (5) C69336865V

40. (1) A56247181D A. 1, 5, 3, 2, 4   40.____
    (2) A56272128P B. 3, 1, 5, 2, 4
    (3) H56247128D C. 3, 2, 1, 5, 4
    (4) H56272288P D. 1, 5, 2, 3, 4
    (5) A56247188D

Questions 41-48.

DIRECTIONS: Questions 41 through 48 are to be answered SOLELY on the basis of the following passage.

Auto theft is prevalent and costly. In 2020, 486,000 autos valued at over $500 million were stolen. About 28 percent of the inhabitants of federal prisons are there as a result of conviction of interstate auto theft under the Dyer Act. In California alone, auto thefts cost the criminal justice system approximately $60 million yearly.

The great majority of auto theft is for temporary use rather than resale, as evidenced by the fact that 88 percent of autos stolen in 2020 were recovered. In Los Angeles, 64 percent of stolen autos that were recovered were found within two days and about 80 percent within a week. Chicago reports that 71 percent of the recovered autos were found within four miles of the point of theft. The FBI estimates that 8 percent of stolen cars are taken for the purpose of stripping them for parts, 12 percent for resale, and 5 percent for use in another crime. Auto thefts are primarily juvenile acts. Although only 21 percent of all arrests for nontraffic offenses in 2020 were of individuals under 18 years of age, 63 percent of auto theft arrests were of persons under 18. Auto theft represents the start of many criminal careers; in an FBI sample of juvenile auto theft offenders, 41 percent had no prior arrest record.

41. In the above passage, the discussion of the reasons for auto theft does NOT include the percent of
  A. autos stolen by prior offenders
  B. recovered stolen autos found close to the point of theft
  C. stolen autos recovered within a week
  D. stolen autos which were recovered

42. Assuming the figures in the above passage remain constant, you may logically estimate the cost of auto thefts to the California criminal justice system over a five-year period beginning in 2020 to have been about _____ million.
  A. $200   B. $300   C. $440   D. $500

43. According to the above passage, the percent of stolen autos in Los Angeles which were not recovered within a week was _____ percent.
  A. 12   B. 20   C. 29   D. 36

44. According to the above passage, MOST auto thefts are committed by
  A. former inmates of federal prisons
  B. juveniles
  C. persons with a prior arrest record
  D. residents of large cities

45. According to the above passage, MOST autos are stolen for
  A. resale
  B. stripping of parts
  C. temporary use
  D. use in another crime

46. According to the above passage, the percent of persons arrested for auto theft who were under 18
    A. equals nearly the same percent of stolen autos which were recovered
    B. equals nearly two-thirds of the total number of persons arrested for nontraffic offenses
    C. is the same as the percent of persons arrested for nontraffic offenses who were under 18
    D. is three times the percent of persons arrested for nontraffic offenses who were under 18

46._____

47. An APPROPRIATE title for the above passage is
    A. How Criminal Careers Begin   B. Recovery of Stolen Cars
    C. Some Statistics on Auto Theft   D. The Costs of Auto Theft

47._____

48. Based on the above passage, the number of cars taken for use in another crime in 2020 was
    A. 24,300   B. 38,880   C. 48,600   D. 58,320

48._____

Questions 49-55.

DIRECTIONS: Questions 49 through 55 are to be answered SOLELY on the basis of the following passage.

Burglar alarms are designed to detect intrusion automatically. Robbery alarms enable a victim of a robbery or an attack to signal for help. Such devices can be located in elevators, hallways, homes and apartments, businesses and factories, and subways, as well as on the street in high-crime areas. Alarms could deter some potential criminals from attacking targets so protected. If alarms were prevalent and not visible, then they might serve to suppress crime generally. In addition, of course, the alarms can summon the police when they are needed.

All alarms must perform three functions: sensing or initiation of the signal, transmission of the signal, and annunciation of the alarm. A burglar alarm needs a sensor to detect human presence or activity in an unoccupied enclosed area like a building or a room. A robbery victim would initiate the alarm by closing a foot or wall switch, or by triggering a portable transmitter which would send the alarm signal to a remote receiver. The signal can sound locally as a loud noise to frighten away a criminal, or it can be sent silently by wire to a central agency. A centralized annunciator requires either private lines from each alarmed point, or the transmission of some information on the location of the signal.

49. A conclusion which follows LOGICALLY from the above passage is that
    A. burglar alarms employ sensor devices; robbery alarms make use of initiation devices
    B. robbery alarms signal intrusion without the help of the victim; burglar alarms require the victim to trigger a switch
    C. robbery alarms sound locally; burglar alarms are transmitted to a central agency
    D. the mechanisms for a burglar alarm and a robbery alarm are alike

49._____

50. According to the above passage, alarms can be located
    A. in a wide variety of settings
    B. only in enclosed areas
    C. at low cost in high-crime areas
    D. only in places where potential criminal will be deterred

51. According to the above passage, which of the following is ESSENTIAL if a signal is to be received in a central office?
    A. A foot or wall switch
    B. A noise producing mechanism
    C. A portable reception device
    D. Information regarding the location of the source

52. According to the above passage, an alarm system can function WITHOUT a
    A. centralized annunciating device   B. device to stop the alarm
    C. sensing or initiating device   D. transmission device

53. According to the above passage, the purpose of robbery alarms is to
    A. find out automatically whether a robbery has taken place
    B. lower the crime rate in high-crime areas
    C. make a loud noise to frighten away the criminal
    D. provide a victim with the means to signal for help

54. According to the above passage, alarms might aid in lessening crime if they were
    A. answered promptly by police   B. completely automatic
    C. easily accessible to victims   D. hidden and widespread

55. Of the following, the BEST title for the above passage is
    A. Detection of Crime By Alarms   B. Lowering the Crime Rate
    C. Suppression of Crime   D. The Prevention of Robbery

KEY (CORRECT ANSWERS)

1. C	11. C	21. D	31. D	41. A	51. D
2. C	12. D	22. B	32. B	42. B	52. A
3. B	13. A	23. C	33. A	43. B	53. D
4. B	14. D	24. A	34. C	44. B	54. D
5. B	15. A	25. B	35. C	45. C	55. A
6. D	16. A	26. C	36. D	46. D	
7. C	17. B	27. D	37. B	47. C	
8. B	18. B	28. A	38. A	48. A	
9. C	19. B	29. B	39. A	49. A	
10. D	20. B	30. D	40. D	50. A	

EXAMINATION SECTION
TEST 1

DIRECTIONS: Each question or incomplete statement is followed by several suggested answers or completions. Select the one that BEST answers the question or completes the statement. *PRINT THE LETTER OF THE CORRECT ANSWER IN THE SPACE AT THE RIGHT.*

1. You answer a phone complaint from a person concerning an improper labeling practice in a shop in his neighborhood. Upon listening to the complaint, you get the impression that the person is exaggerating and may be too excited to view the matter clearly.
   Of the following, your BEST course would be to
   A. tell the man that you can understand his anger but think it is not a really serious problem
   B. suggest to the man that he file a complaint with the Department of Consumer Affairs
   C. tell the man to stay away from the shop and have his friends do the same
   D. take down the information that the man offers so that he will see that the Police Department is concerned

2. Suppose that late at night you receive a call on 911. The caller turns out to be an elderly man who is not able to get out much and who is calling you not because he needs help but because he wants to talk with someone.
   The BEST way to handle such a situation is to
   A. explain to him that the number is for emergencies and his call may prevent others from getting the help they need
   B. talk to him if not many calls are coming in but excuse yourself and cut him off if you are busy
   C. cut him off immediately when you find out he does not need help because this will be the most effective way of discouraging him
   D. suggest that he call train or bus information as the clerks there are often not busy at night

3. While you are on duty, you receive a call from a person whose name your recognize to be that of a person who calls frequently about matters of no importance. The caller requests your name and your supervisor's name so that she can report you for being impolite to her.
   You should
   A. ask her when and how you were impolite to her
   B. tell her that she should not call about such minor matters
   C. make a report about her complaint for your superior
   D. give her the information that she requests

4. Of the following, the MOST important reason for requiring each employ of the Police Department to be responsible for good public relations is that
    A. the Police Department has better morale when employees join in an effort to improve public relations
    B. the public judges the Department according to impressions received at every level in the Department
    C. most employees will not behave well toward the public unless required to do so
    D. employees who improve public relations will receive commendations from superiors

5. Assume that you are in the Bureau of Public Relations. You receive a telephone call from a citizen who asks if a study has been made of the advisability of combining the city's police and fire departments. Assume that you have no information on the subject.
    Of the following, your BEST course would be to
    A. tell the caller that undoubtedly the subject has been studied but that you do not have the information available
    B. suggest to the caller that he telephone the Fire Department's Community Relations section for further information
    C. explain to the caller that the functions of the two departments are distinct and that combining them would be inefficient
    D. take the caller's number in order to call back, and then find information or referrals to give him

6. Suppose that Police Department officials have discouraged representatives of the press from contacting police administrative aides (except aides in the Public Relations Bureau) for information.
    Of the following, the BEST reason for such a policy would be to
    A. assure proper control over information released to the press by the Department
    B. increase the value of official press releases of the Department
    C. make press representatives realize that the Department is not seeking publicity
    D. reduce the chance of crimes being committed in imitation of those reported in the press

7. People who phone the Police Department often use excited, emotional, and sometimes angry speech.
    The BEST policy for you to take when speaking to this type of caller is to
    A. tell the person directly that he must speak in a more civil way
    B. tell the caller to call back when he is in a better mood
    C. give the person time to settle down, by doing most of the talking yourself
    D. speak calmly yourself to help the caller to gradually become more relaxed

8. On a particularly busy evening, the police administrative aide assigned to the telephones had answered a tremendous number of inquiries and complaints by irate citizens. His patience was exhausted when he received a call from a citizen who reported, *Officer, a bird just flew into my bedroom. What should I do?* In a release of tension, the aide responded, *Keep it for seven days; and if no one claims it, it is yours.*
This response by the aide would usually be considered
   A. *advisable*, because the person should see how unusual his question was
   B. *advisable*, because he avoided offering police services that were unavailable
   C. *not advisable*, because such a remark might be regarded as insulting rather than humorous
   D. *not advisable*, because the person might not want a bird for a pet

9. While temporarily assigned to switchboard duty, you receive a call from a man who says his uncle in Pittsburgh has just called him and threatened to commit suicide. The man is convinced his uncle intends to carry out his threat.
Of the following, you should
   A. advise the man to have neighbors of the uncle check to see if the uncle is all right
   B. politely inform the man that such out-of-town incidents are beyond the authority of the local precinct
   C. take the uncle's name, address, and telephone number and immediately contact police authorities in Pittsburgh
   D. get the man's name, address, and telephone number so that you can determine whether the call is a hoax

10. Assume that in the course of your assigned duties you have just taken a necessary action which you feel has angered a citizen. After he has gone, you suddenly realize that the incident might result in an unjustified complaint.
The MOST advisable action for you to take now would be to
   A. contact the person and apologize to him
   B. make complete notes on the incident and on any witnesses who might be helpful
   C. ask your superior what you might expect in case of such a complaint, without giving any hint of the actual occurrence
   D. accept the situation as one of the hazards of your job

11. Your job may bring you in contact with people from the community who are confronted with emergencies,, and are experiencing feelings of tension, anxiety, or hostility. It is good to keep in mind what attitude is most helpful to people who, in such situations like these.
Which of the following would be BEST to do?
   A. Present similar examples of your own problems to make the person feel that his problems are not unusual.
   B. Recognize the person's feelings, present information on available services, and make suggestions as to proper procedures

C. Expect that some of the information is exaggerated and encourage the person to let some time pass before seeking further help.
D. Have the person wait while you try to make arrangements for his problem to be solved.

12. Suppose that while on duty you receive a call from the owner of a gas station which is located within the precinct. The owner is annoyed with a certain rule made by the Police Department which concerns the operation of such stations. You agree with him.
Of the following, the BEST action for you to take is to
    A. make a report on the call and suggest to the owner that he write a letter to the Department about the rule
    B. tell the owner that there is little that can be done since such rules are departmental policy
    C. tell the owner that you agree with his complaint and that you will write a memo of his call
    D. establish good relations with the owner by suggesting how to word a letter that will get action from the department

13. Suppose that you are working at the switchboard when a call comes in late at night from a woman who reports that her neighbors are having a very noisy party. She gives you her first name, surname, and address, and you ask her title is *Miss* or *Mrs.* She replies that her title is irrelevant to her complaint, and wants to know why you ask.
Of the following possible ways of handling this, which is BEST?
    A. Insist that the title is necessary for identification purposes
    B. Tell her that it is merely to find out what her marital status is
    C. Agree that the information is not necessary and ask her how she wants to be referred to
    D. Find out why she shows such a peculiar reaction to a request for harmless information

14. While covering an assignment on the switchboard, you receive a call from a young girl who tells you of rumored plans for a gang fight in her neighborhood. You should
    A. take down the information so that a patrol squad can investigate the area and possibly keep the fight from starting
    B. discourage the girl from becoming alarmed by reminding her that it is only a rumor
    C. realize that this is a teenager looking for attention, humor her, and dismiss the matter
    D. take down the information but tell the girl that you need concrete information, and not just rumors, to take any action on her call

15. The one of the following which would MOST likely lead to friction among police administrative aides in a unit would be for the supervisor in charge of the unit to
    A. defend the actions of the aides he supervises when discussing them with his own supervisor

B. get his men to work together as a team in completing the work of the unit
C. praise each of the aides he supervises *in confidence* as the best aide in the unit
D. consider the point of view of the aides he supervises when assigning unpleasant tasks

16. Suppose that a police administrative aide who had been transferred to your office from another unit in your Department because of difficulties with his supervisor has been placed under your supervision.
The BEST course of action for you to take FIRST is to
    A. analyze the aide's past grievance to determine if the transfer was the best settlement of the problem
    B. advise him of the difficulties his former supervisor had with other employees and encourage him not to feel bad about the transfer
    C. warn him that you will not tolerate any nonsense and that he will be watched carefully while assigned to your unit
    D. instruct him in the duties he will be performing in your unit and make him feel *wanted* in his new position

17. In which of the following circumstances would it be MOST appropriate for you to use an impersonal style of writing rather than a personal style, which relies on the use of personal pronouns and other personal references?
When writing a memorandum to
    A. give your opinion to an associate on the advisability of holding a weekly staff meeting
    B. furnish your superior with data justifying a proposed outlay of funds for new equipment
    C. give your version of an incident which resulted in a complaint by a citizen about your behavior
    D. support your request for a transfer to another division

18. A newly appointed supervisor should learn as much as possible about the backgrounds of his subordinates.
The statement is generally CORRECT because
    A. effective handling of subordinates is based upon knowledge of their individual differences
    B. knowing their backgrounds assures they will be treated objectively, equally, and without favor
    C. some subordinates perform more efficiently under one supervisor than under another
    D. subordinates have confidence in a supervisor who knows all about them

19. You have found it necessary, for valid reasons, to criticize the work of one of the female police administrative aides. She later comes to your desk and accuses you of criticizing her work because she is a woman.
The BEST way for you to deal with this employee is to
    A. ask her to apologize, since you would never allow yourself to be guilty of his kind of discrimination

B. discuss her complaint with her, explaining again and at greater length the reason for your criticism
C. assure her you wish to be fair, and ask her to submit a written report to you on her complaint
D. apologize for hurting her feelings and promise that she will be left alone in the future

20. The following steps are recognized steps in teaching an employee a new skill:
    I. Demonstrate how to do the work
    II. Let the learner do the work himself
    III. Explain the nature and purpose of the work
    IV. Correct poor procedures by suggestion and demonstration
    The CORRECT order for these steps is
    A. III, II, IV, I   B. II, I, III, IV   C. III, I, II, IV   D. I, III, II, IV

21. Suppose you have arranged an interview with a subordinate to try to help him overcome a serious shortcoming in his technical work. While you do not intend to talk to him about his attitude, you have noticed that he seems to be suspicious and resentful of people in authority. You need a record of the points covered in the discussion since further interviews are likely to be necessary.
    Your BEST course would be to
    A. write a checklist of points you wish to discuss and carefully check the points off as the interview progresses
    B. know exactly how you wish to proceed, and then make written notes during the interview of your subordinate's comments
    C. frankly tell your subordinate that you are recording the talk on tape but place the recorder where it will not hinder discussion
    D. keep in mind what you wish to accomplish and make notes on the interview immediately after it is over

22. A police administrative aide has explained a complicated procedure to several subordinates. He has been talking clearly, allowing time for information to sink in. He has also encouraged questions. Yet, he still questions his subordinates after his explanation, with the obvious objective of finding out whether they completely understand the procedure.
    Under these circumstances, the action of the police administrative aide, in asking questions about the procedure, is
    A. *not advisable*, because subordinates who do not now know the procedure which has been explained so carefully can read and study it
    B. *not advisable*, because he endangers his relationship with his subordinates by insulting their intelligence
    C. *advisable*, because subordinate basically resent instructions and seldom give their full attention in a group situation
    D. *advisable*, because the answers to his questions help him to determine whether he has gained his objective

23. The most competent of the police administrative aides is a pleasant, intelligent young woman who breaks the rules of the Department by occasionally making long personal telephone calls during working hours. You have not talked to her up until now about this fault. However, the calls are beginning to increase, and you decide to deal directly with the problem.
The BEST way to approach the subject with her would be to
    A. review with her the history of her infractions of the rules
    B. point out that her conduct is not fair to the other workers
    C. tell her that her personal calls are excessive and discuss it with her
    D. warn her quietly that you intend to apply penalties if necessary

24. Assume that you are supervising eight male police administrative aides who do similar clerical work. A group of four of them work on each side of a row of files which can be moved without much trouble. You notice that in each group there is a clique of three aides, leaving one member isolated. The two isolated members are relative newcomers.
Your BEST course in such a case would be to
    A. ignore the situation because to concern yourself with informal social arrangements of your subordinates would distract you from more important matters
    B. ask each of the cliques to invite the isolated member in their working group to lunch with them from time to time
    C. tell each group that you cannot allow cliques to form as it is bad for the morale of the unit
    D. find an excuse to move the file cabinet to the side of the room and then move the desks of the two isolated members close together

25. Suppose that your supervisor, who has recently been promoted and transferred to your division, asks you to review a certain procedure with a view to its possible revision. You know that several years ago a sergeant made a lengthy and intensive report based on a similar review.
Which of the following would it be BEST for you to do FIRST?
    A. Ask your supervisor if he is aware of the previous report
    B. Read the sergeant's report before you begin work to see what bearing it has on your assignment
    C. Begin work on the review without reading his report so that you will have a fresh point of view
    D. Ask the sergeant to assist you in your review

26. Using form letters in business correspondence is LEAST effective when
    A. answering letters on a frequently recurring subject
    B. giving the same information to many addresses
    C. the recipient is only interested in the routing information contained in the form letter
    D. a reply must be keyed to the individual requirements of the intended reader

27. From the viewpoint of an office administrator, the BEST of the following reasons for distributing the incoming mail before the beginning of the regular work day is that
    A. distribution can be handled quickly and most efficiently at that time
    B. distribution later in the day may be distracting to or interfering with other employees
    C. the employees who distribute the mail can then perform other tasks during the rest of the day
    D. office activities for the day based on the mail may then be started promptly

28. Suppose you have had difficulty locating a document in the files because you could not decide where it should have been filed. You learn that other people in the office have had the same problem. You know that the document will be needed from time to time in the future.
    Your BEST course, when refiling the document, would be to
    A. make a written note of where you found it so that you will find it more easily the next time
    B. reclassify it and file it in the file where you first looked for it
    C. file it where you found it and put cross-reference sheets in the other likely files
    D. make a mental association to help you find it the next time and put it back where you found it

29. Suppose that your supervisor is attending a series of meetings of police captains in Philadelphia and will not be back until next Wednesday. He has left no instructions with you as to how you should handle telephone calls for him.
    In most instances, your BEST course of action would be to say:
    A. He isn't here just now.
    B. He is out of town and won't be back until next Wednesday.
    C. He won't be in today.
    D. He is in Philadelphia attending a meeting of police captains.

30. The one of the following which is USUALLY an important by-product of the preparation of a procedure manual is that
    A. information uncovered in the process of preparation may lead to improvement of procedures
    B. workers refer to the manual instead of bothering their supervisors for information
    C. supervisors use the manual for training stenographers
    D. employees have equal access to information needed to do their jobs

31. You have been asked to organize a clerical job and supervise police administrative aides who will do the actual work. The job consists of removing, from several boxes of data processing cards which are arranged in alphabetical order, the cards of those whose names appear on certain lists. The person removing the card then notes a date on the card. Assume that the work will be done accurately whatever system is used.

Which of the following statements describes both the MOST efficient method and the BEST reasons for using that method? Have
- A. two aides work together, one calling names and the other extracting cards, and dating them, because the average production of any two aides working together should be higher, under these circumstances, than that of any two aides working alone
- B. each aide work alone, because it is easier to check spelling when reading the names than when listening to them
- C. two aides work together, one calling names and the other extracting cards and dating them, because social interaction tends to make work go faster
- D. each aide work alone, because the average production of any two aides, each working alone, should be higher, under these circumstances, than that of any two aides working together

32. The term *work flow*, when used in connection with office management or the activities in an office GENERALLY means the 32.____
- A. rate of speed at which work flows through a single section of an office
- B. use of charts in the analysis of various office functions
- C. number of individual work units which can be produced by the average employee
- D. step-by-step physical routing of work through its various procedures

Questions 33-40.

DIRECTIONS: Name of Offense   V A N D S B R U G H
             Code Letter   c o m p l e x i t y
             File Number   1 2 3 4 5 6 7 8 9 0

Assume that each of the above capital letters is the first letter of the name of an offense, that the small letter directly beneath each capita letter is the code letter for the offense, and that the number directly beneath each code letter is the file number for the offense.
In each of Questions 33 through 40, the code letters and file numbers should correspond to the capital letters.
If there is an error only in Column 2, mark your answer A.
If there is an error only in Column 3, mark your answer B.
If there is an error in both Column 2 and Column, mark your answer C.
If both Columns 2 and 3 are correct, mark your answer D.
Sample Questions:

COLUMN 1	COLUMN 2	COLUMN 3
BNARGHSVVU	emoxtylcci	6357905118

The code letters in Column 2 are correct, but the first 5 in Column 3 should be 2. Therefore, the answer is B.

COLUMN 1	COLUMN 2	COLUMN 3

33. HGDSBNBSVR   ytplxmelcx   0945736517   33._____

10 (#1)

34.	SDGUUNHVAH	lptiimycoy	5498830120	34.____
35.	BRSNAAVUDU	exlmooctpi	6753221848	35.____
36.	VSRUDNADUS	cleipmopil	1568432485	36.____
37.	NDSHVRBUAG	mplycxeiot	3450175829	37.____
38.	GHUSNVBRDA	tyilmcexpo	9805316742	38.____
39.	DBSHVURANG	pesycixomt	4650187239	39.____
40.	RHNNASBDGU	xymnolepti	7033256398	40.____

KEY (CORRECT ANSWERS)

1.	B	11.	B	21.	D	31.	D
2.	A	12.	A	22.	D	32.	D
3.	D	13.	C	23.	C	33.	C
4.	B	14.	A	24.	D	34.	D
5.	D	15.	C	25.	A	35.	A
6.	A	16.	D	26.	D	36.	C
7.	D	17.	B	27.	D	37.	B
8.	C	18.	A	28.	C	38.	D
9.	C	19.	B	29.	B	39.	A
10.	B	20.	C	30.	A	40.	C

MAP READING

EXAMINATION SECTION
TEST 1

DIRECTIONS: Each question or incomplete statement is followed by several suggested answers or completions. Select the one that BEST answers the question or completes the statement. *PRINT THE LETTER OF THE CORRECT ANSWER IN THE SPACE AT THE RIGHT.*

Questions 1-3.

DIRECTIONS: Questions 1 through 3 are to be answered SOLELY on the basis of the map which appears on the next page. The flow of traffic is indicated by the arrow. If there is only one arrow shown, then traffic flows only in the direction indicated by the arrow. If there are two arrows shown, then traffic flows in both directions. You must follow the flow of traffic.

2 (#1)

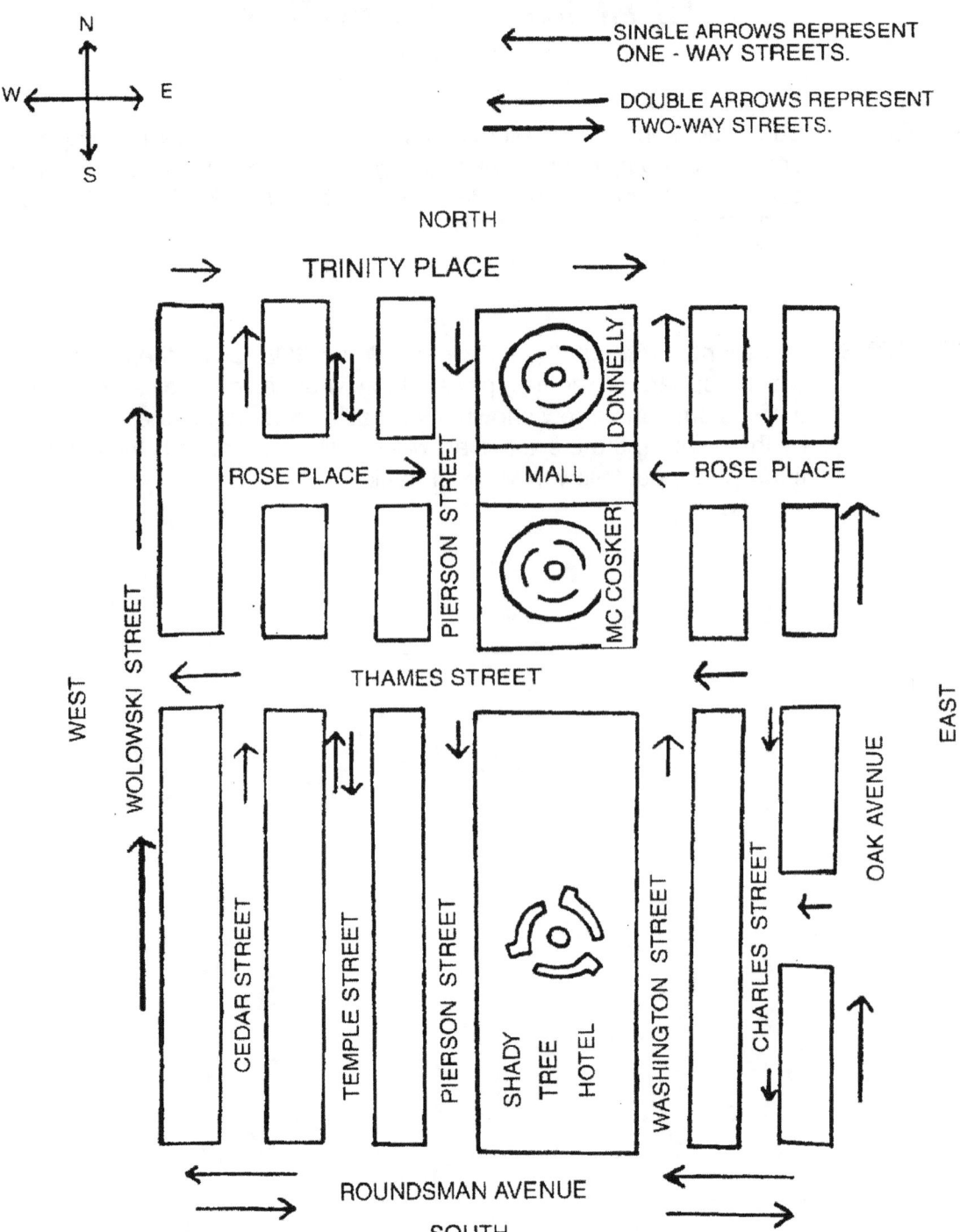

1. Police Officers Simms and O'Brien are located at Roundsman Avenue and Washington Street. The radio dispatcher has assigned them to investigate a motor vehicle accident at the corner of Pierson Street and Rose Place.
   Which one of the following is the SHORTEST route for them to take in their patrol car, making sure to obey all traffic regulations?
   Travel

   A. west on Roundsman Avenue, then north on Temple Street, then east on Thames Street, then north on Pierson Street to Rose Place
   B. east on Roundsman Avenue, then north on Oak Avenue, then west on Rose Place to Pierson Street
   C. west on Roundsman Avenue, then north on Temple Street, then east on Rose Place to Pierson Street
   D. east on Roundsman Avenue, then north on Oak Avenue, then west on Thames Street, then north on Temple Street, then east on Rose Place to Pierson Street

2. Police Officers Sears and Castro are located at Cedar Street and Roundsman Avenue. They are called to respond to the scene of a burglary at Rose Place and Charles Street. Which one of the following is the SHORTEST route for them to take in their patrol car, making sure to obey all traffic regulations?
   Travel

   A. east on Roundsman Avenue, then north on Oak Avenue, then west on Rose Place to Charles Street
   B. east on Roundsman Avenue, then north on Washington Street, then east on Rose Place to Charles Street
   C. west on Roundsman Avenue, then north on Wolowski Street, then east on Trinity Place, then south on Charles Street to Rose Place
   D. east on Roundsman Avenue, then north on Charles Street to Rose Place

3. Police Officer Glasser is in an unmarked car at the intersection of Rose Place and Temple Street when he begins to follow two robbery suspects. The suspects go south for two blocks, then turn left for two blocks, then make another left turn for one more block. The suspects realize they are being followed and make a left turn and travel two more blocks and then make a right turn.
   In what direction are the suspects now headed?

   A. North B. South C. East D. West

Questions 4-6.

DIRECTIONS: Questions 4 through 6 are to be answered SOLELY on the basis of the following map. The flow of traffic is indicated by the arrows. If there is only one arrow shown, then traffic flows only in the direction indicated by the arrow. If there are two arrows shown, then traffic flows in both directions. You must follow the flow of traffic.

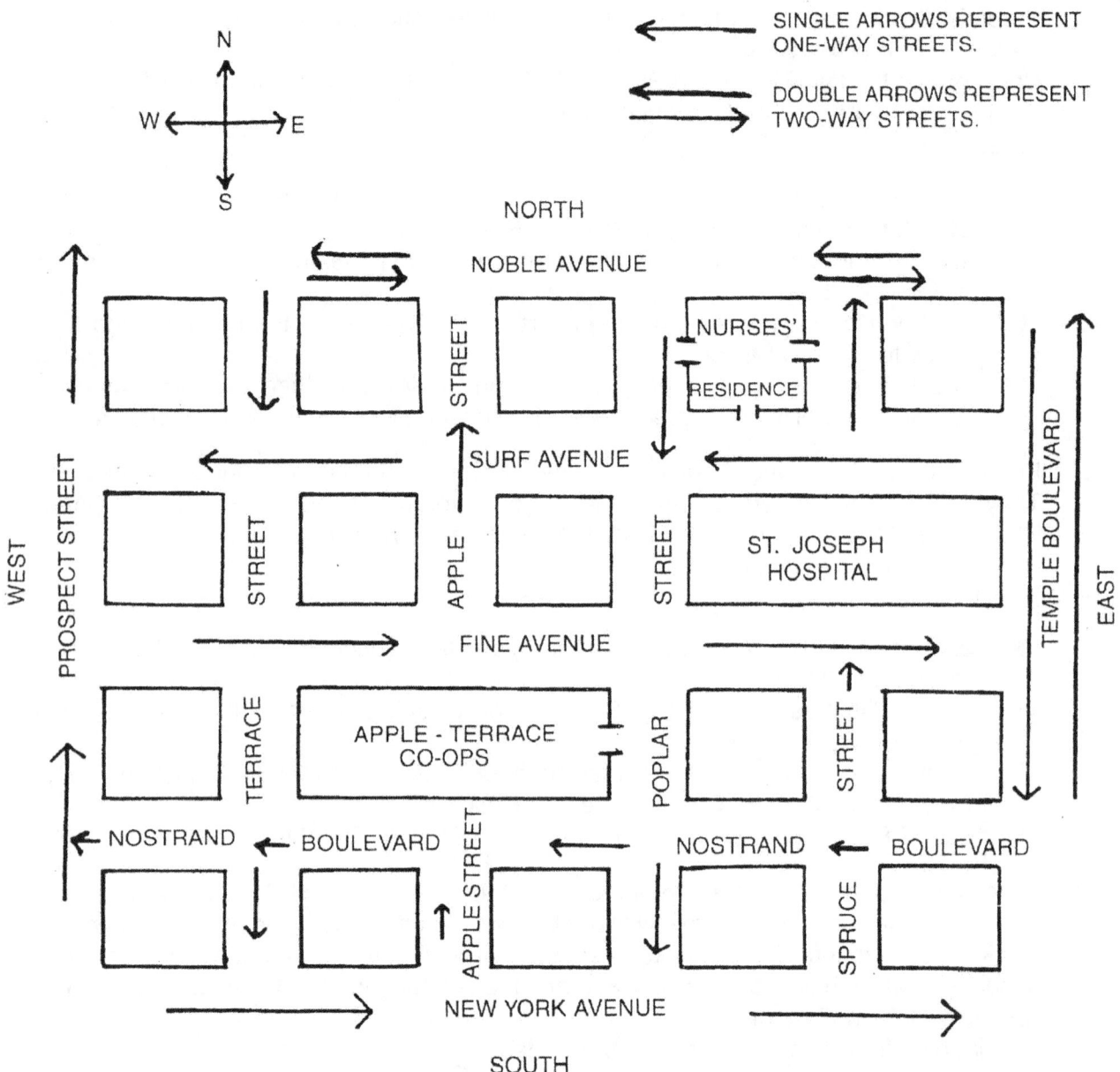

4. Police Officers Gannon and Vine are located at the intersection of Terrace Street and Surf Avenue when they receive a call from the radio dispatcher stating that they need to respond to an attempted murder at Spruce Street and Fine Avenue.
Which one of the following is the SHORTEST route for them to take in their patrol car, making sure to obey all traffic regulations?
Travel _____ to Spruce Street.

- A. west on Surf Avenue, then north on Prospect Street, then east on Noble Avenue, then south on Poplar Street, then east on Fine Avenue
- B. east on Surf Avenue, then south on Poplar Street, then east on Fine Avenue
- C. west on Surf Avenue, then south on Prospect Street, then east on Fine Avenue
- D. south on Terrace Street, then east on Fine Avenue

5. Police Officers Sears and Ronald are at Nostrand Boulevard and Prospect Street. They receive a call assigning them to investigate a disruptive group of youths at Temple Boulevard and Surf Avenue.
   Which one of the following is the SHORTEST route for them to take in their patrol car, making sure to obey all traffic regulations?
   Travel

   A. north on Prospect Street, then east on Surf Avenue to Temple Boulevard
   B. north on Prospect Street, then east on Noble Avenue, then south on Temple Boulevard to Surf Avenue
   C. north on Prospect Street, then east on Fine Avenue, then north on Temple Boulevard to Surf Avenue
   D. south on Prospect Street, then east on New York Avenue, then north on Temple Boulevard to Surf Avenue

6. While on patrol at Prospect Street and New York Avenue, Police Officers Ross and Rock are called to a burglary in progress near the entrance to the Apple-Terrace Co-ops on Poplar Street midway between Fine Avenue and Nostrand Boulevard.
   Which one of the following is the SHORTEST route for them to take in their patrol car, making sure to obey all traffic regulations?
   Travel _____ Poplar Street.

   A. east on New York Avenue, then north
   B. north on Prospect Avenue, then east on Fine Avenue, then south
   C. north on Prospect Street, then east on Surf Avenue, then south
   D. east on New York Avenue, then north on Temple Boulevard, then west on Surf Avenue, then south

Questions 7-8.

DIRECTIONS: Questions 7 and 8 are to be answered SOLELY on the basis of the map which appears below. The flow of traffic is indicated by the arrows. If there is only one arrow shown, then traffic flows only in the direction indicated by the arrow. If there are two arrows shown, then traffic flows in both directions. You must follow the flow of traffic.

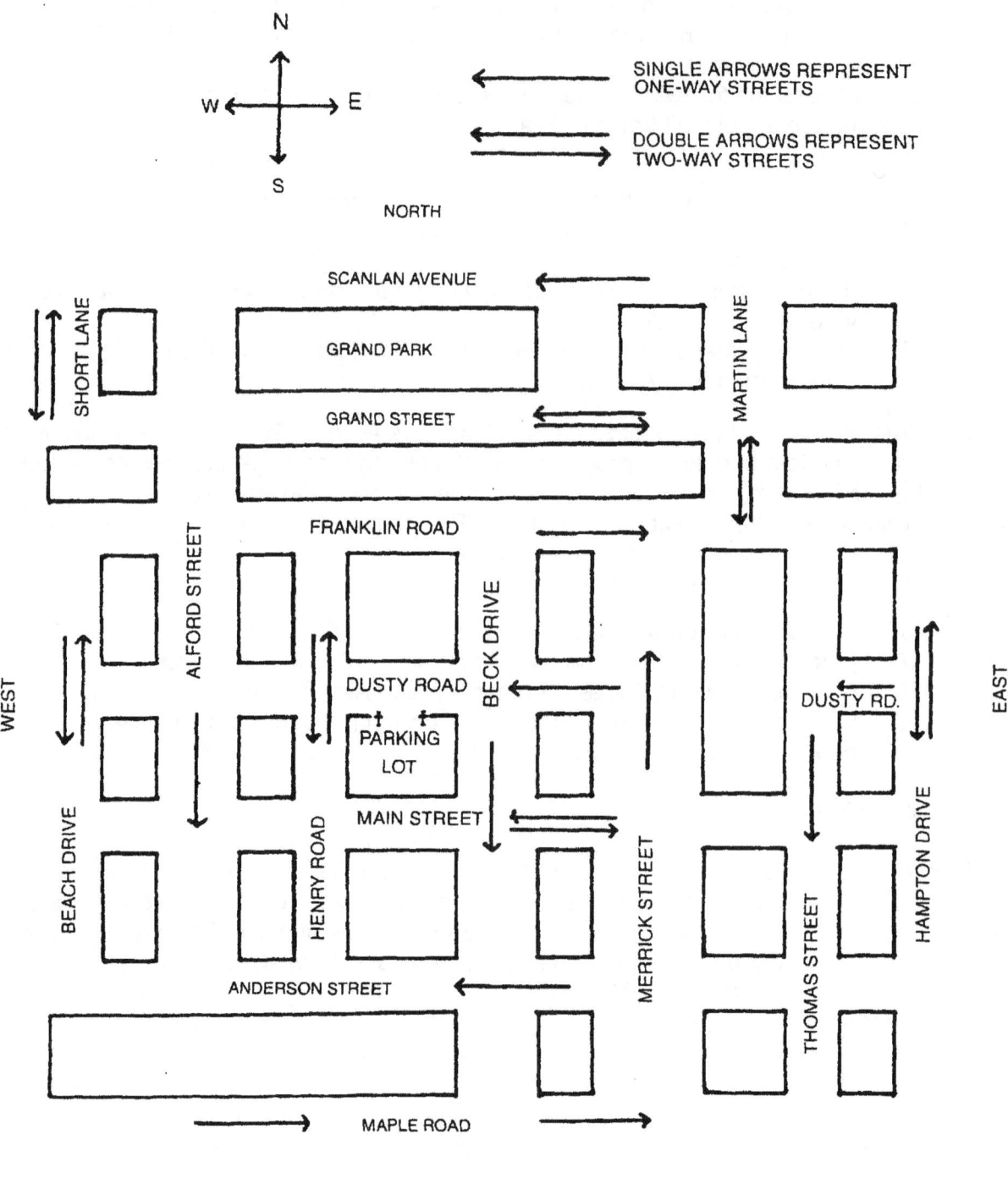

7. Police Officers Gold and Warren are at the intersection of Maple Road and Hampton Drive. The radio dispatcher has assigned them to investigate an attempted auto theft in the parking lot on Dusty Road.
Which one of the following is the SHORTEST route for the officers to take in their patrol car to get to the entrance of the parking lot on Dusty Road, making sure to obey all traffic regulations?
Travel _____ to the parking lot entrance.

7. ___

A. north on Hampton Drive, then west on Dusty Road
B. west on Maple Road, then north on Beck Drive, then west on Dusty Road
C. north on Hampton Drive, then west on Anderson Street, then north on Merrick Street, then west on Dusty Road
D. west on Maple Road, then north on Merrick Street, then west on Dusty Road

8. Police Officer Gladden is in a patrol car at the intersection of Beach Drive and Anderson Street when he spots a suspicious car. Police Officer Gladden calls the radio dispatcher to determine if the vehicle was stolen. Police Officer Gladden then follows the vehicle north on Beach Drive for three blocks, then turns right and proceeds for one block and makes another right. He then follows the vehicle for two blocks, and then they both make a left turn and continue driving. Police Officer Gladden now receives a call from the dispatcher stating the car was reported stolen and signals for the vehicle to pull to the side of the road.
In what direction was Police Officer Gladden heading at the time he signaled for the other car to pull over?

A. North   B. East   C. South   D. West

Questions 9-10.

DIRECTIONS: Questions 9 and 10 are to be answered SOLELY on the basis of the map which appears on the following page. The flow of traffic is indicated by the arrows. If there is only one arrow shown, then traffic flows only in the direction indicated by the arrow. If there are two arrows shown, then traffic flows in both directions. You must follow the flow of traffic.

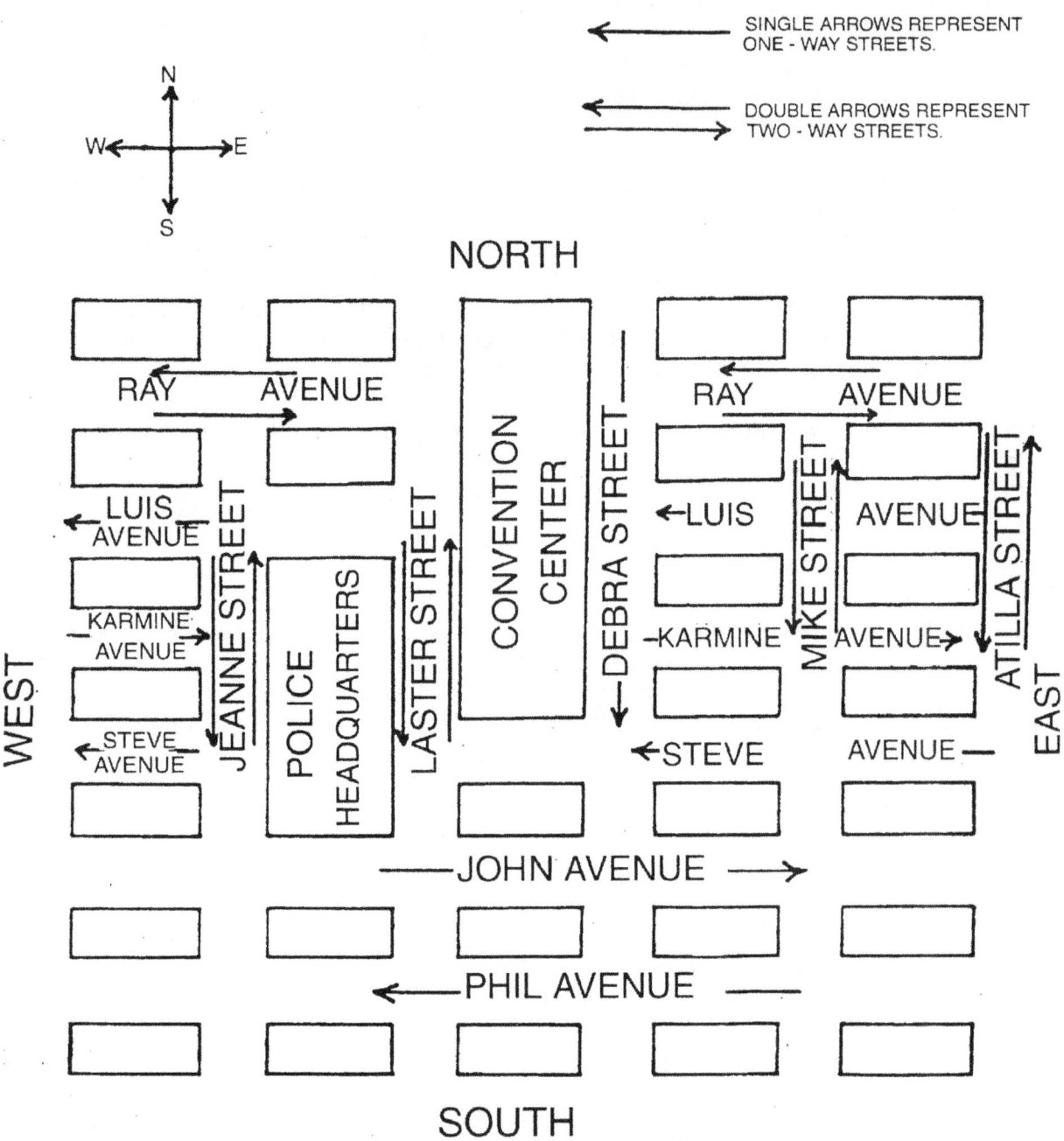

9. While in a patrol car located at Ray Avenue and Atilla Street, Police Officer Ashley receives a call from the dispatcher to respond to an assault at Jeanne Street and Karmine Avenue.
Which one of the following is the SHORTEST route for Officer Ashley to follow in his patrol car, making sure to obey all traffic regulations?
Travel

   A. south on Atilla Street, west on Luis Avenue, south on Debra Street, west on Steve Avenue, north on Lester Street, west on Luis Avenue, then one block south on Jeanne Street
   B. south on Atilla Street, then four blocks west on Phil Avenue, then north on Jeanne Street to Karmine Avenue

C. west on Ray Avenue to Debra Street, then five blocks south to Phil Avenue, then west to Jeanne Street, then three blocks north to Karmine Avenue
D. south on Atilla Street, then four blocks west on John Avenue, then north on Jeanne Street to Karmine Avenue

10. After taking a complaint report from the assault victim, Officer Ashley receives a call from the dispatcher to respond to an auto larceny in progress at the corner of Debra Street and Luis Avenue.
Which one of the following is the SHORTEST route for Officer Ashley to follow in his patrol car, making sure to obey all traffic regulations?
Travel 10.____

A. south on Jeanne Street to John Avenue, then east three blocks on John Avenue, then north on Mike Street to Luis Avenue, then west to Debra Street
B. south on Jeanne Street to John Avenue, then east two blocks on John Avenue, then north on Debra Street to Luis Avenue
C. north on Jeanne Street two blocks, then east on Ray Avenue for one block, then south on Lester Street to Steve Avenue, then one block east on Steve Avenue, then north on Debra Street to Luis Avenue
D. south on Jeanne Street to John Avenue, then east on John Avenue to Atilla Street, then north three blocks to Luis Avenue, then west to Debra Street

Questions 11-13.

DIRECTIONS: Questions 11 through 13 are to be answered SOLELY on the basis of the following map. The flow of traffic is indicated by the arrows. You must follow the flow of traffic.

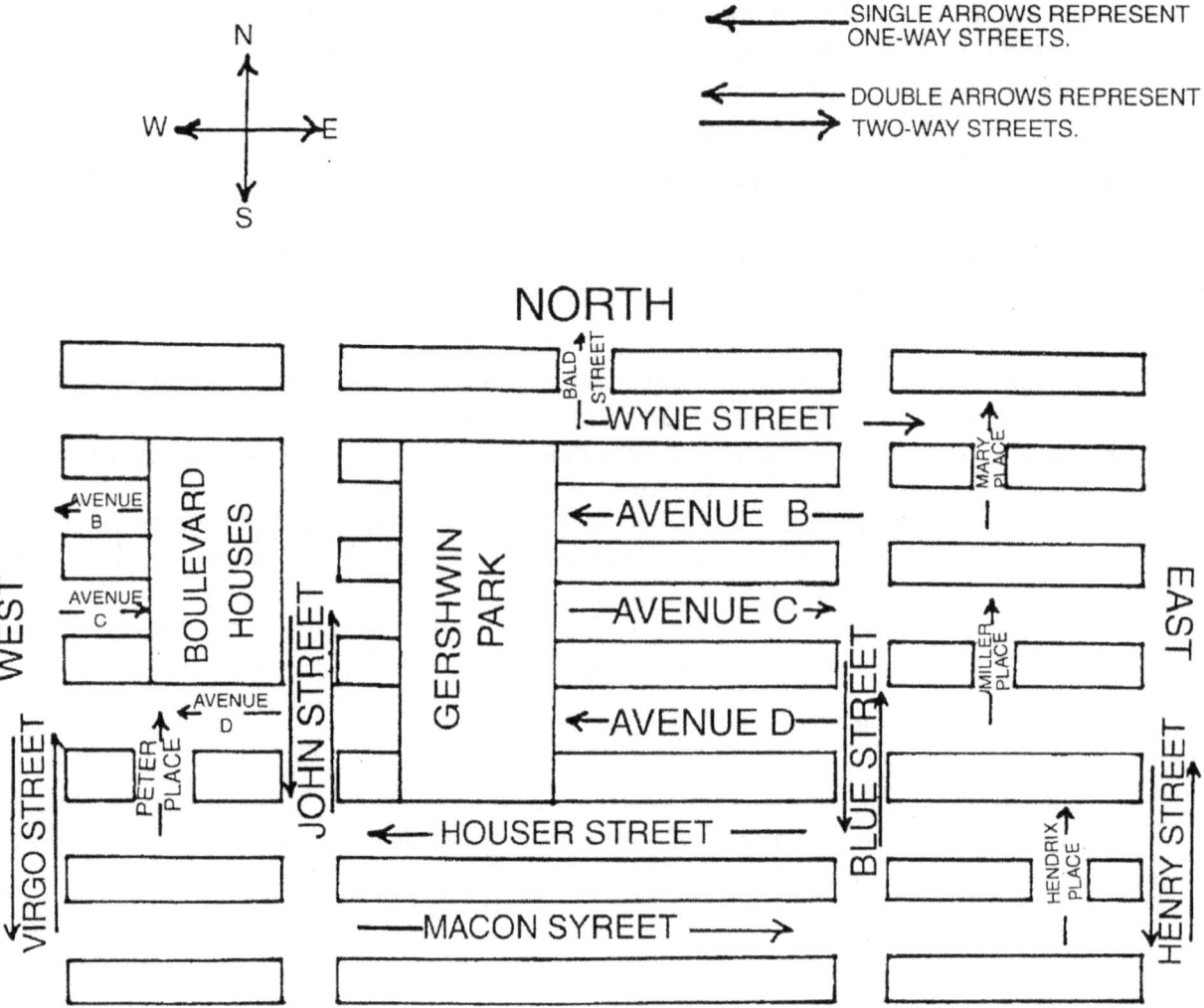

11. Police Officers Ranking and Fish are located at Wyne Street and John Street. The radio dispatcher has assigned them to investigate a motor vehicle accident at the corner of Henry Street and Houser Street.
Which one of the following is the SHORTEST route for them to take in their patrol car, making sure to obey all traffic regulations?
Travel

    A. four blocks south on John Street, then three blocks east on Houser Street to Henry Street
    B. two blocks east on Wyne Street, then two blocks south on Blue Street, then two blocks east on Avenue C, then two blocks south on Henry Street
    C. two blocks east on Wyne Street, then five blocks south on Blue Street, then two blocks east on Macon Street, then one block north on Henry Street
    D. five blocks south on John Street, then three blocks east on Macon Street, then one block north to Houser Street

11._____

12. Police Officers Rizzo and Latimer are located at Avenue B and Virgo Street. They respond to the scene of a robbery at Miller Place and Avenue D.
    Which one of the following is the SHORTEST route for them to take in their patrol car, making sure to obey all traffic regulations?
    Travel _____ to Miller Place.

    A. one block north on Virgo Street, then four blocks east on Wyne Street, then three blocks south on Henry Street, then one block west on Avenue D
    B. four blocks south on Virgo Street, then two blocks east on Macon Street, then two blocks north on Blue Street, then one block east on Avenue D
    C. three blocks south on Virgo Street, then east on Houser Street to Henry Street, then one block north on Henry Street, then one block west on Avenue D
    D. four blocks south on Virgo Street, then four blocks east to Henry Street, then north to Avenue D, then one block west

13. Police Officer Bendix is in an unmarked patrol car at the intersection of John Street and Macon Street when he begins to follow a robbery suspect. The suspect goes one block east, turns left, travels for three blocks, and then turns right. He drives for two blocks and then makes a right turn. In the middle of the block, the suspect realizes he is being followed and makes a u-turn. In what direction is the suspect now headed?

    A. North   B. South   C. East   D. West

Questions 14-15.

DIRECTIONS: Questions 14 and 15 are to be answered SOLELY on the basis of the following map. The flow of traffic is indicated by the arrows. If there is only one arrow shown, then traffic flows only in the direction indicated by the arrow. If there are two arrows shown, then traffic flows in both directions. You must follow the flow of traffic.

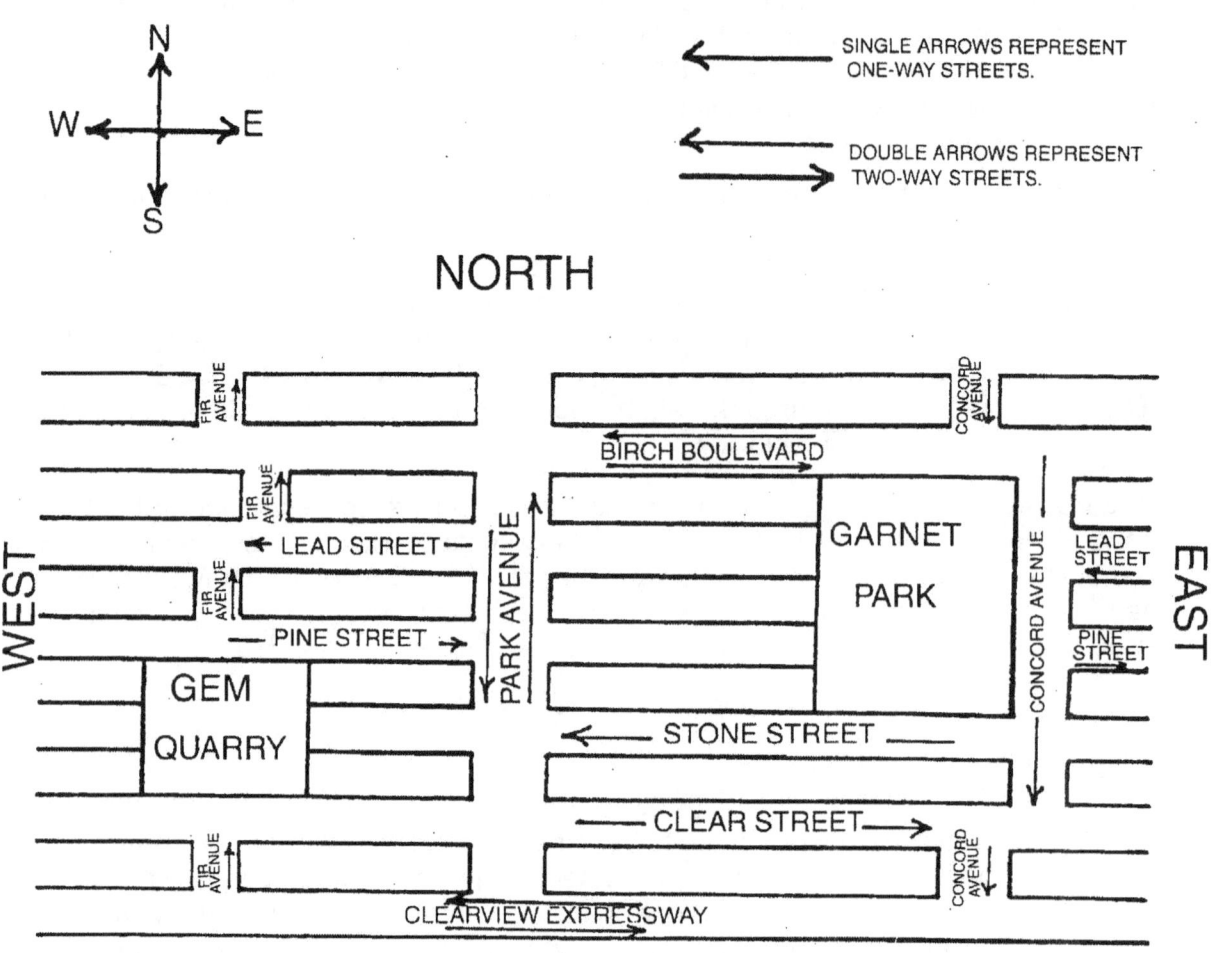

14. You are located at Fir Avenue and Birch Boulevard and receive a request to respond to a disturbance at Fir Avenue and Clear Street.
Which one of the following is the MOST direct route for you to take in your patrol car, making sure to obey all traffic regulations?
Travel

    A. one block east on Birch Boulevard, then four blocks south on Park Avenue, then one block east on Clear Street
    B. two blocks east on Birch Boulevard, then three blocks south on Concord Avenue, then two blocks west on Stone Street, then one block south on Park Avenue, then one block west on Clear Street
    C. one block east on Birch Boulevard, then five blocks south on Park Avenue, then one block west on the Clearview Expressway, then one block north on Fir Avenue
    D. two blocks south on Fir Avenue, then one block east on Pine Street, then three blocks south on Park Avenue, then one block east on the Clearview Expressway, then one block north on Fir Avenue

15. You are located at the Clearview Expressway and Concord Avenue and receive a call to respond to a crime in progress at Concord Avenue and Pine Street. Which one of the following is the MOST direct route for you to take in your patrol car, making sure to obey all traffic regulations?
Travel

15.____

    A. two blocks west on the Clearview Expressway, then one block north on Fir Avenue, then one block east on Clear Street, then four blocks north on Park Avenue, then one block east on Birch Boulevard, then two blocks south on Concord Avenue
    B. one block north on Concord Avenue, then one block west on Clear Street, then one block north on Park Avenue, then one block east on Stone Street, then one block north on Concord Avenue
    C. one block west on the Clearview Expressway, then four blocks north on Park Avenue, then one block west on Lead Street, then one block south on Fir Avenue
    D. one block west on the Clearview Expressway, then five blocks north on Park Avenue, then one block east on Birch Boulevard, then two blocks south on Concord Avenue

Questions 16-20.

DIRECTIONS: Questions 16 through 20 are to be answered SOLELY on the basis of the following map. The flow of traffic is indicated by the arrows. You must follow the flow of traffic.

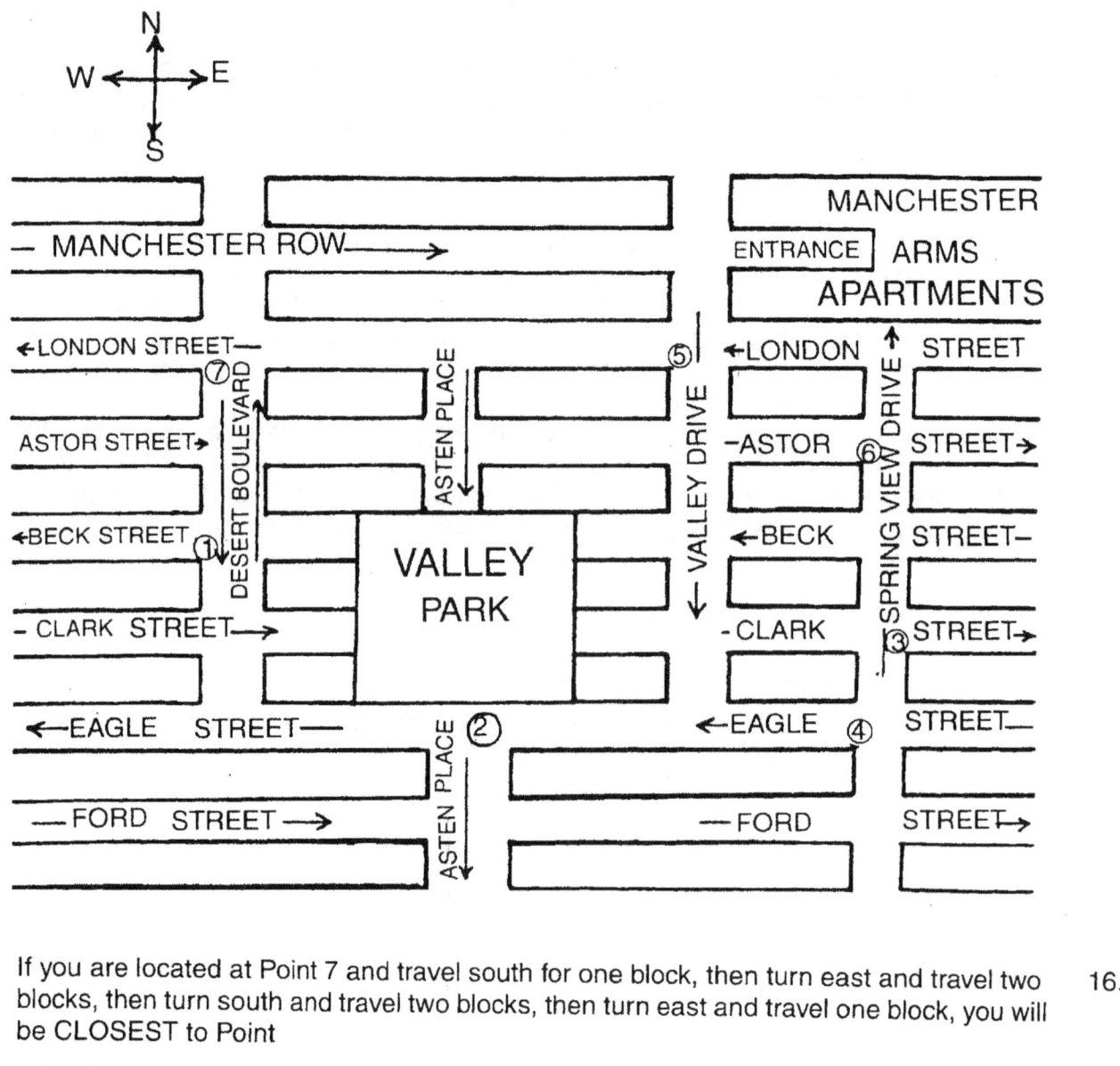

16. If you are located at Point 7 and travel south for one block, then turn east and travel two blocks, then turn south and travel two blocks, then turn east and travel one block, you will be CLOSEST to Point

    A. 2   B. 3   C. 4   D. 6

17. If you are located at Point 3 and travel north for one block, and then turn west and travel one block, and then turn south and travel two blocks, and then turn west and travel one block, you will be CLOSEST to Point

    A. 1   B. 2   C. 4   D. 6

18. You are located at Astor Street and Spring View Drive. You receive a call of a crime in progress at the intersection of Beck Street and Desert Boulevard.
    Which one of the following is the MOST direct route for you to take in your patrol car, making sure to obey all traffic regulations?
    Travel

    A. one block north on Spring View Drive, then three blocks west on London Street, then two blocks south on Desert Boulevard
    B. three blocks west on Astor Street, then one block south on Desert Boulevard

C. one block south on Spring View Drive, then three blocks west on Beck Street
D. three blocks south on Spring View Drive, then three blocks west on Eagle Street, then two blocks north on Desert Boulevard

19. You are located on Clark Street and Desert Boulevard and must respond to a disturbance at Clark Street and Spring View Drive.
Which one of the following is the MOST direct route for you to take in your patrol car, making sure to obey all traffic regulations?
Travel

19.____

A. two blocks north on Desert Boulevard, then three blocks east on Astor Street, then two blocks south on Spring View Drive
B. one block south on Desert Boulevard, then three blocks east on Eagle Street, then one block north on Spring View Drive
C. two blocks north on Desert Boulevard, then two blocks east on Astor Street, then three blocks south on Valley Drive, then one block east on Eagle Street, then one block north on Spring View Drive
D. two blocks north on Desert Boulevard, then two blocks east on Astor Street, then two blocks south on Valley Drive, then one block east on Clark Street

20. You are located at Valley Drive and Beck Street and receive a call to respond to the corner of Asten Place and Astor Street.
Which one of the following is the MOST direct route for you to take in your patrol car, making sure to obey all traffic regulations?
Travel _____ on Astor Street.

20.____

A. one block north on Valley Drive, then one block west
B. two blocks south on Valley Drive, then one block east on Eagle Street, then three blocks north on Spring View Drive, then two blocks west
C. two blocks south on Valley Drive, then two blocks west on Eagle Street, then three blocks north on Desert Boulevard, then one block east
D. one block south on Valley Drive, then one block east on Clark Street, then two blocks north on Spring View Drive, then two blocks west

KEY (CORRECT ANSWERS)

1.	C	11.	B
2.	A	12.	A
3.	A	13.	A
4.	D	14.	C
5.	C	15.	D
6.	B	16.	B
7.	C	17.	B
8.	B	18.	A
9.	A	19.	D
10.	A	20.	C

EXAMINATION SECTION
TEST 1

DIRECTIONS: Each question or incomplete statement is followed by several suggested answers or completions. Select the one that BEST answers the question or completes the statement. *PRINT THE LETTER OF THE CORRECT ANSWER IN THE SPACE AT THE RIGHT.*

1. Of the following, the MOST direct way of driving from Citi Field to Yankee Stadium would include using

    A. Northern Boulevard, the Queensborough Bridge, the Bruckner Expressway, and Fordham Road
    B. Northern Boulevard, the Third Avenue Bridge, and the Cross Bronx Expressway
    C. the Grand Central Parkway, the Triborough Bridge, and the Major Deegan Expressway
    D. the Grand Central Parkway, the Whitestone Expressway, the Bronx-Whitestone Bridge, and the Cross Bronx Expressway.

   1.____

2. The one of the following which is CLOSEST to the Queensborough Bridge is

    A. 41st Street, Manhattan   B. 59th Street, Manhattan
    C. 178th Street, Bronx   D. Ferry Point Park, Bronx

   2.____

3. A driver is going from Coney Island to Prospect Park. If he takes the most direct route, he will be traveling MOSTLY on

    A. Ocean Parkway   B. the Shore Parkway
    C. Fort Hamilton Parkway   D. the Prospect Expressway

   3.____

4. Which one of the following leads MOST directly to the Throgs Neck Bridge?

    A. Hutchinson River Parkway   B. Pelham Parkway
    C. Bruckner Expressway   D. Clearview Expressway

   4.____

5. At what corner of Central Park is Columbus Circle located?

    A. Northeast   B. Northwest   C. Southeast   D. Southwest

   5.____

6. When driving the most direct route from John F. Kennedy International Airport to LaGuardia Airport, you should use

    A. the Belt Parkway and the Brooklyn-Queens Expressway
    B. Southern Parkway and Ocean Parkway
    C. the Van Wyck Expressway and the Grand Central Parkway
    D. the Cross Island Parkway and the Clearview Expressway

   6.____

7. Which one of the following passes CLOSEST to Belmont Park Race Track?

    A. Cross Island Parkway   B. Southern Parkway
    C. Long Island Expressway   D. Interborough Parkway

   7.____

8. If a driver wishes to go from Battery Park to Long Island City, he would be LEAST likely to use the

   A. Belt Parkway
   B. Brooklyn Battery Tunnel
   C. Manhattan Bridge
   D. FDR Drive

9. City Island is a part of

   A. Brooklyn   B. Manhattan   C. Queens   D. the Bronx

10. The one of the following streets which runs parallel to and one block east of Central Park is _____ Avenue.

    A. Madison   B. Fifth   C. Columbus   D. Park

11. Of the following streets, the one which is CLOSEST to the Queens Borough Hall is

    A. Atlantic Avenue
    B. Queens Boulevard
    C. Roosevelt Avenue
    D. Woodhaven Boulevard

12. Which one of the following bridges connects the Bronx to Manhattan? The _____ Bridge.

    A. Washington
    B. Pelham
    C. Williamsburg
    D. Goethals

13. Which one of the following roads MOST NEARLY cuts through the middle of Staten Island in a generally north-south direction?

    A. Richmond Avenue
    B. Hylan Boulevard
    C. Richmond Terrace
    D. Henderson Avenue

14. Of the following, the MOST direct way of driving from Hunter College at 68th Street and Lexington Avenue, Manhattan to New York University at West 180th Street in the Bronx would include using the

    A. FDR Drive, the Williamsburg Bridge, and the Bronx Pelham Parkway
    B. FDR Drive, the Willis Avenue Bridge, and the Major Deegan Expressway
    C. Henry Hudson Parkway, Dyckman Street, and the Mosholu Parkway
    D. Henry Hudson Parkway, the Alexander Hamilton Bridge, and Westchester Avenue

15. Which one of the following streets is CLOSEST to both Brooklyn Marine Park and the Manhattan Bridge? _____ Avenue.

    A. Flatbush   B. Utica   C. Atlantic   D. New Lots

16. Of the following, the section of Brooklyn that is CLOSEST to Brownsville is

    A. Bensonhurst
    B. Brooklyn Heights
    C. East New York
    D. Red Hook

17. Lincoln Center for the Performing Arts is located

    A. below 42nd Street
    B. between Rockefeller Center and the UN Building
    C. near Washington Square
    D. west of Central Park

18. The current Madison Square Garden was built at   18._____

    A. Columbus Circle
    B. 8th Avenue and 50th Street
    C. the site of Pennsylvania Station on 8th Avenue
    D. the site of the former Steeplechase Park, on Surf Avenue in Coney Island

19. Which one of the following does NOT connect the Borough of Queens with The Bronx?   19._____
    _____ Bridge.

    A. Throgs Neck   B. Triborough
    C. Queensboro   D. Bronx-Whitestone

20. If you were planning to take a distinguished visitor on a tour of Uptown Manhattan, some   20._____
    of the highlights you would select would be

    A. American Museum of Natural History, Hayden Planetarium, Gracie Mansion, Hunter College, and Grand Central Terminal
    B. Central Park, Columbia University, Columbia-Presbyterian Medical Center, George Washington Bridge, and Metropolitan Museum of Art
    C. Temple Emanu-El, Solomon R. Guggenheim Museum, Columbus Circle, Barnard College, and Port Authority Bus Terminal
    D. Triborough Bridge, Lincoln Center for the Performing Arts, Cathedral of St. John the Divine, New York Hospital - Cornell Medical Center, and New York Botanical Gardens

21. If you were arranging an itinerary for a distinguished visitor that covered some of the   21._____
    highlights of Downtown Manhattan, you would select

    A. Battery Park, Wall Street, City Hall, Chinatown, and Trinity Church
    B. Brooklyn Bridge, Greenwich Village, New York University, New York Aquarium, and Grace Church
    C. LaGuardia Airport, Bowling Green, Fulton Fish Market, St. Paul's Chapel, and Woolworth Building
    D. Statue of Liberty, New York Stock Exchange, Woolworth Building, The Bowery, and Coney Island

22. If the itinerary you planned for a distinguished visitor were to cover some of the highlights   22._____
    of Midtown Manhattan, you would select

    A. New York Public Library, Radio City Music Hall, Empire State Building, St. Thomas Church, and Manhattan College
    B. Pennsylvania Station, Chrysler Building, Times Square, Carnegie Hall, and St. John's University
    C. Rockefeller Center, United Nations, Metropolitan Opera House, Museum of Modern Art, and Madison Square Garden
    D. United Nations, Rockefeller Center, Metropolitan Opera House, St. Patrick's Cathedral, and Hall of Fame for Great Americans

23. If you wished to escort a distinguished visitor on a tour of the City which included a hospital, the world's largest futures market, an exhibition hall, and the largest Gothic Cathedral in the world, you would take him to   23.____

    A. Lenox Hill Hospital, American Stock Exchange, National Design Center, and Trinity Church
    B. Mount Sinai Hospital, New York Cotton Exchange, New York Coliseum, The Cathedral of St. John the Divine
    C. St. Vincent's Hospital, New York City Markets, Conference House, Riverside Church
    D. The New York Hospital, New York Stock Exchange, Tea Center, and St. Patrick's Cathedral

24. If you planned to escort a distinguished visitor to the Cloisters, you would be taking him to a(n)   24.____

    A. branch of the Metropolitan Museum of Art devoted to European medieval art and architecture
    B. Off Broadway theatre notable for its avant-garde productions
    C. restaurant specializing in Greek and Armenian dishes
    D. supper club featuring jam sessions in modern jazz

25. Generally regarded as the oldest building in Manhattan, as well as a museum of revolutionary relics and Washington memorabilia, is   25.____

    A. Fraunces Tavern   B. Jumel Mansion
    C. Lefferts Homestead   D. Voorlezer's House

KEY (CORRECT ANSWERS)

1.	C		11.	B
2.	B		12.	A
3.	A		13.	A
4.	D		14.	B
5.	D		15.	A
6.	C		16.	C
7.	A		17.	D
8.	A		18.	C
9.	D		19.	C
10.	A		20.	B

21.	A
22.	C
23.	B
24.	A
25.	A

TEST 2

DIRECTIONS: Each question or incomplete statement is followed by several suggested answers or completions. Select the one that BEST answers the question or completes the statement. *PRINT THE LETTER OF THE CORRECT ANSWER IN THE SPACE AT THE RIGHT.*

1. Grand Central Station is located in Manhattan at

    A. 34th Street and 7th Avenue
    B. Union Square
    C. Columbus Circle
    D. 42nd Street and Vanderbilt Avenue

    1._____

2. Shea Stadium/Citi Field is located in

    A. Manhattan
    B. The Bronx
    C. Brooklyn
    D. Queens

    2._____

3. The Empire State Building is located in Manhattan at

    A. Lenox Avenue and 125th Street
    B. Broadway and 42nd Street
    C. Fifth Avenue and 34th Street
    D. West 4th Street and Broadway

    3._____

4. If a passenger asks you how to get to the Statue of Liberty, you should direct him to

    A. South Ferry
    B. the Verrazano Bridge
    C. the Port Authority Bus Terminal
    D. Penn Station

    4._____

5. Lincoln Center for the Performing Arts is located in Manhattan at

    A. Broadway and 64th Street
    B. Central Park West and 86th Street
    C. Wall Street and Broadway
    D. 6th Avenue and 50th Street

    5._____

6. City Hall is located NEAREST to

    A. South Ferry
    B. the Brooklyn Bridge
    C. Union Square
    D. Greenwich Village

    6._____

7. The World Trade Center is located in

    A. The Bronx
    B. Brooklyn
    C. Manhattan
    D. Queens

    7._____

8. Madison Square Garden is located

    A. in Central Park
    B. at Penn Station
    C. near Borough Hall
    D. at Coney Island

    8._____

9. On which street in Manhattan is Macy's Department Store located? _____ Street.

   A. 14th B. 34th C. 42nd D. 59th

10. Which of the following bridges is CLOSEST to City Hall?

    A. Brooklyn B. Williamsburg
    C. 59th Street D. George Washington

11. At which of the following is the New York Aquarium located?

    A. Coney Island B. South Ferry
    C. Lincoln Center D. Central Park

12. In which borough is Grand Central Terminal located?

    A. The Bronx B. Brooklyn
    C. Manhattan D. Queens

13. In which borough is Forest Hills located?

    A. The Bronx B. Brooklyn
    C. Staten Island D. Queens

14. In which borough is Yankee Stadium located?

    A. The Bronx B. Brooklyn
    C. Manhattan D. Queens

15. In which borough is Flatbush Avenue located?

    A. The Bronx B. Brooklyn
    C. Manhattan D. Queens

16. Times Square is located at the intersection of Broadway, Sixth Avenue, and _____ Street.

    A. 14th B. 23rd C. 34th D. 42nd

17. There is NOT a direct subway route between

    A. Queens and Brooklyn B. Manhattan and The Bronx
    C. Manhattan and Brooklyn D. The Bronx and Queens

Questions 18-25.

DIRECTIONS: Questions 18 through 25 involve various places of interest in New York City. Column I lists the place of interest, while Column II lists four of the boroughs of New York City. For the question number involved, indicate the letter preceding the borough where the place of interest is located.

3 (#2)

COLUMN I	COLUMN II	
18. New York Aquarium	A. Bronx	18.____
19. Carnegie Hall	B. Brooklyn	19.____
20. Citi Field	C. Manhattan	20.____
21. Lincoln Center	D. Queens	21.____
22. Sheepshead Bay		22.____
23. Van Cortlandt Park		23.____
24. LaGuardia Airport		24.____
25. Union Square		25.____

KEY (CORRECT ANSWERS)

1.	D	11.	A
2.	D	12.	C
3.	C	13.	D
4.	A	14.	A
5.	A	15.	B
6.	B	16.	D
7.	C	17.	D
8.	B	18.	B
9.	B	19.	C
10.	A	20.	D

21. C
22. B
23. A
24. D
25. C

READING COMPREHENSION
UNDERSTANDING AND INTERPRETING WRITTEN MATERIAL
EXAMINATION SECTION
TEST 1

DIRECTIONS: Each question or incomplete statement is followed by several suggested answers or completions. Select the one that BEST answers the question or completes the statement. *PRINT THE LETTER OF THE CORRECT ANSWER IN THE SPACE AT THE RIGHT.*

Questions 1-4.

DIRECTIONS: Questions 1 through 4 are to be answered SOLELY on the basis of the following passage.

On April 6, at 5:25 A.M., while patrolling the #8 train southbound to Brooklyn, Transit Police Officer O'Rourke noticed a young woman at the end of the car who appeared to be ill. Officer O'Rourke approached the woman and asked her if she was feeling all right. The woman was crying and began speaking incoherently. Officer O'Rourke escorted the woman off the train at the next southbound #8 platform in order to obtain information from her. After speaking with her for fifteen minutes, Officer O'Rourke learned that her name was Carol Rivers and that she had been assaulted and sexually molested while waiting for the southbound #8 train about a half hour before meeting the Officer. Miss Rivers described the suspect as a white male, in his forties, with gray hair, glasses, a red shirt, black pants, and a brown hat. The suspect fled on a northbound #8 train with the victim's pocketbook. Officer O'Rourke then radioed for an ambulance to respond to the location to assist Miss Rivers.

The next day at approximately 5:30 A.M., while Officer O'Rourke was standing on the subway platform waiting to board the uptown #7 train to Queens, he noticed an individual coming down the steps from the southbound platform. The man was in his forties, with gray hair, dark glasses, and the same clothing described by Miss Rivers the day before, except for his shirt, which was white. Officer O'Rourke, believing the man to be the same perpetrator, decided to follow him in order to observe the suspect's actions. The man was walking alongside a woman on the northbound platform and attempted to snatch her pocketbook. The woman held onto her purse and started to yell for the police. The man immediately released his hold on the pocketbook and ran down the platform onto an awaiting #7 train to Manhattan. Officer O'Rourke pursued the man onto the train and subsequently placed him under arrest two stations later.

1. Officer O'Rourke requested that the ambulance respond to the subway platform of the _____ train. 1._____

    A. northbound # 8 B. uptown # 7
    C. downtown # 7   D. southbound # 8

2. At approximately what time was Miss Rivers assaulted? _____ A.M. 2._____

    A. 4:55   B. 5:10   C. 5:25   D. 5:40

3. The suspect arrested by Officer O'Rourke was wearing a shirt _____ and _____ pants.

   A. red; blue
   B. white; black
   C. red; black
   D. white; red

4. On April 7, Officer O'Rourke boarded a train to

   A. Manhattan
   B. Queens
   C. the Bronx
   D. Brooklyn

Questions 5-7.

DIRECTIONS: Questions 5 through 7 are to be answered SOLELY on the basis of the following passage.

Police Officers Ryder and Brown respond to a call concerning a past burglary in a private house located at 1296 Brentwood Road. When the Officers arrive, they are met by William Parker, who owns the house. Mr. Parker tells the Officers that he had been out of town for the entire weekend and, upon his return twenty minutes ago, discovered that the lock on his back door was broken. He also discovered that several items were missing from around his house. At this point, Officer Ryder asks Mr. Parker to show her where the burglars entered. Meanwhile, Officer Brown makes a search of the immediate area. Officer Ryder's investigation reveals that the burglars had cut a wire located by the front basement window in order to disable the alarm system. The burglars then forced open the lock with a metal bar of some kind. Officer Brown's search of the area uncovers no evidence. Officer Ryder then asks Mr. Parker to describe the items which are missing. Mr. Parker says that his 19" plasma television and clock radio are gone, along with several items which were borrowed from various friends. Among the missing items are a compact disc player owned by David Mills, a videotape recorder owned by Samantha Burns, and a portable tape player with headphones owned by Roger Denning. Officer Ryder lists the missing items and the owners' names in her report and tells Mr. Parker to call the station house in the morning to obtain a report number which he can use if he files an insurance claim.

5. The thieves broke the lock of which entrance?

   A. Side   B. Front   C. Basement   D. Back

6. Which of the missing items were owned by William Parker?

   A. Color television and clock radio
   B. Compact disc player and tape player
   C. Videotape recorder and compact disc player
   D. Portable tape player and headphones

7. What crime is this passage PRIMARILY concerned with?

   A. Arson   B. Assault   C. Burglary   D. Fraud

Questions 8-10.

DIRECTIONS: Questions 8 through 10 are to be answered SOLELY on the basis of the following passage.

Police Officers Wilson and Mills receive a radio call to investigate an auto accident involving injuries. Upon their arrival, Officer Mills approaches a Mustang convertible which had been driven into the side of an Oldsmobile sedan. There is also a small Dodge truck several feet away which had crashed into a fire hydrant. Officer Mills immediately determines that no one is injured and radios the dispatcher to cancel the ambulance. Meanwhile, Officer Wilson interviews Sam Thomas, who is the owner and driver of the Mustang. Mr. Thomas states that he was driving south on Bedford Avenue when a large Oldsmobile pulled out of a parking lot in front of him. Mr. Thomas goes on to say that he immediately hit his brakes but slid into the side of the Oldsmobile. Officer Mills interviews Thomas Parker, who is the driver of the Oldsmobile. Mr. Parker admits that he drove out of the parking lot without looking for oncoming traffic. He tells Officer Mills that he is not used to driving and borrowed the Oldsmobile from his brother, Harold Parker, who is the owner of the car. Finally, Officer Wilson interviews Rutger Schmidt, who is the driver of the Dodge truck. Mr. Schmidt indicates that, in an attempt to avoid the accident, he swerved out of the way, lost control of the truck, and ran into a fire hydrant. Mr. Schmidt tells Officer Wilson that he works for the Acme Exterminating Company, which owns the truck. Following the interviews, the two Officers write their accident report and indicate the damage to each vehicle. The Mustang had a damaged front bumper and grill, and broken headlights; the Oldsmobile had a dented driver's side quarter panel; the Dodge truck had a crumpled bumper and blown right front tire.

8. Who was the owner of the Oldsmobile sedan?

    A. Sam Thomas   B. Thomas Parker
    C. Harold Parker   D. Rutger Schmidt

9. What was damaged on the Dodge truck?

    A. Driver's side quarter panel
    B. Bumper and right front tire
    C. Tailgate and tail lights
    D. Front bumper, grill, and headlights

10. The driver of which vehicle was the PRIMARY cause of the accident?

    A. Mustang convertible   B. Patrol car
    C. Dodge truck   D. Oldsmobile sedan

Questions 11-13.

DIRECTIONS: Questions 11 through 13 are to be answered SOLELY on the basis of the following passage.

Police Officer Lombardo was dispatched to the scene of an apparently dead human body. His supervisor and another Officer were at the scene, as were two paramedics. The paramedics, Pete Lizzo and Erick Clark, had just pronounced the body dead at 6:55 P.M. There were no relatives present, and a neighbor, Eddie Torres, told Officer Lombardo that the dead person lived alone and had no family. Mr. Torres agreed to be a witness to the search of the premises. Officer Lombardo knew that the police were required to voucher or hold all valuables and important papers for safekeeping if a close relative did not live with the dead person. The apartment was filled with a large number of possessions, including two gold rings, a gold watch, $200 in cash, and kitchen and living room furniture. They also found an old black and white television set, old clothing, and numerous kitchen utensils. In a tin box, the Officer found a birth certificate, social security card, and the dead person's diary. After the search was completed, the jewelry, cash, birth certificate, and social security card were vouchered. Eddie Torres signed Officer Lombardo's Memo Book.

11. Of the following, which items were vouchered by Officer Lombardo?

    A. Two gold rings, a gold watch, a social security card, birth certificate, and $200 in cash
    B. A gold watch, two gold rings, $200 cash, a diary, and a social security card
    C. A birth certificate, social security card, diary, jewelry, and $200 in cash
    D. A social security card, two gold watches, a gold ring, a birth certificate, and $200 cash

12. The search was witnessed by a

    A. neighbor
    B. relative
    C. police officer
    D. paramedic

13. Officer Lombardo vouchered the dead person's property because

    A. the paramedics were present
    B. a supervisor was not available
    C. there was only one witness
    D. there was no relative living with the dead person

Question 14.

DIRECTIONS: Question 14 pertains to the following section of the Penal Law.

A person who, after having been three times convicted within this state, of felonies or attempts to commit felonies, or under the law of any other state, government or country, of crimes which if committed within this state would be felonious, commits a felony, other than murder, first or second degree, or treason, within this state, shall be sentenced upon conviction of such fourth, or subsequent offense to imprisonment in a state prison for an indeterminate term the minimum of which shall be not less than the maximum term provided for first offenders for the crime for which the individual has been convicted but, in any event, the minimum term upon conviction for a felony as the fourth or subsequent offense, shall be not less than fifteen years, and the maximum thereof shall be his natural life.

14. Under the terms of the above quoted portion of the section of the Penal Law a person must receive the increased punishment therein provided, if

    A. he is convicted of a felony and has been three times previously convicted of felonies
    B. he has been three times previously convicted of felonies, regardless of the nature of his present conviction
    C. his fourth conviction is for murder, first or second degree, or treason
    D. he has previously been convicted three times of murder, first or second degree, or treason

Questions 15-17.

DIRECTIONS: Questions 15 through 17 are to be answered SOLELY on the basis of the following passage.

At 11:30 P.M., while parked in front of 945 Howard Street, Police Officers Abbott and Johnson received a radio call of a family dispute at 779 Seward Street, Apartment 1928. The radio dispatcher informed the Officers that the call came from Mrs. Debra Lacoste who lives in Apartment 1930. The Officers arrived at the location and heard yelling and screaming. When the Officers knocked on the door, a woman crying hysterically opened the door. The woman, Gloria Ross, informed the Officers that her husband, Sam Ross, was in her apartment. She said he was drunk, had yelled at her, and had made threats to hurt her if she did not let him see his children. Mrs. Ross then presented a letter to Officer Abbott, which he recognized as being an Order of Protection issued by Family Court. The Order of Protection stated that Mr. Ross was not to be seen anywhere near his wife, including her residence and place of employment. Furthermore, the Order stated that he had no right to see the children or to yell at his wife or use obscene language in his wife's presence. Mrs. Ross told the Officer that she wanted her husband arrested for violating the Order of Protection. Officer Johnson quickly read the Order of Protection and informed Officer Abbott that the Order was valid. Officer Abbott ordered Sam Ross to turn around with his hands behind his back, and Officer Abbott handcuffed him and placed him under arrest.

15. Which of the following persons FIRST made the authorities aware of the family dispute?

    A. A neighbor
    B. The victim
    C. A police officer
    D. The suspect

16. The Police Officers responded to a report of a disturbance at _____ Street, Apartment _____.

    A. 945 Howard; 1928
    B. 779 Seward; 1930
    C. 779 Seward; 1928
    D. 945 Howard; 1930

17. Which of the following actions caused Mr. Ross to be arrested? He

    A. called his children on the telephone
    B. tried to visit his children
    C. waited for his wife in front of her job
    D. yelled at his children

Questions 18-19.

DIRECTIONS: Questions 18 and 19 are to be answered SOLELY on the basis of the following passage.

As a result of numerous interviews of complainants and witnesses of violent crimes, Officer Wells has noticed a serious rise in the number of certain crimes in his patrol area over the past three months. He has observed that most of the rapes take place on E. 98th Street between Lott Avenue and Herk Place; assaults happen on Lott Avenue between Chester Avenue and E. 98th Street; and the majority of the robberies occur on Lott Avenue between E. 98th Street and Hughes Place. The assaults take place between 1:00 A.M. and 3:00 A.M. All of the robberies happen between 1:00 A.M. and 6:00 A.M., and most of the rapes happen between 8:00 A.M. and 11:00 A.M. The rapes usually occur on Mondays and Wednesdays, the robberies oh Fridays and Saturdays, and the assaults on Saturdays and Sundays.

18. Officer Wells would MOST effectively reduce the number of robberies by patrolling

    A. Lott Avenue between E. 98th Street and Hughes Place on Fridays and Saturdays between 1:00 A.M. and 8:00 A.M.
    B. Lott Avenue between E. 98th Street and Chester Avenue on Saturdays and Sundays between 1:00 A.M. and 6:00 A.M.
    C. E. 98th Street between Lott Avenue and Herk Place on Saturdays and Sundays between 1:00 A.M. and 3:00 A.M.
    D. E. 98th Street between Herk Place and Chester Avenue on Mondays and Wednesdays between 8:00 A.M. and 11:00 A.M.

19. Officer Wells has been informed by his supervisor that he will be assigned to a patrol each week that would allow him to concentrate on reducing the number of rapes. What would be the MOST appropriate patrol for Officer Wells to work?

    A. Tuesday through Saturday, 8:00 P.M. to 4:00 P.M.
    B. Monday through Friday, 7:30 A.M. to 3:30 P.M.
    C. Wednesday through Sunday, noon to 8:00 P.M.
    D. Monday through Friday, 3:00 P.M. to 11:00 P.M.

Questions 20-23.

DIRECTIONS: Questions 20 through 23 are to be answered SOLELY on the basis of the following passage.

Police Officers Grice and Sexton were working a 4:00 P.M. to Midnight tour of duty on Friday, December 5, when they were assigned to investigate a burglary. They were told to respond to 355 Grand Street, the 14th floor, Apartment 1402, and to speak to the complainant, Ms. Starr. Upon arrival, Officer Sexton interviewed Ms. Starr, who stated that when she returned home from work at approximately 6:10 P.M., she was unable to unlock her door because the keyhole had been stuffed with toothpicks. After the door was opened by building maintenance, she entered her apartment and saw that her jewelry box had been emptied and was laying on the floor.

Officer Grice, who is qualified in the recovery of fingerprints, dusted the jewelry box and the front door in an attempt to recover any fingerprints that the burglar may have left. The Officers also interviewed Mrs. Caputo, who lives in Apartment 1404, and Mr. Babbit, who lives in Apartment 1407. Both individuals stated that they neither saw nor heard anything unusual.

The next night, Saturday, December 6, Officers Grice and Sexton responded to Apartment 1514 in the same building on a call of a burglary. The complainant, Ms. Chung, stated that when she returned home from shopping she discovered that her lock had been stuffed with chewing gum and that her apartment had been burglarized. Officer Grice dusted the front door and a dresser, which had been opened, for prints.

Ten days after the last burglary, Detective Carrano, who had been assigned to investigate the burglaries, was informed by Mr. Hunt of the fingerprint identification unit that the prints recovered from both apartments belonged to Peter Remo of 355 Gravel Street, Apartment 1705. Later that evening, after obtaining an arrest warrant, Detective Carrano arrested Peter Remo for the burglaries.

20. Who lived on the same floor as Ms. Starr? 20.____

    A. Ms. Chung B. Peter Remo
    C. Mr. Babbit D. Mr. Hunt

21. Who was responsible for recovering the fingerprints that were used to identify Peter Remo? 21.____

    A. Officer Grice B. Mr. Hunt
    C. Detective Carrano D. Officer Sexton

22. When was Peter Remo arrested? December 22.____

    A. 5 B. 6 C. 15 D. 16

23. Why was Ms. Starr unable to unlock her door? 23.____

    A. She lost her keys.
    B. Chewing gum had been stuffed into the lock.
    C. Her keys had been taken from her jewelry box.
    D. The lock was stuffed with toothpicks.

Questions 24-25.

DIRECTIONS: Questions 24 and 25 are to be answered SOLELY on the basis of the following passage.

While working an 8:00 A.M. to 4:00 P.M. shift on January 14, Police Officers Jones and Smith received a radio call at 1:45 P.M. to investigate a report of a man with a gun in front of 103 Lexington Avenue. Mary Holmes had called 911 from her home at 1:43 P.M. and explained that two days ago while on her way home from work, she had been threatened by a man with a gun in front of her home at 113 Lowell Street. She told the police operator that the same man was now standing in front of Harry's Lounge at 103 Lexington Avenue, drinking a beer. She described him as being 30-40 years old, 5'6", 160 lbs., wearing a gray coat, gray brim hat, and gold wire-rimmed glasses. The Officers responded to the location and observed a male fitting the description given by Miss Holmes. The Officers approached the suspect and, while searching his right front waistband, Officer Jones found a chromeplated .38 caliber revolver licensed and registered under the name of Joseph Fitz. Miss Holmes was brought to the scene and identified the suspect as the person who had threatened her earlier. Officer Smith then placed the man, identified as Joseph Fitz, under arrest.

24. On what day did the suspect threaten Miss Holmes? January 24.____

    A. 10 B. 12 C. 14 D. 16

25. Officer Jones recovered the gun from the suspect's waistband. 25.____

    A. left front B. right rear
    C. left rear D. right front

KEY (CORRECT ANSWERS)

1. D
2. A
3. B
4. A
5. D

6. A
7. C
8. C
9. B
10. D

11. A
12. A
13. D
14. A
15. A

16. C
17. B
18. A
19. B
20. C

21. A
22. D
23. D
24. B
25. D

TEST 2

DIRECTIONS: Each question or incomplete statement is followed by several suggested answers or completions. Select the one that BEST answers the question or completes the statement. *PRINT THE LETTER OF THE CORRECT ANSWER IN THE SPACE AT THE RIGHT.*

Questions 1-4.

DIRECTIONS: Questions 1 through 4 are to be answered SOLELY on the basis of the following passage.

On May 10, at 5:30 P.M., Police Officers Swift and Monroe were on routine patrol when they were dispatched to 1180 Albany Avenue, Apartment 3C, on an assault in progress. They arrived at the apartment at 5:40 P.M. and were met by Mr. Raymond Ambrose. Mr. Ambrose said he called the police because he heard yelling and screaming coming from Apartment 3A, but it had since stopped. Mr. Ambrose told the Officers that the tenant in 3A, Helen Gray, lived alone ever since her divorce.

Officer Monroe knocked on the door of Apartment 3A and noticed that the door was partially opened. The Officers cautiously entered the apartment, which appeared to have been ransacked. Officer Swift checked the fire escape while his partner searched the bedroom, where he found Mrs. Gray, unconscious, lying on the floor and bleeding heavily from the head. A blood-covered baseball bat was found next to her. The Officer called for an ambulance to respond while Officer Swift tried to gather information from neighbors.

Mary Grable, age 68, of Apartment 3B, Ben Grim, age 16 of Apartment 1A, and Angela Arnold, age 27, of 1162 Albany Avenue were standing in the hallway. Ms. Arnold stated that she and Mrs. Gray are close friends, and she became concerned when she saw Stuart Gray in the neighborhood around 5:10 P.M. Ms. Arnold told Officer Swift, *Since they've been divorced, Stuart visits Helen to get money to support a "crack" habit, and it always leads to an argument.* Grable said she heard a commotion, but didn't know who was involved. Grim told Officer Swift that he saw Stuart Gray running from the building at about 5:35 P.M. with blood on his hands and shirt.

Paramedics arrived at 5:50 P.M. and transported Mrs. Gray to the hospital, where she died at 6:30 P.M. without regaining consciousness. Stuart Gray was arrested at 7:15 the next morning at the home of his mother, Valerie Gray, and was charged with the homicide.

1. From the information given, it is MOST likely that the crime was committed between   1._____

   A. 5:10 A.M. - 5:35 A.M.   B. 5:10 P.M. - 5:35 P.M.
   C. 5:30 P.M. - 5:35 P.M.   D. 5:30 P.M. - 5:50 P.M.

2. Who was the FIRST person to find Mrs. Gray?   2._____

   A. Officer Monroe   B. Mr. Ambrose
   C. Officer Swift   D. Ms. Arnold

3. Whose information tied Stuart to the crime?   3._____

   A. Ms. Arnold and Ben Grim   B. Mr. Ambrose and Ms. Arnold
   C. Ben Grim and Valerie Gray   D. Ms. Arnold and Ms. Grable

4. Stuart Gray was arrested on May

   A. 10 at 6:30 P.M.
   B. 11 at 7:15 P.M.
   C. 10 at 7:15 A.M.
   D. 11 at 7:15 A.M

Questions 5-8.

DIRECTIONS: Questions 5 through 8 are to be answered SOLELY on the basis of the following passage.

While returning to the 15th Precinct from court, Police Officer Moody encountered an armed robbery in progress outside of 238 Madison Street. When the perpetrator saw the Officer, he fled into the building and attempted to enter the second floor apartment of Maria Vasquez. Ms. Vasquez had previously opened the door when she heard the noise downstairs. When Ms. Vasquez saw the perpetrator approaching her with a gun in his hand, she immediately closed and locked the door. Since the perpetrator was not able to gain entrance to the apartment, he jumped out of the hallway window and hid in the courtyard. When Officer Moody arrived at the bottom of the second floor stairway, he heard Ms. Vasquez crying hysterically from inside the apartment. He banged on the door and called to her to see if she was all right. Ms. Vasquez did not speak English and, thinking it was the perpetrator, she refused to open the door. As a result, Officer Moody assumed that the woman was being held hostage by the perpetrator. Officer Moody immediately stepped away from the door, advised the radio dispatcher of the circumstances, and requested back-up assistance.

Every sector car in the precinct responded to assist Officer Moody; and each, with the exception of sectors Adam and Charlie, took up a strategic location outside of the building. Officers O'Connor and Torres, of sector Adam, went up to the second floor to guard the apartment door with Officer Moody. Officer Perez, of sector Charlie, went up to the roof. Officer Donadio, also of sector Charlie, started to enter the courtyard when he observed the perpetrator hiding in the bushes. Officer Donadio quickly took cover behind the cement wall entrance of the courtyard and ordered the perpetrator at gunpoint to surrender. The perpetrator surrendered his weapon and allowed himself to be easily apprehended. Officer Donadio then advised the other Officers by radio that the perpetrator was in custody and that Ms. Vasquez was not being held hostage.

5. Which Officer went up to the roof?

   A. O'Connor   B. Perez   C. Donadio   D. Moody

6. Officer Moody chased the perpetrator because he

   A. was trying to get into the apartment of Maria Vasquez
   B. was holding Maria Vasquez hostage
   C. was attempting to commit an armed robbery
   D. jumped out the second floor hallway window

7. Which Officer was NOT on the second floor?

   A. Moody   B. Torres   C. O'Connor   D. Donadio

8. While Officer Moody was standing at the bottom of the stairs, the suspect was 8._____

   A. in Ms. Vasquez's apartment
   B. in the courtyard
   C. on the roof
   D. on the second floor fire escape

Questions 9-11.

DIRECTIONS: Questions 9 through 11 are to be answered SOLELY on the basis of the following passage.

    Police Officer Berman has been assigned to a steady post from Hartman Boulevard to Bement Street on Forest Avenue for the past two years. Officer Berman's duties involve walking along Forest Avenue and in and out of stores talking with the people on his post to ensure that everything is all right. While on duty at 11:30 on Saturday morning, Officer Berman walks into Pete Arturo's Boutique, which is normally filled with female customers because of the type of merchandise sold there. Today, the Officer sees only three young men in the store. Officer Berman looks around and notices that Pete is not in sight. Officer Berman notices a thin man whom he has never seen behind the register. Officer Berman decides to ask for Mrs. Arturo, knowing that Pete is not married, because he suspects that something is wrong. The thin man replies with a smile, *She will be in a little later.* Officer Berman then walks out of the boutique and calls for back-up assistance on a possible robbery in progress. At 11:40, Police Officers Fernandez and Heck arrive at the side of Arturo's Boutique. Five minutes later, Police Officer Jones arrives in his scooter. The Officers are now waiting for a Supervisor to arrive so they can proceed with the plan of action, which they have already discussed. Two minutes after Officer Jones arrives, Sgt. Demond pulls up with his driver, Police Officer Ricco, and gathers all of the information. Sgt. Demond then calls the boutique by phone, identifies himself, and advises the man who answers to give himself up so that nobody will get hurt. Sgt. Demond also tells the man on the phone that he has the store surrounded and will give them five minutes to surrender. The three men walk out of the boutique with Mr. Arturo, who is unharmed. Officer Berman recovers three loaded .38 caliber revolvers from the suspects.

9. How many police personnel responded to Officer Berman's call for assistance? 9._____

   A. Four   B. Five   C. Six   D. Seven

10. At what time did Sergeant Demond arrive at the boutique? _____ A.M. 10._____

    A. 11:40   B. 11:42   C. 11:45   D. 11:47

11. Which of the following Officers arrived in the scooter? 11._____

    A. Berman   B. Fernandez   C. Jones   D. Heck

Questions 12-14.

DIRECTIONS: Questions 12 through 14 are to be answered SOLELY on the basis of the following passage.

    Police Officer Smith was reassigned to the Parkhill Housing Complex, which consists of nine 8-story buildings. He was told that nine rapes had occurred in the last eight days in the complex and all had taken place between 9:00 A.M. and 6:00 P.M. On May 2, Officer Smith was working the 10:00 A.M. to 6:00 P.M. shift. At the beginning of Officer Smith's shift, his Supervisor, Sergeant Larry, gave him the suspected rapist's description, which had been obtained on April 27 from Nancy Lewis, one of the rape victims. The suspect was described as a male, Black, 6'2", approximately 210 lbs., having a light complexion and the word *Budda* tattooed on his left forearm.

While on patrol several blocks from the Parkhill Complex at Noon of the same day, Officer Smith was called by the dispatcher and told to respond to a complaint at 110 Park Avenue, Apartment 3C, located in the complex. Upon his arrival at the apartment, he was met by Mary Wilson, who told him that her 16-year-old daughter Tammy had just been raped in the building elevator. Tammy stated that when she entered her building, a Black male, approximately 26 years old, about 6'1", wearing a suit, had been waiting for the elevator. She also told Officer Smith that when she entered the elevator with this man, he forced her to the floor, raped her, and pushed her out of the elevator on the 7th floor.

On May 3, at 8:00 A.M., an individual fitting the description given by Ms. Lewis was apprehended in front of 55 Hill Street, another building in the Parkhill Complex. The suspect's name was John Jones. At 12:30 P.M. of the same day, Ms. Wilson and Ms. Lewis went to the precinct station house and identified John Jones as the person who raped them.

12. Who was the FIRST person to give Officer Smith a description of the rapist?

   A. Sergeant Larry
   B. Tammy Wilson
   C. Mary Wilson
   D. Nancy Lewis

13. Where was Tammy Wilson raped?

   A. In the elevator at 55 Hill Street
   B. On the 5th floor at 110 Park Avenue
   C. In the elevator at 110 Park Avenue
   D. On the 7th floor at 55 Hill Street

14. John Jones was apprehended the

   A. same day as the rape of Nancy Lewis
   B. day after the rape of Nancy Lewis
   C. same day as the rape of Tammy Wilson
   D. day after the rape of Tammy Wilson

Questions 15-17.

DIRECTIONS: Questions 15 through 17 are to be answered SOLELY on the basis of the following passage.

Police Officers Wilson and Jost are assigned to a patrol car and receive a call from the dispatcher to respond to a shooting at 236 Bever Street between Hoyt and Clinton Avenues. The two Officers arrive at the scene at 5:20 P.M. and see a man, later identified as David Smith of 242 Bever Street, lying on the sidewalk and bleeding from the chest. An ambulance arrives at 5:35 P.M., and the attendant, Peter Johnson, pronounces Mr. Smith dead from a gunshot wound on the left side of the chest. Officer Jost begins to walk along Bever Street looking for witnesses. Suddenly, William Jones comes out of his store, located at 239 Bever Street, and tells Officer Jost that he heard a gunshot at 5:15 P.M. and saw two White males going through the victim's pockets. Meanwhile, Walter Garvey, of 247 Bever Street, approaches Officer Wilson and tells him that he saw the victim fall to the ground and then observed two White males search the victim before they ran west on Bever Street toward Clinton Avenue. Mr. Garvey describes one suspect as having blonde hair and wearing a blue jacket with black jeans, and the other suspect as having brown hair and wearing a white jacket and blue jeans.

After interviewing Mr. Jones, Officer Jost is approached by Doris Finkle, owner of the Sweet Shop located at 238 Bever Street. She tells him that the victim was walking along Bever Street when two White males came from behind and pushed Mr. Smith against the wall. She also says that a man with blonde hair started talking to the victim when suddenly a man wearing a white jacket fired a gun and Mr. Smith fell to the ground. Mrs. Finkle tells the Officer that the two suspects searched the victim and then ran away.

15. Who pronounced David Smith dead?

    A. William Jones
    B. Doris Finkle
    C. Peter Johnson
    D. Walter Garvey

16. Which of the following persons was the FIRST to report hearing a gunshot?

    A. Police Officer Jost
    B. Walter Garvey
    C. Peter Johnson
    D. William Jones

17. Who was the FIRST witness to give a description of the suspects' clothing?

    A. Mrs. Finkle
    B. Mr. Garvey
    C. Mr. Jones
    D. Mr. Johnson

Questions 18-22.

DIRECTIONS: Questions 18 through 22 are to be answered SOLELY on the basis of the following passage.

At 10:30 P.M., while parked in front of a clothing store at 1925 First Avenue, Police Officers Cole and Reese received a radio call to investigate a possible burglary at 1423 Second Avenue. The Officers were to meet the complainant in front of the location given by the dispatcher.

Upon arriving at the scene, the Officers were met by Mr. Rivers, the owner of the Melody Grocery Store, located at 1425 Second Avenue. He explained that he had called the police because he noticed the bicycle shop next door had been left open. Mr. Rivers further stated that the shop owner, Mr. Rose, usually closes at 9:00 P.M. Mr. Reyes, who lives at 1923 First Avenue and works with Mr. Rivers, noticed that the store gate had been partially closed and upon checking saw that the lights were off and the door was not locked.

At 10:40 P.M., Police Officer Reese radioed for a Supervisor before entering the premises. Sgt. Parker arrived ten minutes later and supervised a search to find out if the owner was sick, injured, or incapacitated somewhere in the store. The results proved negative. Apparently nothing had been taken or disturbed, and there were no visible signs of forced entry. The Sergeant instructed Officer Reese to guard the premises while his partner contacted Police Officer Craig, the Precinct Telephone Switchboard Operator, who would check the precinct merchant index file and then notify Mr. Rose of the situation.

18. The Sergeant supervised a search to determine if the

   A. store was being burglarized
   B. owner was sick or injured
   C. store had been ransacked
   D. owner was working late

19. The police dispatcher received a call regarding a possible burglary at _____ Avenue.

   A. 1423 Second   B. 1923 First
   C. 1425 Second   D. 1925 First

20. What type of business was left unsecured?

   A. Florist shop   B. Bicycle shop
   C. Grocery store   D. Clothes store

21. At what time did the Sergeant arrive? _____ P.M.

   A. 10:30   B. 10:40   C. 10:45   D. 10:50

22. Which Police Officer would attempt to contact the store owner?

   A. Reese   B. Parker   C. Craig   D. Cole

Questions 23-25.

DIRECTIONS: Questions 23 through 25 are to be answered SOLELY on the basis of the following passage.

Housing Police Officer Lewis is patrolling Woodrow Houses, a housing project consisting of ten 14-story apartment buildings. Officer Lewis is working a Midnight to 8 A.M. tour of duty. Before going to his assigned post, Officer Lewis was told by Sergeant Smith that there has been an increase in the number of apartment burglaries on his post. Sergeant Smith also stated that the burglaries are occurring between 10 P.M. and 6 A.M. A male Hispanic, 5'5" tall, dark complexion, tattoo of a cross on right forearm, large black mustache, and wearing dark sunglasses has been seen in the area just prior to a number of the burglaries. At 3:00 A.M., Officer Lewis is patrolling his post and notices a male Hispanic, 5'5", dark complexion, no mustache, no sunglasses, a tattoo of a cross on his right forearm, exiting an apartment building carrying a portable TV and a Sony radio. Officer Lewis stops the man and asks him where he was coming from. The man says that he was just coming from his friend's 6th floor apartment and that he was going to have the TV and radio repaired in the morning. Officer Lewis asks the man to return to the apartment with him. The man then drops the TV and radio and starts to run. Officer Lewis pursues and apprehends the man and places him under arrest.

A short time later, Officer Lewis learns that a burglary had occurred in a 6th floor apartment in the same building that the male Hispanic was seen leaving. Among the items stolen were a TV and radio.

23. What did the male Hispanic have in his possession when he was stopped by Officer Lewis? A

    A. portable radio and a Sony TV
    B. portable TV and a Sony radio
    C. Sony TV and a Zenith radio
    D. Zenith TV and a Sony radio

24. Sergeant Smith informed Officer Lewis of burglaries occurring on his post

    A. late evening and early morning
    B. early morning and early afternoon
    C. early afternoon and late afternoon
    D. late morning and early evening

25. The man Officer Lewis stopped to question

    A. was about 5'5" tall and wore dark sunglasses
    B. had a dark complexion and a large black mustache
    C. had a large black mustache and a tattoo on his forearm
    D. had a tattoo on his forearm and was about 5'5" tall

KEY (CORRECT ANSWERS)

1.	B/C	11.	C
2.	A	12.	A
3.	A	13.	C
4.	D	14.	D
5.	B	15.	C
6.	C	16.	D
7.	D	17.	B
8.	B	18.	B
9.	B	19.	A
10.	D	20.	B

21. D
22. C
23. B
24. A
25. D

REPORT WRITING

EXAMINATION SECTION
TEST 1

DIRECTIONS: Each question or incomplete statement is followed by several suggested answers or completions. Select the one that BEST answers the question or completes the statement. *PRINT THE LETTER OF THE CORRECT ANSWER IN THE SPACE AT THE RIGHT.*

1. Upon coming into possession of found property, a police officer should do the following in the order given: 1.____
    - I. Issue a receipt to person delivering property if other than a police officer.
        - a. If property is turned in at station house, Station House Clerk will prepare a Property Clerk's Invoice and give finder a copy as a receipt.
        - b. If property is delivered to a police officer on patrol, prepare a receipt including a description of the property and signature of receiving officer.
    - II. Enter facts in Memo Book.
    - III. Prepare worksheet of Property Clerk's Invoice.
    - IV. Deliver property and worksheet to Station House Officer.
    - V. Verify accuracy of Property Clerk's Invoice by signing name in the appropriate box.

    Police Officer Bestwell, while on patrol, finds a black leather purse near a subway entrance. The bag contains a wallet with personal papers and other miscellaneous items. After logging the items that were contained in the bag into his Memo Book, Officer Bestwell asks Mrs. Robinson, a witness, to sign the book to verify that he found the property and that he was going to deliver it to the station house. Officer Bestwell's NEXT step should be to

    A. give Mrs. Robinson a receipt describing the property
    B. have the Station House Clerk prepare a Property Clerk's Invoice and give a copy to Mrs. Robinson
    C. prepare a worksheet of the Property Clerk's Invoice
    D. deliver property and Property Clerk's Invoice to the Station House Officer

2. Police Officer Rogers was dispatched to investigate a report of drugs being sold. The Officer obtained the following information: 2.____

    Place of Occurrence: In front of 109-30 Hollis Avenue
    Time of Occurrence: Between 3:00 P.M. and 6:00 P.M.
    Reporter: Mrs. Williams, who resides at 109-30 Hollis Avenue
    Crime: Drug sales
    Suspects: Male students from PS 182

    Officer Rogers is preparing a report on the investigation.
    Which one of the following expresses the above information MOST clearly and accurately?

A. Mrs. Williams reports between the hours of 3:00 P.M. and 6:00 P.M. drugs are sold. She lives at 109-30 Hollis Avenue where a group of boys from PS 182 sell drugs outside of her home.
B. Male students selling drugs from PS 182 are creating a problem for Mrs. Williams. She reports this takes place in front of her home. She resides at 109-30 Hollis Avenue. The sales take place from 3:00 P.M. to 6:00 P.M.
C. Drugs are being sold in front of 109-30 Hollis Avenue. Mrs. Williams reported a group of boys from PS 182 are responsible in front of her home at 109-30 Hollis Avenue. The drugs sell from 3:00 P.M. to 6:00 P.M.
D. Mrs. Williams reports that a group of boys from PS 182 are selling drugs in front of her home at 109-30 Hollis Avenue. She further reports that the drug sales occur between 3:00 P.M. and 6:00 P.M.

3. While on patrol, Police Officer Willis responds to a report of unusual odors at an apartment complex. The following information was obtained by the Officer:
Place of Occurrence: 173 Concord Avenue, Apt. 17
Time of Occurrence: 1:10 A.M.
Caller: Mrs. Denise Mathis
Odors: Gas and ammonia
Source of Odors: Janitor's supply room
Action Taken: Fire Department called
Officer Willis is completing a report on the incident. Which one of the following expresses the above information MOST clearly and accurately?

A. At 173 Concord Avenue, Apt. 17, the smell of gas and ammonia prompted Mrs. Denise Mathis to call 911. The Fire Department responded to the scene of the janitor's supply room. It was 1:10 A.M.
B. Mrs. Denise Mathis smelled gas and ammonia from her home at 173 Concord Avenue, Apt. 17. She called 911. The source was found in the janitor's supply room after being noticed at 1:10 A.M., and the Fire Department was called.
C. At 1:10 A.M., Mrs. Denise Mathis of 173 Concord Avenue, Apt. 17, smelled gas and ammonia, and called 911. The odors were found to be coming from the janitor's supply room. The Fire Department was called to the scene.
D. Unusual odors of gas and ammonia were noticed by Mrs. Denise Mathis at 173 Concord Avenue, Apt. 17 at 1:10 A.M. The janitor's supply room was responsible. She called 911. The Fire Department was called.

4. Police Officer Kelly responds to a call from the radio dispatcher regarding a small boy who has fallen down while running in a schoolyard. Officer Kelly has obtained the following information:
Time of Incident: 8:00 A.M.
Place of Incident: PS 27 schoolyard at 1313 Thorn Lane
Victim: Henry Ruiz
Injury: Broken right index finger
Officer Kelly is writing a report on the incident.
Which one of the following expresses the above information MOST clearly and accurately?

- A. While running in the PS 27 schoolyard, Henry Ruiz broke his right index finger. At 8:00 A.M., an accident occurred at 1313 Thorn Lane.
- B. At 8:00 A.M., a little boy broke his finger in the schoolyard at 1313 Thorn Lane. Henry Ruiz was running and it was his right index finger he broke at PS 27.
- C. Henry Ruiz fell down while running at 8:00 A.M. at 1313 Thorn Lane. The small boy broke his right index finger in the schoolyard of PS 27.
- D. At 8:00 A.M. in the schoolyard of PS 27, 1313 Thorn Lane, Henry Ruiz fell down while running and broke his right index finger.

5. Police Officer Covatti was on patrol when he received the following information relating to a person in need of assistance:

   Place of Occurrence: Canal Street and Ludlow Place
   Date of Occurrence: May 25
   Person Aided: Unidentified woman, unconscious and bleeding from the head
   Reporter: Laura Gallo
   Disposition: Victim transported by ambulance to Beth Israel Hospital

   Officer Covatti is about to enter the details regarding this incident in his Memo Book. Which one of the following expresses the above information MOST clearly and accurately?

   - A. An unconscious woman was transported to Beth Israel Hospital by ambulance. Laura Gallo reported that she was bleeding from the head at the corner of Canal Street and Ludlow Place on May 25th. She was unidentified.
   - B. On May 25th, Laura Gallo reported that there was an unconscious woman bleeding from the head on the corner of Canal Street and Ludlow Place. An ambulance responded and transported the woman, who was unidentified, to Beth Israel Hospital.
   - C. Laura Gallo reported that there was an unconscious unidentified woman bleeding from the head on the corner of Canal Street and Ludlow Place. On May 25th, an ambulance transported the woman to Beth Israel Hospital.
   - D. An ambulance transported an unconscious woman, bleeding from the head, to Beth Israel Hospital. On May 25th, Laura Gallo reported that an unidentified woman was on the corner of Canal Street and Ludlow Place.

6. Police Officers Carrano and Lee have responded to the scene of a burglary and obtained the following information:

   Place of Occurrence: 289 Orchard Street
   Time of Occurrence: 1:35 A.M.
   Witness: Ms. Perez
   Suspect: A female Hispanic, 5'10", 140 lbs., wearing a black jacket and blue jeans
   Crime: Burglary of a clothing store, three coats taken

   Officers Lee and Carrano are filing the initial report on the incident. Which one of the following expresses the above information MOST clearly and accurately?

A. At 1:35 A.M., Ms. Perez reported a woman stole three coats while wearing a black jacket and blue jeans in the store at 289 Orchard Street. The Hispanic is 5'10" and 140 lbs.
B. A female Hispanic witnessed by Ms. Perez was wearing blue jeans and a black jacket. A store at 289 Orchard Street was robbed of three coats by a suspect weighing 140 lbs. at 5'10" at 1:35 A.M.
C. Ms. Perez witnessed a burglary when she saw a woman steal three coats. She was wearing blue jeans and a black jacket. At 1:35 A.M. she burglarized a store at 289 Orchard Street. The Hispanic suspect was 5'10" and 140 lbs.
D. At 1:35 A.M., Ms. Perez reportedly saw a female Hispanic steal three coats from a store at 289 Orchard Street. The suspect was described as being 5'10", 140 lbs., wearing blue jeans and a black jacket.

7. Police Officer Sanchez has just finished investigating a report of a rape and has obtained the following information:
Time of Occurrence: 9:10 A.M.
Place of Occurrence: Tony's Bodega, 109 Victory Boulevard
Victim: Joyce Rivera, employee
Crime: Rape
Suspect: Male, white, carrying a gun
Officer Sanchez is completing a report on the incident.
Which one of the following expresses the above information MOST clearly and accurately?

A. Joyce Rivera is an employee at Tony's Bodega located at 109 Victory Boulevard. She reported that at 9:10 A.M. a white male went into the Bodega and raped her at gunpoint.
B. While working in Tony's Bodega, located at 100 Victory Boulevard, Joyce Rivera reported at 9:10 A.M. she was raped at gunpoint by a male white.
C. The time was 9:10 A.M. when a white male went into Tony's Bodega and pointed a gun at an employee. He then raped Joyce Rivera. The Bodega is located at 109 Victory Boulevard.
D. At 9:10 A.M. Joyce Rivera reported that she was in Tony's Bodega, located at 109 Victory Boulevard. A white male went in and raped her while she was working at gunpoint.

8. Police Officer Mercardo has been assigned to inspect Patrol Car #785 for its equipment and general condition.
The following information has been obtained by the Officer:
   I. Total mileage of car: 76,561
   II. Exterior of car: Poor
      A. Broken right headlight
      B. Dents on right fender and right door
      C. Front tires flat
   III. Interior or car: Poor
      A. Seats ripped
      B. Dashboard lights broken
      C. Glove compartment door missing
Officer Mercado is completing a report on his inspection of the car.
Which one of the following expresses the above information MOST clearly and accurately?

A. Patrol Car #785 has a total mileage of 76,561 miles and is in poor condition in that the exterior of the car has a broken right headlight. It also has flats on both front tires and dents are on right fender and door. The interior of the car shows ripped seats and no glove compartment door with the dashboard lights broken.
B. Patrol Car #785, which is in poor condition, has a total mileage of 76,561 miles. The exterior of the car has a broken right headlight and dents on the right fender and right door. Both front tires are flat. The interior of the car reveals that the seats are ripped, the dashboard lights don't work, and the door to the glove compartment is missing.
C. Patrol Car #785 has on the exterior a broken right headlight, dents to the fender and door which can be found on the right side, and two flat tires in the front. For the interior, the seats are ripped, the dashboard lights are broken, and the glove compartment needs to be fixed. The general condition of the car is poor, which has a total mileage of 76,561.
D. Patrol Car #785 has in the interior ripped seats and a missing glove compartment door. Also the dashboard lights don't come on. The condition of the car is poor, it has a total mileage of 76,561 miles on it. The exterior of the car has two front tires that are flat, a broken right headlight and dents to the right fender. The door is also dented.

9. Police Officer Cohen is on patrol and receives a call to respond to a disturbance at a local grocery store. The following information is given to the Officer at the scene:
Place of Occurrence: Joe's Mini-Mart
Complainant: Tom Callas
Crime: Loitering and using abusive language
Suspect: Male, Hispanic
Action Taken: The suspect was removed from premises
Officer Cohen is completing a report on the incident. Which one of the following expresses the above information MOST clearly and accurately?

A. Tom Callas called the police because a male Hispanic was loitering and using abusive language in Joe's Mini-Mart. The male Hispanic was removed from the premises by police.
B. A male Hispanic was removed from Joe's Mini-Mart. Tom Callas called the police. He was loitering and using abusive language when he was removed from the premises.
C. At Joe's Mini-Mart, a male Hispanic was loitering and using abusive language. Tom Callas called the police. They removed him from the premises.
D. The police removed a male Hispanic from Joe's Mini-Mart. Tom Callas called them because he was loitering and using abusive language.

10. Police Officer Roach responded to the home of Audrey Seager regarding a past burglary. Ms. Seager reported that, while she was at work, someone broke into her home and stole the property listed below. She further stated that a piece of her luggage worth approximately $150.00 was also taken and was probably used by the robber to carry the following property out of her apartment:

2 35mm cameras, each valued at	$289.00
2 televisions, each valued at	$329.00
Miscellaneous jewelry valued at	$455.00
Cash	$350.00
Stock certificates valued at	$1500.00

    Officer Roach is completing a Complaint Report.
    Which one of the following is the TOTAL value of the property and cash stolen from Ms. Seager?

    A. $2,923 B. $3,073 C. $3,691 D. $3,991

11. While on patrol, Police Officer Richardson receives a call to respond to a grand larceny. The following information relating to the crime is obtained by the Officer:

    Time of Occurrence: Between 3:00 A.M. and 4:00 A.M.
    Place of Occurrence: In front of 1122 Dumont Avenue
    Victim: Bart Edwards
    Crime: Car theft
    Type of Car: 2005 Chrysler 300

    Officer Richardson is completing a report on the incident. Which one of the following expresses the above information MOST clearly and accurately?

    A. Reported stolen at 3:00 A.M. and 4:00 A.M. in front of 1122 Dumont Avenue was Bart Edwards' 2005 Chrysler 300.
    B. Bart Edwards reported that at some time between 3:00 A.M. and 4:00 A.M., his 2005 Chrysler 300 was stolen from in front of 1122 Dumont Avenue.
    C. Between 3:00 A.M. and 4:00 A.M., Bart Edwards reported that his 2005 Chrysler 300 was stolen in front of 1122 Dumont Avenue.
    D. In front of 1122 Dumont Avenue between 3:00 A.M. and 4:00 A.M., Bart Edwards reported that his 2005 Chrysler 300 was stolen.

12. While on patrol, Police Officers Coates and Hall respond to a complaint about a stolen vehicle. The following information relating to the incident is obtained by the Officers:

    Time of Occurrence: 3:00 A.M.
    Stolen Vehicle: 2006 Corvette
    Witness: Mark Wondon
    Place: In front of 12-14 Diamond Street
    Victim: John Silber
    Suspect: James Frank

    Officer Hall is completing a report on the incident.
    Which one of the following expresses the above information MOST clearly and accurately?

A. Mark Wondon reports that at 3:00 A.M. he witnessed James Frank steal a 2006 Corvette from in front of 12-14 Diamond Street. Mr. Wondon states that the car belongs to John Silber.
B. Mark Wondon reports that the 2006 Corvette taken was for John Silber. In front of 12-14 Diamond Street it was taken. The car was robbed by James Frank at 3:00 A.M.
C. At 3:00 A.M. a 2006 Corvette stolen by James Frank was reported. Mark Wondon saw it in front of 12-14 Diamond Street. It was owned by John Silber.
D. At 12-14 Diamond Street, a 2006 Corvette was reported by Mark Wondon at 3:00 A.M. John Silber, the car owner, was the victim. It was done by James Frank.

13. While on patrol in the subway, Police Officer Conway is notified, via radio, to respond to the northbound platform to investigate a crime. The following information relating to the crime was obtained by the Officer:
Time of Occurrence: 5:30 P.M.
Place: Northbound A train
Witness: Gertrude Stern
Victim: Matilda Jones
Crime: Chain snatch
Officer Conway is completing a report on the incident.
Which one of the following Memo Book entries expresses the above information MOST clearly and accurately?

A. There was a chain snatching incident on the Northbound A train at 5:30 P.M. involving Matilda Jones and Gertrude Stern. There was a witness.
B. Gertrude Stern, while traveling on the Northbound A train, witnessed a chain snatching with Matilda Jones at 5:30 P.M.
C. Matilda Jones and Gertrude Stern were on the Northbound A train at 5:30 P.M. when Gertrude witnessed a chain snatching.
D. Matilda Jones informed me that her chain was snatched aboard a Northbound A train at 5:30 P.M. Gertrude Stern witnessed the chain snatching.

14. Police Officers Quinn and Dunn receive a call to respond to a reported robbery. The following information relating to the crime is obtained by the Officers:
Time of Occurrence: 10:00 P.M.
Place of Occurrence: 31-42 Maplewood Avenue, Liquor Store
Victim: Donna Miller, store owner
Witness: Thomas White, customer
Suspect: Michael Wall
Crime: Money stolen from cash register
Officers Quinn and Dunn are completing a report on the incident.
Which one of the following expresses the above information MOST clearly and accurately?

A. The witness said that he got to the liquor store at 10:00 P.M.; and when he got there; the place was being held up. His name was Michael Wall. He took the money from Donna Miller, the owner of the liquor store on 31-42 Maplewood Avenue out of the store cash register. Thomas White reported these facts to us.
B. At 10:00 P.M., Thomas White, the witness, states that after entering the liquor store at 31-42 Maplewood Avenue, he saw the suspect take money from the cash register which belongs to Donna Miller, the owner. Michael Wall is suspected.

C. Thomas White reports that at 10:00 P.M. he went to the liquor store at 31-42 Maplewood Avenue and saw Michael Wall take money from the cash register. The store is owned by Donna Miller.

D. Donna Miller, the owner, was robbed at 10:00 P.M. when the money from her cash register was taken at 31-42 Maplewood Avenue. Thomas White was in the liquor store at the time and saw Michael Wall do it.

15. Police Officers Mains and Jacobs respond to a report of an assault and obtain the following information:

Time of Occurrence:	8:00 P.M.
Place of Occurrence:	Lobby of 165 E. 210th Street
Victim:	Charles Rayes, stabbed in chest
Witness:	John McNam
Suspect:	Lydon Syms
Weapon:	Large kitchen knife

The Officers are completing a report on the incident.
Which one of the following expresses the above information MOST clearly and accurately?

A. Mr. John McNam states that at 8:00 P.M. he observed Lydon Syms stab Charles Rayes in the chest while entering the lobby of 165 E. 210th Street with a large kitchen knife.

B. At 8:00 P.M., John McNam stated he saw Lydon Syms use a large kitchen knife on Charles Rayes in the chest in the lobby of 165 E. 210th Street.

C. At 8:00 P.M., John McNam stated he observed Lydon Syms stab him in the chest with a kitchen knife while in the lobby of 165 E. 210th Street with Charles Rayes.

D. Mr. John McNam stated that at 8:00 P.M. he observed Lydon Syms stab Charles Rayes in the chest with a large kitchen knife in the lobby of 165 E. 210th Street.

16. While on patrol, Police Officers Murray and Crown receive a radio call to respond to a reported assault. The following information is given to them at the scene:

Time of Occurrence:	6:00 P.M.
Victim:	Sarah Schwartz, wife
Witness:	Cathy Morris, Sarah's sister
Suspect:	Raymond Schwartz, husband
Crime:	Assault with a knife

The Officers are completing a report on the incident.
Which one of the following expresses the above information MOST clearly and accurately?

A. Cathy Morris stated that she was visiting her sister, Sarah Schwartz. They were cooking dinner when Raymond Schwartz, Sarah's husband, came home at 6:00 P.M. Raymond was drunk and started an argument with Sarah. During the argument, Raymond picked up a knife and cut Sarah.

B. Sarah Schwartz stated that she was making dinner with her sister, Cathy Morris. Her husband Raymond came home real angry and was drunk at 6:00 P.M. They had an argument and Raymond cut her with a knife.

C. According to Cathy Morris, her sister Sarah Schwartz was cooking dinner with her. Sarah's husband Raymond came home. They got into an argument. He was drunk and had a knife in his hand and cut her. This happened when he arrived at 6:00 P.M.

D. Sarah Schwartz' sister reported to me that at 6:00 P.M. her husband Raymond came home drunk. Cathy Morris was with her making dinner. Raymond got mad at her, picked up a knife, and cut her.

17. Police Officer Allan responds to the scene of a robbery. The following information relating to the incident is obtained by the Officer:

Time of Occurrence: 2:00 A.M.
Victim: Michael Harper
Perpetrator: Unknown
Description of Crime: Victim was grabbed around neck from behind while walking home; money and jewelry taken.

Police Officer Allan is preparing a report on the robbery.
Which one of the following expresses the above information MOST clearly and accurately?

A. At 2:00 A.M. while walking home, Michael Harper observed someone he could not identify. The victim was grabbed around the neck, and his money and jewelry were stolen,
B. At 2:00 A.M. while walking home, Michael Harper was grabbed around the neck from behind. His money and jewelry were stolen. Mr. Harper is unable to identify the perpetrator.
C. Michael Harper is unable to identify the perpetrator because he grabbed him around the neck while walking home. The victim was robbed of money and jewelry at 2:00 A.M.
D. Michael Harper was robbed of money and jewelry. The unknown perpetrator was not identified; however, he grabbed him from behind while walking home.

18. While on patrol, Police Officer Silas responds to a report of a robbery. The following information is obtained by the Officer:

Time of Occurrence: 5:00 P.M.
Place of Occurrence: 40 Forman Street
Victim: Floyd Joy
Witness: Paul Clay
Suspect: Joe Lister
Crime: Robbery

Officer Silas is completing a report on the incident.
Which one of the following expresses the above information MOST clearly and accurately?

A. At 5:00 P.M., Paul Clay witnessed a robbery at 40 Forman Street. Floyd Joy was robbed by Joe Lister.
B. At 5:00 P.M., Joe Lister was observed committing a robbery with Floyd Joy on 40 Forman Street by Paul Clay.
C. At 40 Forman Street, Paul Clay stated to me that he had seen Floyd Joy getting robbed. The perpetrator, Joe Lister, committed the robbery at 5:00 P.M.
D. Paul Clay stated that he witnessed a robbery taking place at 40 Forman Street at 5:00 P.M. with Joe Lister. The subject of the robbery was Floyd Joy.

19. While on patrol, Police Officer Wright receives a call to respond to a robbery. The following information relating to the crime is obtained by the Officer:

Place of Occurrence: Corner of Rockaway and New York Avenues
Victim: Frank Holt
Suspect: Male white
Weapon: .357 Magnum

Officer Wright is completing a report on the incident. Which one of the following expresses the above information MOST clearly and accurately?

- A. On the corner of Rockaway and New York Avenues, Frank Holt reported that he was robbed with a .357 Magnum by a white male.
- B. Armed with a .357 Magnum on the corner of Rockaway and New York Avenues, Frank Holt reported that he was robbed by a white male.
- C. A white male on the corner of Rockaway and New York Avenues who was armed with a .357 Magnum committed a robbery, reported Frank Holt.
- D. Frank Holt reported that he was robbed on the corner of Rockaway and New York Avenues by a white male armed with a .357 Magnum.

20. Police Officer Daniels has just finished investigating a report of criminal mischief and has obtained the following information:

Place of Occurrence: In front of victim's residence
Time of Occurrence: Between 5:15 A.M. and 5:30 A.M.
Victim: Carl Burns, of 1856 Lenox Street, owner of vehicle
Crime: Criminal mischief
Damage: Paint poured onto his vehicle

Officer Daniels is preparing a report on the incident. Which one of the following expresses the above information MOST clearly and accurately?

- A. While parked in front of his residence, Carl Burns stated between 5:15 A.M. and 5:30 A.M. that paint was poured onto his vehicle at 1856 Lenox Street.
- B. Carl Burns, of 1856 Lenox Street, stated that between 5:15 A.M. and 5:30 A.M. paint was poured onto his vehicle while it was parked in front of his residence.
- C. Between 5:15 A.M. and 5:30 A.M., Carl Burns of 1856 Lenox Street stated, while parked in front of his residence, that paint was poured on his vehicle.
- D. Carl Burns between 5:15 A.M. and 5:30 A.M. while parked at 1856 Lenox Street, his residence, stated that paint was poured onto his vehicle.

21. At 10:20 A.M., Police Officer Medina responds to a report of a robbery. The Officer obtains the following information regarding the incident:

Time of Occurrence: 10:15 A.M.
Place of Occurrence: Mike's Deli
1700 E. 9th Street
Victim: Chuck Baker, owner of Mike's Deli
Amount Stolen: $500.00
Suspects: 3 male whites

Officer Medina is completing a report on the incident. Which one of the following expresses the above information MOST clearly and accurately?

11 (#1)

    A. Chuck Baker, the owner of Mike's Deli, located at 1700 E. 9th Street, reported that at 10:15 A.M. three white males robbed his deli of $500.00.
    B. At 10:15 A.M., Chuck Baker, deli owner, reported that Mike's Deli, located at 1700 E. 9th Street, was robbed of $500.00 by three white males.
    C. Chuck Baker reported that $500.00 had been taken from the owner of Mike's Deli, located at 1700 E. 9th Street at 10:15 A.M. by three white males.
    D. At 10:15 A.M., it was reported by the deli owner that three white males robbed $500.00 from Chuck Baker. Mike's Deli is located at 1700 E. 9th Street.

22. While on patrol, Police Officers Rydell and Francis receive a call to respond to a reported robbery. The following information related to the crime is obtained by the Officers: 22.____

Time of Occurrence:	10:00 A.M.
Place of Occurrence:	8012 Liberty Street
Victim:	Leslie Reese, friend of witness
Witness:	Lorraine Mitchell
Suspect:	Bill Clark
Crime:	Money and jewelry stolen

Officer Francis is completing a report on the incident.
Which one of the following expresses the above information MOST clearly and accurately?

    A. Lorraine Mitchell stated that while responding to a robbery, at 10:00 A.M., she was a witness at 8012 Liberty Street. Her friend, Leslie Reese, had her jewelry and money taken from her by Bill Clark.
    B. Lorraine Mitchell stated that at 10:00 A.M. she saw Bill Clark approach her friend, Leslie Reese, and take money and jewelry from her. The crime took place at 8012 Liberty Street.
    C. At 8012 Liberty Street, stolen money and jewelry were reported. This was witnessed by Lorraine Mitchell and her friend, Leslie Reese, who was also robbed of her money and jewelry. The incident occurred at 10:00 A.M. The suspect is Bill Clark.
    D. At 10:00 A.M., Lorraine Mitchell saw Bill Clark enter 8012 Liberty Street. At that point, Leslie Reese owned jewelry and money which were stolen.

23. While on patrol, Police Officer York responds to a case of a missing child. The following information relating to this case was obtained by the Officer: 23.____

Name of Missing Child:	Susan Spencer
Age:	7 years old
School:	Mountainside School
Information Provided By:	Mary Templeton, Principal
Disposition of Case:	Child is all right; she arrived at school five minutes before Officer York arrived

Officer York is completing a report on the incident.
Which one of the following expresses the above information MOST clearly and accurately?

A. Only five minutes before my arrival she was at the school and was all right. Mary Templeton, the Principal of Mountainside School said that the missing child, Susan Spencer, was seven years old.
B. I arrived at Mountainside School and spoke with Mary Templeton, the Principal. She informed me that the missing child, Susan Spencer, age seven, had arrived five minutes before I did and is fine.
C. She arrived five minutes before I did. The Principal of Mountainside School, Mary Templeton, informed me that the missing child was seven years old, Susan Spencer, and was fine.
D. Seven-year-old Susan Spencer was missing. Mary Templeton, Principal, Mountainside School said that only five minutes before my arrival she was at the school and was fine.

24. The following details were obtained by Police Officer Talbert at the scene of a shooting:

Place of Occurrence: 77 Greene Street, inside the Video Arcade
Victim: Mr. Gerald Jackson, Video Arcade customer
Suspect: Mr. Michael Benton, Video Arcade owner
Crime: Shooting
Action Taken: Suspect arrested

Officer Talbert is completing a report on the incident.
Which one of the following expresses the above information MOST clearly and accurately?

A. Gerald Jackson was present in the Video Arcade when Michael Benton, the Arcade owner, was involved in a shooting. The shooting occurred at 77 Greene Street. An arrest was made.
B. Michael Benton and Gerald Jackson were in a shooting at the Video Arcade located at 77 Greene Street. The person shot by the owner was a customer. An arrest was made.
C. Gerald Jackson, a customer at the Video Arcade, located at 77 Greene Street, was shot by Michael Benton, the Arcade owner. Mr. Benton was arrested.
D. Michael Benton, owner of the Video Arcade, located at 77 Greene Street and Gerald Jackson, an Arcade customer were involved in a shooting. An arrest was made.

25. While on patrol, Police Officers Cando and Poppy receive a call to respond to a reported burglary. The following information relating to the crime is obtained by the Police Officers:

Time of Occurrence: 4:00 A.M.
Place of Occurrence: 81-31 Mitts Street
Witness: Jennifer Wink
Victim: Bette Miller, neighbor
Suspect: John Haysport, neighbor
Crime: House burglarized; TV set stolen

The Officers are completing a report on the incident.
Which one of the following expresses the above information MOST clearly and accurately?

A. Jennifer Wink, while on patrol, stated to me that the house next to her house at 81-31 Mitts Street was burglarized. The crime was committed by John Haysport. The crime was the TV set was no longer there. Bette Miller, a neighbor could not find her TV.
B. At 4:00 A.M. Jennifer Wink, the witness, reported to me that before she had seen John Haysport, a neighbor, go into 81-31 Mitts Street and steal a TV set. The TV belonged to Bette Miller who also lives nearby.
C. Jennifer Wink, the witness, states that John Haysport, burglarized her neighbor's house at 81-31 Mitts Street. She saw her neighbor leaving her neighbor's house at 4:00 A.M. with a TV set. The house was Bette Miller's house.
D. Jennifer Wink, the witness, states that her neighbor's house located at 81-31 Mitts Street was burglarized. Mrs. Wink further states that at 4:00 A.M. she saw a neighbor, John Haysport, leave Mrs. Miller's house with a TV set.

KEY (CORRECT ANSWERS)

1. C
2. D
3. C
4. D
5. B

6. D
7. A
8. B
9. A
10. C

11. B
12. A
13. D
14. C
15. D

16. A
17. B
18. A
19. D
20. B

21. A
22. B
23. B
24. C
25. D

TEST 2

DIRECTIONS: Each question or incomplete statement is followed by several suggested answers or completions. Select the one that BEST answers the question or completes the statement. *PRINT THE LETTER OF THE CORRECT ANSWER IN THE SPACE AT THE RIGHT.*

1. While on tow truck duty, Bridge and Tunnel Officer McNeil responded to an accident and obtained the following information at the scene:
   Place of Occurrence: Lamppost, York Ave. Bridge
   Time of Occurrence: 2:25 A.M.
   Make and License No. of Car: Dodge, license no. 427-ABM
   Cause of Accident: Wet roadway
   Action Taken: Hoisted and towed vehicle to disabled area of bridge
   Officer McNeil is completing an accident report.
   Which one of the following expresses the above information MOST clearly and accurately? 1.___

   A. On a wet roadway, a vehicle struck a lamppost and was hoisted and towed to a disabled area. The Dodge, license no. 427-ABM, was on the York Avenue Bridge at 2:25 A.M.
   B. A Dodge, license no. 427-ABM, drove into a lamppost on the York Avenue Bridge due to a wet roadway that had to be hoisted and towed off of the bridge at 2:25 A.M.
   C. A Dodge, license no. 427-ABM, drove into a lamppost at 2:25 A.M. on the York Avenue Bridge due to a wet roadway. The car was hoisted and towed off the bridge to the disabled area.
   D. A Dodge, license no. 427-ABM, hoisted and towed to a disabled area after 2:25 A.M. when it drove into a lamppost on the wet roadway of the York Avenue Bridge.

2. On February 15, 2004, Joyce Wright arrived at the facility building of the Army Memorial Bridge to file a complaint about being short-changed. Details of the incident are listed below:
   Date Reported: February 15, 2004
   Date of Occurrence: February 14, 2004
   Time of Occurrence: 8:20 A.M.
   Lane: 7
   Direction Traveling: West
   Amount of Toll $3.00
   Amount Given: $20.00 bill
   Change Returned: $7.00
   Bridge and Tunnel Officer Sanford is completing a report on the incident.
   Which one of the following expresses the above information MOST clearly and accurately? 2.___

A. On February 15, 2004, Joyce Wright reported in Lane 7 that she was given only $7.00 for change when she paid the $3.00 toll with a $20.00 bill while traveling west on February 14, 2004 at 8:20 A.M.
B. On February 15, 2004, while traveling west, Joyce Wright reported at 8:20 A.M. she was short-changed on February 14, 2004. She paid $20.00 for a $3.00 toll. She received $7.00 in Lane 7.
C. On February 15, 2004, Joyce Wright reported that she was short-changed on February 14, 2004 at 8:20 A.M. in Lane 7 while traveling westbound. She received $7.00 in change after paying the $3.00 toll with a $20.00 bill.
D. Joyce Wright reported on February 14, 2004 she was short-changed in westbound Lane 7 at 8:20 A.M. She paid the toll with a $20.00 bill and received $7.00 in change for the $3.00 toll according to the complainant on February 15, 2004.

3. While on duty at a bridge toll plaza, Bridge and Tunnel Officer White was told by a motorist that she realized she was off her intended route and was going the wrong way. The woman did not want to pay the toll or go over the bridge. Officer White recorded the following information:

Toll Lane: 10
License Plate Number: 627-AIB
Make of Car: Ford
Motorist's Name: Joan Semoore
Number of Occupants: Three
Time of Occurrence: 10:27 A.M.

Officer White is completing an Off-Route report on this incident.
Which one of the following expresses the above information MOST clearly and accurately?

A. Joan Seemoore was off-route in a Ford in Lane 10, license plate number 627-AIB, at 10:27 A.M., with three occupants.
B. At 10:27 A.M., a Ford, license plate number 627-AIB, was off-route with Joan Seemoore and three occupants in Lane 10.
C. At 10:27 A.M., a Ford, license plate number 627-AIB, driven by Joan Seemoore, was off-route in Lane 10. There were three occupants in the car.
D. Joan Seemoore drove three occupants and a Ford, license plate number 627-AIB, off-route in Lane 10, at 10:27 A.M.

4. Bridge and Tunnel Officer Grummund responds to an accident and obtains the following information:

Place of Occurrence: Andrea Bridge
Number of Vehicles Involved: Three
Type of Accident: Rear-end collision
Number of Injured: Four
Direction of Travel: Southbound
Witness: Mrs. Angela Court

Officer Grummund is reporting the accident to the Sergeant.
Which one of the following expresses the above information MOST clearly and accurately?

A. At the Andrea Bridge, three vehicles had a rear-end collision accident with four injuries, reported Mrs. Angela Court.
B. At the Andrea Bridge, three vehicles were involved in a rear-end collision accident. This information, obtained by Mrs. Angela Court, included four injured.
C. Southbound on the Andrea Bridge, three vehicles were involved in a rear-end collision involving four injuries and witnessed by Mrs. Angela Court.
D. At the Andrea Bridge, three vehicles were involved in a rear-end collision resulting in four injuries. The accident occurred in the southbound roadway and was witnessed by Mrs. Angela Court.

5. At 4:40 P.M., Bridge and Tunnel Officer Rasmon responds to the scene of an accident. The following information was obtained by the Officer:

Vehicles Involved: 2001 Ford
                     1999 GMC truck
                     1998 Volkswagen
Time of Occurrence: 4:35 P.M.
Place of Occurrence: Brownsville Bridge
Vehicle Needing a Tow: 2001 Ford
Witness: Sheila Norris

Officer Rasmon is reporting this information to the sergeant on duty.
Which one of the following expresses the above information MOST clearly and accurately?

A. Sheila Norris reported at 4:35 P.M. she witnessed an accident involving a 2001 Ford, which needed to be towed, a 1999 GMC truck, and a 1998 Volkswagon on the Brownsville Bridge. I responded to the scene at 4:40 P.M.
B. At 4:40 P.M., I responded to an accident on the Brownsville Bridge. The accident occurred at 4:35 P.M. and was witnessed by Sheila Norris. A 2001 Ford, a 1999 GMC truck, and a 1998 Volkswagon were involved in the accident. A tow was required for the 2001 Ford.
C. I responded to an accident on the Brownsville Bridge at 4:40 P.M. A 2001 Ford needed a tow, as well as a 1999 GMC truck and a 1998 Volkswagon, which were involved in the accident witnessed by Sheila Norris at 4:35 P.M.
D. I responded at 4:40 P.M. to an accident with a 1999 GMC truck, a 2001 Ford that needed a tow, and a 1998 Volkswagon that was witnessed by Sheila Norris at 4:35 P.M.

6. While collecting tolls at the Whitehouse Bridge, Bridge and Tunnel Officer Smith observed a vehicle pass through his toll lane without paying the toll. The following details were obtained by Officer Smith:

Vehicle Year and Make: 2005 Ford
Vehicle Color: Black
License Plate Number: BIX-621, New York
Driver Description: Male, white, blonde hair
Time of Occurrence: 8:50 A.M.
Place of Occurrence: Toll Lane 6

Officer Smith is completing a report on the situation.
Which one of the following expresses the above information MOST clearly and accurately?

A. Toll Lane 6 was not payed a toll by a black Ford, New York license plate number BIX-621. A white male, driving the 2005 vehicle at 8:50 A.M., had blonde hair.
B. A white male did not stop at Toll Lane 6. The blonde-haired driver of a black 2005 Ford did not pay the toll at 8:50 A.M. He was driving with New York plates, license number BIX-621.
C. At 8:50 A.M., a white male with blonde hair failed to pay the toll in Lane 6. He was driving a black 2005 Ford with New York license plates BIX-621.
D. Driving a black 2005 Ford at 8:50 A.M., a white male with blonde hair did not stop in Toll Lane 6. His black 2005 Ford with New York plates BIX-621 failed to pay the toll.

7. Bridge and Tunnel Officer Gallo has been called to court to testify about two summonses he issued on December 4, 2008. Officer Gallo refers to his memo book entries on the incident to prepare himself for the testimony. The relevant memo book entries are listed below:

Date of Occurrence: December 4, 2008
Time of Occurrence: 12:40 P.M.
Name of Driver: Vincent Bourne
Vehicle Year and Make: 2001 Pontiac
Violations: Uninspected vehicle, uninsured vehicle
Officer Assignment: Post B

Officer Gallo must testify on the incident, based on the prepared report.
Which one of the following expresses the above information MOST clearly and accurately?

A. On December 4, 2008, Vincent Bourne was driving at 12:40 P.M. The 2001 Pontiac was uninspected and uninsured. Summonses were issued while I was assigned to Post B.
B. A 2001 Pontiac driven by Vincent Bourne received two summonses for being uninsured and unregistered at 12:40 P.M. while I was assigned to Post B on December 4, 2008.
C. While assigned to Post B on December 4, 2008, at 12:40 P.M., I issued two summonses to Vincent Bourne. One of the summonses issued was for driving an uninsured vehicle and the other was for driving an unregistered vehicle. Vincent Bourne was driving a 2001 Pontiac.
D. On December 4, 2008, Vincent Bourne was issued two summonses for driving a 2001 Pontiac at 12:40 P.M. While I was assigned to Post B, he received them for driving an uninsured and unregistered vehicle.

8. In preparing a report which will be released to the public, a District Superintendent should FIRST be sure that the report

A. has no irrelevant material
B. includes only statements which conform to the Department's policy
C. is free of all hackneyed and stereotyped phrases
D. presents ideas in a most logical order

9. The MAJOR function of prompt, accurate reports in an agency is to

   A. be available for future reference
   B. expedite the official business of the agency
   C. indicate the efficient employee
   D. provide excellent research material

10. Fire Marshal Davis is training Fire Marshal Jones, who recently graduated from Fire Marshal school. Fire Marshal Davis has completed a physical examination of a 10-41 Code 1 and has obtained the following information:

Time Out:	2305 hours
Box:	3-3-6502
Place of Occurrence:	Apple Food Store located at 123 1st Avenue
Examination Showed:	Two separate and distinct fires
Damage:	Confined to basement storage room

    Fire Marshal Davis asks Fire Marshal Jones to prepare a report.
    Of the following statements Fire Marshal Jones might include in the report, which one MOST clearly and accurately expresses the information obtained by Fire Marshal Davis?

    A. At 3rd alarm box 6502, at 2305 hours, a fire occurred in the basement storage room of the Apple Food Store located at 123 1st Avenue.
    B. At 3rd alarm box 6502, at 2305 hours, two separate and distinct fires occurred in the basement storage room of the Apple Food Store located at 123 1st Ave.
    C. At 2305 hours, at box 6502, two separate and distinct fires occurred in the Apple Food Store located at 123 1st Avenue in the basement.
    D. At 2305 hours, at box 6502 which went to a 3rd alarm, a fire occurred in the basement room of the Apple Food Store located at 123 1st Avenue.

11. A fire marshal has just finished investigating a report of arson in the third degree and has obtained the following information:

Name of Auto Owner:	John Brown (interviewed in his residence)
Place of Occurrence:	2805 White Ave. in front of owner's residence
Crime:	Arson third degree (heavy scorching to vinyl roof of auto)
Time of Occurrence:	0300 hours (vehicle unoccupied)

    In preparing a report on the incident, which one of the following statements should the fire marshal include to express the above information MOST clearly and accurately?

    A. While parked in front of his residence, John Brown stated that at 0300 hours, his vehicle was set on fire at 2805 White Ave.
    B. John Brown of 2805 White Avenue stated that at 0300 hours, his vehicle was set on fire while it was parked in front of his residence.
    C. John Brown at 0300 hours while parked at 2805 White Ave., his residence, stated that his vehicle was set on fire.
    D. At 0300 hours, John Brown of 2805 White Ave. stated that while he was parking in front of his residence, his vehicle was set on fire.

12. A fire marshal arrives at the West Park Synagogue thirty minutes after it was firebombed by an arsonist. The following are details provided by eyewitnesses:

    Suspect: Male
    Ethnicity: White
    Height: 6'2" to 6'4"
    Weight: 220 lbs. to 240 lbs.
    Hair Color: Black
    Clothing: Blue dungaree jacket, brown pants
    Ignition Device: Molotov cocktail

    In completing a report on the incident, which one of the following statements should the fire marshal include to express the above information MOST clearly and accurately?

    A. A white male firebombed the West Park Synagogue with a Molotov cocktail. The perpetrator was described as being between 220-240 lbs., 6'2" to 6'4", with black hair. He was wearing a blue dungaree jacket and brown pants.
    B. A white male with black hair weighing 220-240 lbs. firebombed the West Park Synagogue. He was very tall and wore a blue dungaree jacket and brown pants. He used a Molotov cocktail.
    C. A heavy set white male was wearing a blue dungaree jacket and brown pants. He had black hair and a Molotov cocktail, and was 6'2" to 6'4". He fire-bombed the West Park Synagogue.
    D. A white male was 6'2" to 6'4" and weighed between 220-240 lbs., firebombed the West Park Synagogue with a Molotov cocktail. He was wearing brown pants, a blue dungaree jacket with black hair.

13. While on patrol, Traffic Enforcement Agent Scott witnessed an incident. He recorded the following information:

    Place of Incident: Grand Central Parkway
    Time of Incident: 4:50 A.M.
    Cause of Incident: Falling debris struck a vehicle
    Vehicle Type: Buick
    License Plate Number: 403-QRM

    Agent Scott is about to radio Traffic Control regarding this incident.
    Which one of the following expresses the above information MOST clearly and accurately?

    A. A Buick, license plate number 403-QRM, was struck by falling debris on the Grand Central Parkway at 4:50 A.M.
    B. License plate number 403-QRM is a Buick. Falling debris struck the Grand Central Parkway at 4:50 A.M.
    C. On the Grand Central Parkway, falling debris struck license plate number 403-QRM at 4:50 A.M. The car was a Buick.
    D. Debris was falling at 4:50 A.M. A Buick, license plate number 403-QRM was on the Grand Central Parkway.

14. Before beginning her patrol, Traffic Enforcement Agent Flores inspects her patrol vehicle. She obtains the following information:

Vehicle Number: 147
Exterior Condition: Poor
(A) Dent in right front door
(B) Left front tire flat
Interior Condition: Poor
(A) Seatbelts broken
(B) Rear seat ripped

Agent Flores is completing a report on her vehicle inspection.
Which one of the following expresses the above information MOST clearly and accurately?

A. The rear seat is ripped and the exterior is in poor condition of vehicle 147. The seatbelts are broken. The interior is also in poor condition. The front tire on the left side is flat and the right front door is dented.
B. The exterior shows a dented right front door and ripped rear seat. Vehicle 147 has a flat left front tire and broken seatbelts. The vehicle's interior and exterior are both in poor condition.
C. Vehicle 147 has a flat left front tire. The interior and exterior are in poor condition. Inside, the vehicle has a ripped rear seat and its seatbelts are broken. There is also a dent on the right front door.
D. Vehicle 147 is in poor condition. The exterior of the vehicle has a dent in the right front door and a flat left front tire. The interior of the vehicle shows that the rear seat is ripped and the seatbelts are broken.

15. While on patrol, Traffic Enforcement Agent Gates observes the following:

Violation: Parked in a *No Standing 7:00 A.M. to 7:00 P.M.* zone
Place of Occurrence: 29-29 Park Lane
License Plate Number: XZC-410
Vehicle Type: Blue Dodge
Assistance Needed: Tow truck

Agent Gates is about to radio Traffic Control with this information.
Which one of the following expresses the above information MOST clearly and accurately?

A. At 29-29 Park Lane, a tow truck is needed between 7:00 A.M. and 7:00 P.M. A blue Dodge, license plate number XZC-410 is parked in a *No Standing* zone.
B. A blue Dodge, license plate number XZC-410, is parked in a *No Standing 7:00 A.M. to 7:00 P.M.* zone at 29-29 Park Lane. A tow truck is needed.
C. License plate number XZC-410 is parked in a *No Standing 7:00 A.M. to 7:00 P.M.* zone. A tow truck is needed for a blue Dodge, at 29-29 Park Lane.
D. A tow truck is needed in a *No Standing 7:00 A.M. to 7:00 P.M.* zone at 29-29 Park Lane. License plate number XZC-410 is parked. It's a blue Dodge.

16. The following information relates to an accident observed by Traffic Enforcement Agent Taylor:

    Place of Accident: 625 Hollings Avenue
    Time of Accident: 2:00 P.M.
    Drivers Involved: Mrs. Jean Rodgers and Mr. John Cruz
    Violation: Failure to Obey a Stop Sign
    Action Taken: Summons served to Mrs. Jean Rodgers

    Agent Taylor is informing his Lieutenant about the facts of the accident.
    Which one of the following expresses the above information MOST clearly and accurately?

    16._____

    A. A summons was issued to Mrs. Jean Rodgers for driving at 2:00 P.M. in front of 625 Hollings Avenue. Mrs. Rodgers and Mr. John Cruz were involved in an accident and failed to obey a stop sign.
    B. Mrs. Jean Rodgers was issued a summons at 2:00 P.M. For failure to obey a stop sign, Mrs. Rodgers and Mr. John Cruz were involved in an accident at 625 Hollings Avenue.
    C. Mrs. Jean Rodgers and Mr. John Cruz were involved in an accident at 2:00 P.M. in front of 625 Hollings Avenue, and Mrs. Rodgers was issued a summons for failure to obey a stop sign.
    D. It was 2:00 P.M. when a summons was issued to Mrs. Jean Rodgers. For failure to obey a stop sign, Mrs. Rodgers and Mr. Cruz were involved in an accident. It was at 625 Hollings Avenue.

17. While directing traffic, Traffic Enforcement Agent Ross observed an accident and recorded the following information at the scene:

    Place of Accident: Intersection of White Plains
                               Road and Pelham Parkway
    Time of Accident: 4:48 P.M.
    Name of Injured: Kim Johnson
    Name of Driver: Kim Johnson
    Description of Accident: Car slid on ice and crashed into
                               an elevated train support beam
    Action Taken: Notified Traffic Control to
                               request police and ambulance

    Agent Ross is informing his Lieutenant about the accident.
    Which one of the following expresses the above information MOST clearly and accurately?

    17._____

    A. At the intersection of White Plains Road and Pelham Parkway, Kim Johnson injured herself on an elevated train support beam. When Traffic Control was notified that at 4:48 P.M. her car slid on the ice, police and an ambulance were requested.
    B. Kim Johnson was injured at the intersection of White Plains Road and Pelham Parkway. She injured herself and notified Traffic Control that her car hit a support beam at 4:48 P.M. when she slid on the ice into the train. A request for police and an ambulance was made.
    C. At the intersection of White Plains Road and Pelham Parkway, Kim Johnson injured herself and Traffic Control was notified. Her car hit a support beam at 4:48 P.M., and she slid on the ice into the train. Traffic Control requested the police and an ambulance.

D. At 4:48 P.M., Kim Johnson was injured at the intersection of White Plains Road and Pelham Parkway when her car slid on the ice and crashed into an elevated train support beam. Traffic Control was notified to request police and an ambulance.

18. Traffic Enforcement Agent Gilmore is required to testify in court regarding a moving violation. The following facts were recorded at the scene of the incident:

    Date of Occurrence: May 26, 2004
    Place of Occurrence: Intersection of W. 125th Street and Broadway
    Operator of Vehicle: George Underwood
    Charge: Failure to stop for a red light
    Vehicle: A blue 2004 Chevrolet sedan
    Action Taken: Summons issued

    Agent Gilmore needs to be accurate and clear when testifying.
    Which one of the following expresses the above information MOST clearly and accurately?

    A. On May 26, 2004, I issued a summons to George Underwood while driving a 2004 blue Chevrolet sedan. He received the summons for failure to stop for a red light. This happened at the intersection of W. 125th Street and Broadway.
    B. For failure to stop a blue 2004 Chevrolet sedan for a red light, I issued a summons. George Underwood was at the intersection of W. 125th Street and Broadway on May 26, 2004.
    C. A 2004 blue Chevrolet sedan was driven by George Underwood, and I issued him a summons on May 26, 2004. He was on W. 125th Street when he failed to stop for a red light at the intersection of Broadway.
    D. On May 26, 2004, I issued a summons to George Underwood, who was driving a 2004 blue Chevrolet sedan, for failure to stop for a red light at the intersection of W. 125th Street and Broadway.

19. Traffic Enforcement Agent Cohen witnessed an accident. He recorded the following information:

    Accident: Hit and run of a pedestrian
    Vehicle Make and Model: Plymouth station wagon
    License Plate Number: IJD-689
    Description of Driver: Male, white, black hair
    Time of Occurrence: 3:15 P.M.
    Place of Occurrence: Intersection of McLean Avenue and W. 249th Street

    Agent Cohen is preparing a report on this incident. Which one of the following expresses the above information MOST clearly and accurately?

    A. At 3:15 P.M., a Plymouth station wagon, license plate number IJD-689, driven by a white male with black hair, struck a pedestrian at the intersection of McLean Avenue and W. 249th Street.
    B. A Plymouth station wagon, license plate number IJD-689, struck a pedestrian. A white male with black hair was at the intersection of McLean Avenue and W. 249th Street at 3:15 P.M.
    C. A pedestrian struck a Plymouth station wagon, license plate number IJD-689, at the intersection of McLean Avenue and W. 249th Street. The driver was a white male with black hair.

D. A white male with black hair struck a pedestrian. At 3:15 P.M., he was driving a Plymouth station wagon, license plate number IJD-689 at the intersection of McLean Avenue and W. 249th Street.

20. The following facts relate to a vehicular accident observed by Traffic Enforcement Agent Webb:

    Date of Accident: February 13, 2004
    Time of Accident: 11:55 A.M.
    Place of Accident: Corner of Haven and Ridge Streets
    Driver in Violation: Mrs. Levin
    Violation: Driving the wrong way on a one-way street
    Other Driver: Mrs. Chang

    Agent Webb is preparing a report on the accident. Which one of the following expresses the above information MOST clearly and accurately?

    A. Driving the wrong way on a one-way street on February 13, 2004 was Mrs. Levin. At the corner of Haven and Ridge Streets the other driver, was Mrs. Chang, caused an accident at 11:55 A.M.
    B. Mrs. Chang was at the corner of Haven and Ridge Streets. On February 13, 2004 at 11:55 A.M., Mrs. Levin drove the wrong way on a one-way street and caused an accident with another driver.
    C. On February 13, 2004 at 11:55 A.M., Mrs. Levin drove the wrong way on a one-way street and caused an accident with another driver, Mrs. Chang, on the corner of Haven and Ridge Streets.
    D. Mrs. Chang was the other driver in an accident. Mrs. Levin drove the wrong way on a one-way street on February 13, 2004 on the corner of Haven and Ridge Streets at 11:55 A.M.

KEY (CORRECT ANSWERS)

1. C	11. B
2. C	12. A
3. C	13. A
4. D	14. D
5. B	15. B
6. C	16. C
7. A	17. D
8. B	18. D
9. B	19. A
10. B	20. C

POLICE SCIENCE NOTES

POLICE COMMUNICATIONS

Communication can be defined as the transfer of information from one person to another. It can be accomplished in a variety of ways including the spoken word, written message, signal or electrical device. Geographically, communication involves the transmission of messages from one point to another, either interdepartmentally or intradepartmentally. Any exchange of words, messages, or signals in connection with police action may be classified as police communications.

History

Police communications, contrary to many modern beliefs, are as old as the police service itself. In 17th century England, policemen carried bells or lanterns for identification and as signal devices to give warnings or to summon assistance. The 18th century saw little improvement in police signaling equipment. Police officers in the 19th century utilized whistles, night sticks, and even their pistols as signal devices. The 20th century brought the introduction of electrical devices to the field of police communications. The horn, bell, light, telegraph, telephone, radio-telegraph, radio, radar, and now television, afford communications with infinitely increased efficiency. These developments also have produced great strides in the area of speed, range, and area coverage.

Along with these developments in the technical aspects of police communications, the written reporting system of law enforcement agencies have become considerably more sophisticated with the use of automatic and electronic data storage and processing equipment becoming more and more common. This progress has resulted in more accurate, complete, and easily recoverable information for police use.

The rapid growth of police communication probably is the best indication of its success in police administration. It has enabled a remarkable increase in the promptness and effectiveness of police action, especially in emergencies where time is of utmost importance, and closer and more effective control over patrolmen in the field. Most recently developed and available are: two-way radios small enough to be carried on an officer's belt; printout or screen display devices mounted in patrol cars with computer inquiry capability; and automatic query/response devices which show dispatchers or supervisors the geographic locations of patrol cars by radio direction finding systems. Advances in radio communication render perhaps the most important innovations in police methods since the introduction of fingerprinting.

Present Practice

Today's tools of communication are allowing police departments, both large and small, to increase the extent and efficiency of their service. Hardly a single police action is taken that does not involve some sort of communication. Original complaints are usually made to the police department by use of citizen-placed telephone calls. The information is relayed to police dispatchers or other appropriate personnel by use of interoffice phones or by use of mechanical devices, such as the pneumatic tube. In many cases two-way radio is used to relay information to patrol vehicles or to other police departments.

Also helping to stretch the police potential are systems of communication involving teletype, radiotelegraph, land-wire telegraph, long-distance phone circuits, interconnected computer and photo transmitting machines.

These are but a sample of what make up the network of communication found in most police departments. These tools plus proper techniques are invaluable in accomplishing the necessary steps to deal with natural disasters or nuclear attacks. Therefore, knowledge of such tools and techniques are imperative to successful actions of local police auxiliary units.

Telephone Procedures

The citizen's first contact with the police department is often a telephone conversation with an officer. On the telephone you are the police department's voice and whatever you say and how you say it creates for the citizen an impression of the department to that citizen. Every time you pick up the phone you are doing a public relations job. It may be good, bad, or indifferent. Why not always try for the good public relations job?

When considering proper procedures for the use of the telephone, courtesy and consideration are always the keywords. Even when receiving calls from persons who are agitated or excited the proper action remains much the same as in normal telephone calls. Since a large part of police telephone work is receiving calls the following procedures are essential ones.

1. Identify yourself immediately after answering.
2. Speak courteously.
3. Have pad and pencil handy-makes notes when necessary.

On the other hand, when *you* make a call follow the same basic guides of courtesy and consideration. This may be stated as follows:

1. Have in mind what you wish to know or say when your call is answered.
2. Identify yourself and state your business.
3. Have pad and pencil available-make notes when necessary.

Reaching for a telephone is one of our most frequent and familiar gestures. However, this does not guarantee good telephone usage. Proper procedures can result in good telephone usage and are important to proper police work.

Radio Procedure

Two-way radio might well be considered the backbone of police communications. In many instances the proper use of this instrument may well mean the difference between success or failure in any given situation. In general, the same guides apply as did to good telephone procedures, namely, courtesy and consideration. However, a few specific guides are identified for your use.

To transmit a message:
1. Be certain the dispatcher is not busy transmitting other messages.
2. Contact dispatcher, giving your identification, and then wait for dispatcher to answer.
3. Begin your message after the dispatcher has answered you.

While transmitting a message:
1. Speak distinctly into the microphone as in ordinary conversation. Too loud a voice distorts the reception.
2. Speak slowly.
3. Keep messages brief.
4. Mentally rehearse your message before transmitting.
5. Never use vulgar language.

The final rule cannot be overemphasized. Not only is such language in poor taste, but is prohibited by regulations of the FCC. Furthermore, any excess language used, and vulgar language is excess, may well confuse or distort the meaning of your message.

In learning to use radio communications effectively it is necessary to master the codes and specific procedures in effect in your local police department. Appendix II gives some samples of such procedures.

Emergency Information Media

In addition to the telephone and radio communications of the police service, during a CD emergency the auxiliary policeman will need to receive and act on messages disseminated by public information media (radio and television broadcasts, newspapers, etc.) as part of the emergency information program. Although these messages will be intended for the general public, they will also convey information of value to the auxiliary policeman in the performance of his duties. For example, in many local civil defense plans provision is made for certain radio stations to remain on the air as part of the Emergency Broadcasting System, and their broadcasts will convey official information on such matters as warning conditions and last-minute instructions regarding movement to shelters or relocation areas.

POLICE COMMUNICATIONS & TELETYPE OPERATIONS

TABLE OF CONTENTS

	Page
I. COMMUNICATIONS	1
a. Radio in Automobiles	1
b. Police Radio Messages	1
c. Tampering with Private Communications	1
d. Failing to Report Criminal Telephone or Telegraph Communications	1
e. Unlawfully Obtaining Communications Information	2
f. Tampering with Letters, Mail, etc.	2
II. OFFENSES IN USE OF COMMUNICATION MEDIA	2
a. Party Lines	2
b. Annoying or Alarming Communications	2
c. Jamming, Other Non-Legitimate Phone Calls	3
d. Theft of Services (Telephone, Telegraph)	3
III. INVESTIGATIONS	3
IV. POLICE RADIO COMMUNICATIONS	4
a. General Requirements for Proper Transmissions	4
i. Ten-Signal Code	5
ii. Word Code	6
b. Headquarters Transmissions	7
c. Field Transmissions	7
d. Listeners	7
e. Authority	7
f. Radio Logs	7
V. POLICE TELETYPE NETWORKS	8
a. Description of "cops"	8
b. Computer Control	8
c. Operating Rules and Procedures	9
d. Teletype Messages Required by Law	9
e. Persons Wanted	9
f. Warrant and Extradition	10
g. Retention of Teletype Message Copies	11
h. Cases Involving Property	11
i. Stolen Cars	11
j. Emergency Messages	11
k. Criminal Record Requests – New York State	11
l. Firearms Records	11
m. Definitions	12
n. Authorized Abbreviations	13

VI. PREPARING TELETYPE MESSAGES		15
a.	Message Form	15
b.	Message Example	15
c.	File 1 and File 16 Messages	17
d.	Punctuation	19
e.	Numbers in Messages	20
f.	Added Information, Correction, Reply, Cancellation	20
g.	Code Signals	20
h.	Fifth Line, Other Original Messages	20
i.	Body of Message	20
j.	Authority for Messages	21
k.	File Classification Chart	22
l.	Data Available on Persons or Property	25
m.	Comparison of NCIC, NYIIS, COPS Data	25
n.	Entering Data and Making Inquiries	26
o.	Message Record Sheet	26
p.	Cancellations and Corrections	27

POLICE COMMUNICATIONS & TELETYPE OPERATIONS

I. COMMUNICATIONS

A. RADIOS IN AUTOMOBILES

It is an Unclassified misdemeanor for any person who is not a peace officer to either equip an automobile with or knowingly use an automobile equipped with a radio receiving set capable of receiving signals on the frequencies allocated to police use. Excepted are holders of Federal amateur radio operator's licenses operating a receiver in connection with a mobile transmitter (V&T Sec. 397).

B. POLICE RADIO MESSAGES

It is a like misdemeanor to in any way knowingly interfere with the transmission of radio messages by police without first having secured a permit to do so from the person authorized to issue such a permit by the local municipal governing body or board. Offenses are punishable by fine not over $1,000, imprisonment not more than 6 months, or both (V&T Sec. 397).

The law excepts persons who hold a valid amateur radio operator's license issued by the Federal Communications Commission and who operate a duly licensed portable transmitter-receiver on frequencies allocated by the Federal Communications Commission to licensed radio amateurs (V&T Sec. 397).

C. TAMPERING WITH PRIVATE COMMUNICATIONS

A person is guilty of Tampering with Private Communications when, knowing that he does not have the consent of the sender or receiver, he obtains or attempts to obtain from an employee, officer or representative, of a telephone or telegraph corporation, by connivance, deception, intimidation or in any other manner, information with respect to the contents or nature thereof of a telephonic or telegraphic communication (P.L. Sec. 250.25, subd. 3).

A person is also guilty of Tampering with Private Communications when, knowing that he does not have the consent of the sender or receiver, and being an employee, officer or representative of a telephone or telegraph corporation, he knowingly divulges to another person the contents or nature thereof of a telephonic or telegraphic communication. The provisions of this subdivision do not apply to such person when he acts to report a criminal communication under the requirements of Penal Law Section 250.35 (see next paragraph) (P.L. Sec. 250.25, subd. 4). Tampering with Private Communications is a Class B misdemeanor.

D. FAILING TO REPORT CRIMINAL TELEPHONE OR TELEGRAPH COMMUNICATIONS

It is the duty of a telephone or telegraph corporation and of any employee, officer or representative thereof having knowledge that the facilities of such corporation are being used to conduct any criminal business, traffic or transaction, to furnish or attempt to furnish to an appropriate law enforcement officer or agency, all pertinent information within his possessionrelating to such matter, and to cooperate fully with any law enforcement officer or agency investigating such matter. A person is guilty of Failing to Report Criminal Communications when he knowingly violates any duty prescribed in this section (P.L. Sec. 250.35).

Failing to Report Criminal Communications is a Class B misdemeanor.

The prohibitions in Section 250.25, Penal Law do not apply to a law enforcement officer who obtains information from a telephone or telegraph corporation pursuant to Section 250.35 of the Penal Law (P.L. Sec. 250.25, subd.3).

E. UNLAWFULLY OBTAINING COMMUNICATIONS INFORMATION

A person is guilty of Unlawfully Obtaining Communications Information when, knowing that he does not have the authorization of a telephone or telegraph corporation, he obtains or attempts to obtain, by deception, stealth or in any other manner, from such corporation or from any employee, officer or representative thereof:

1. Information concerning identification or location of any wires, cables, lines, terminals or other apparatus used in furnishing telephone or telegraph service; or
2. Information concerning a record of any communication passing over telephone or telegraph lines of any such corporation (P.L. Sec. 250.30).

Unlawfully Obtaining Communications Information is a Class B misdemeanor.

F. TAMPERING WITH LETTERS, MAIL, ETC.

A person is guilty of Tampering with Private Communications when:

1. Knowing that he does not have the consent of the sender or receiver, he opens or reads a sealed letter or other sealed private communication (P.L. Sec. 250.25, subd. 1); or
2. Knowing that a sealed letter or other sealed private communication has been opened or read in violation of subdivision one of this section, he divulges, without the consent of the sender or receiver, the contents of such letter or communication, in whole or in part, or a resume of any portion of the contents thereof (P.L. Sec. 250.25, subd. 2).

Tampering with Private Communications is a Class B misdemeanor.

It is a Federal crime, punishable by $2,000 fine or 5 years imprisonment or both, to take a letter, postcard or package out of any post office or authorized depository or from a mail carrier or to take such thing which has been in the mails before it is delivered to a person to whom directed, with intent to obstruct the correspondence or to pry into the business or secrets of another. This violation includes taking mail left by the carrier, including from private mail boxes where deposited by the carrier.

It is also a Federal violation to steal or obtain mail by fraud from the post office or any postal facility.

These Federal violations are investigated by U.S. Postal Inspectors, who should be promptly notified of offenses (Title 18 U.S. Code, Secs. 1703, 1708).

II. OFFENSES IN USE OF COMMUNICATION MEDIA

A. PARTY LINES

A person commits the crime of Unlawfully Refusing to Yield a Party Line when being informed that a party line is needed for an emergency call, he refuses to immediately relinquish the line (P.L. Sec 270.15, subd. 2).

Unlawfully Refusing to Yield a Party Line is a Class B misdemeanor. A "party line" is a subscriber's line telephone circuit, consisting of two or more main telephone stations connected therewith, each station with a distinctive ring or telephone number (P.L. Sec. 270.15, subd. 1-a). An "emergency call" is a telephone call to a police or fire department, or for medical aid or ambulance service, necessitated by a situation in which human life or property is in jeopardy and prompt summoning of aid is essential (P.L. Sec. 270.15, subd. 1-b).

B. ANNOYING OR ALARMING COMMUNICATIONS

It is the crime of Aggravated Harassment to communicate with a person anonymously or otherwise, by telephone, telegraph, mail or any other form of communication, in a manner likely to cause annoyance or alarm, with intent to harass, annoy or alarm another (P.L. Sec. 240.30, subd.1). Aggravated Harassment is a Class A misdemeanor.

C. JAMMING, OTHER NON-LEGITIMATE PHONE CALLS

It is also Aggravated Harassment for any person to make a telephone call, whether or not a conversation ensues, with no purpose of legitimate communication and with intent to harass, annoy or alarm another (P.L. Sec. 240.30, subd. 2).

D. THEFT OF SERVICES (TELEPHONE, TELEGRAPH)

A person is guilty of Theft of Services when, with intent to avoid payment by himself or another person of the lawful charge for any telecommunications service, he obtains or attempts to avoid payment therefor by himself or another person by means of:
1. Tampering or making connection with the equipment of the supplier, whether by mechanical, electrical, acoustical, or other means, or
2. Any misrepresentation of fact which he knows to be false, or
3. Any other artifice, trick, deception, code or device (P.L. Sec. 165.15, subd. 4).

Theft of Services is a Class A misdemeanor. It includes use of illicit credit cards

III. INVESTIGATIONS

In any case involving police-frequency radio in automobiles, care must be taken to ensure that an actual test of the illicit receiver is made, to establish receipt of police frequencies. In addition, an expert in radio matters should make an examination of the radio, for expert testimony that the radio could receive police frequencies.

In taking complaints dealing with Tampering with Private Communications, the officer must be certain to pin down specific facts and details of the matter divulged, with exact times, dates and facts as to identification of violators.

In cases involving *"jamming"* telephones, it is proper to take detailed written statements from complaints, setting down the time and date of the calls and specific words said. Any factual information the victim may have to identify the offender should be obtained in detail. Where positive proof of identity is lacking, obtain permission to monitor the victim's telephone and consider obtaining an order to monitor the telephone of any suspect. Telephone companies may be able to offer valuable technical assistance in respect to crimes of this kind and the possibilities should be explored with ranking telephone company officals in proper cases.

In party line telephone cases, the officer must establish that the offender was in fact informed that the line was needed for an emergency call and that the emergency met the terms of the statute. A factor of identification of the offender is always present and if the complainant is not familiar with the offender, arrangements may be made for telephone and personal confrontation of the complainant and each potential user of the party line who could be the offender, for identification purposes. Officers should not overlook the value of proper interrogation of suspects in this kind of case.

In cases involving Theft of Services, officers should always work closely with telephone company sections assigned responsibility for attempting to determine to whom calls should properly be billed, since these persons are frequently able to make associations of persons and numbers which cannot be done by anyone not constantly working with such things.

IV. POLICE RADIO COMMUNICATIONS

Police radio transmitters must be licensed by the Federal Communications Commission (FCC). Each Base Station transmitter must be licensed. All mobile stations are included under the main license. The FCC will assign appropriate frequencies and call letters. Police radio falls in the category of "Public Safety Radio Services" in FCC terminology and is covered by FCC Rules and Regulations, Part 89.

All adjustments and tests which may affect the proper operation of police radios must be made only by holders of first or second class commercial radio operator's licenses. Such license holders may be either a department member or an outsider, such as a radio shop owner or employee.

Police officers and dispatchers broadcasting over police voice radios are not required to have individual licenses.

FCC Rules and Regulations, Sec. 89.151, require that all police transmissions, regardless of their nature, shall be restricted to the minimum practical transmission time.

In all police agencies with radio broadcasting systems, clear general instructions should be in effect to ensure that the headquarters transmitter is in charge of the air and may order other units silenced for priority messages, regardless of the rank of persons using mobile equipment, including radio cars, in the field.

In an emergency, the headquarters transmitter can temporarily transfer command of the air to a ranking officer in the field. This should be a rare occasion and should be done on a formal basis. There should be no informal monopolizing of the air by mobile units in the field.

A list of emergency telephone numbers should be maintained at the dispatcher's desk. The list should be regularly checked and kept current and complete. It should include hospitals, ambulance service, doctors available for emergencies, fire departments, coroner and medical examiners, garages, etc.

A. GENERAL REQUIREMENTS FOR PROPER TRANSMISSIONS

All transmission must be clearly enunciated. The microphone should be held exactly in front of the speaker's lips and about two inches away. The voice should always be free of emotion or stress. The speaker must be certain that a very brief pause is made after pressing the transmitter button and before speaking and that another very brief pause is made before releasing the button after speaking, to avoid chopping off parts of the transmission.

Inexperienced officers commonly fail to clearly enunciate and often chop off parts of their transmissions by pressing or releasing the transmitter button too late or too soon. All officers using any transmitter should receive substantial training to ensure that they use it properly. (A microphone-amplifier-loudspeaker or a tape recorder set-up should be used in training and not any actual radio transmissions.)

Training should include practice in the use of established radio procedure of the department and in brief, clear wording of transmissions, whether information messages, requests for information or instructions.

Headquarters radio transmitters are distinguishable by sound from the mobile transmitters. It is thus not necessary for headquarters to always identify itself. FCC rules require only that the main station shall identify itself with its assigned call letters at least once each thirty minutes during each period of operation. Mobile transmitters (radio cars, walkie-talkies, etc.) must identify themselves with the geographic name of the governmental subdivision under whose name the main station is licensed (e.g., car two of the Southton, N.Y., Police Department would call itself "Southton two").

A usual, clear and brief routine would thus be: "Car two" (from headquarters); "Southton two" (from the mobile unit), "Compliant, Mrs. John Doe, one Main Street, family disturbance" (from Headquarters); "Southton two okay" (from the mobile unit). With these brief messages, headquarters has located car two "in service," issued instructions to investigate a family disturbance based on a complaint, given the identity of the complainant and the location of the disturbance and has been informed by car two that the message was understood and that the instructions would be complied with.

Established procedures should also include routing for mobile units to inform headquarters when they go into service at the beginning of a tour of duty and when they go out of service from time to time during the tour. The initial call at the beginning of the tour will automatically give a check of the operating condition of the mobile units' radio equipment. The officer or officers using the equipment during the tour should be identified in this initial call.

A usual routing would be: "Southton two" (from the mobile unit); "Car two" (from headquarters); "In service, occupant 113" (from the mobile unit); "'Okay two" (acknowledgment from headquarters, specifying which car is being acknowledged).

"Occupant 113" identifies the officers in Southton Car two in the preceding example. It is best to use numbers, usually badge or shield numbers, to identify officers on the air. It is more secure against unauthorized listeners and is more accurate and brief than using names. The headquarters radioman should of course have a complete list of officers' names and numbers, arranged in numerical sequence and also in name order. He should record the mobile units in use and the officers using them, as they call in.

In larger departments, where air-time is limited, due to the large number of mobile units requiring air-time, it is desirable to use a code to save time on the air. The *"ten-signal"* code is widely used. It provides codes for a major part of the information constituting police radio traffic, thus cutting down words and saving substantial amounts of air-time. Some departments may add security to their use of radio by assigning numbers "post numbers") to key locations in their territory and then describing locations by giving distance and direction from a post number. The following are frequently used *"ten-signals"* of the system recommended by the Associated Public Safety Communications Officers, Inc. (APCO);

TEN-SIGNAL CODE

10-1	Unable to copy, change your location	10-8	In Service
10-2	Signals good	10-9	Repeat, please
10-3	Stop transmitting	10-10	Fight in progress at
10-4	Acknowledgment	10-11	Dog case (describe - e.g., *"fight,"* *"biting," "rabid"*)
10-5	Relay		
10-6	Busy, stand by unless urgent	10-12	Stand by (or "stop")
		10-13	Weather and road
10-7	Out of service atreport (give location or telephone number)	10-14	Report of prowler at
		10-15	Civil disturbance at
10-16	Domestic trouble at	10-48	Traffic standard needs repairs at
10-17	Meet complainant at		
10-18	Complete assignment quickly	10-49	Traffic light out at
		10-50	Accident (Kind, location)
10-19	Return to		
10-20	My location is (or what is your location)	10-51	Wrecker needed at

10-21	Call by telephone	10-52	Ambulance needed at
10-22	Disregard	10-53	Road blocked at
10-23	Arrived at scene	10-54	Livestock on highway
10-24	Assignment completed	10-55	Intoxicated driver
10-25	Report in person to (meet)	10-56	Intoxicated pedestrian
10-26	Holding subject - expedite reply	10-57	Hit-and-run (fatal personal injury, property damage)
10-27	Diver's license information	10-58	Direct traffic at
		10-59	Convoy or escort (specify)
10-29	Check records for wanted	10-62	Reply to message
10-30	Illegal use of radio	10-63	Prepare to make written copy
10-31	Crime in progress at		
10-32	Man with gun at	10-64	Message for local delivery
10-33	Emergency		
10-36	Correct time is	10-65	Net message assignment
10-37	Investigate suspicious vehicle (describe)	10-66	Message cancellation
10-38	Stopping suspicious vehicle (Give description and location before stopping)	10-67	Clear to read net message
		10-68	Dispatch information
		10-69	Message received
10-41	Beginning tour of duty	10-70	Fire alarm at
10-42	Ending tour of duty	10-74	Negative
10-43	Inform me about	10-75	In contact with
10-44	Request permission to leave patrol for	10-76	En Route
		10-77	Estimated time of arrival
10-45	Animal carcass in lane at	10-78	Need assistance at
10-46	Assist motorist at	10-90	Bank alarm at
10-47	Emergency road repairs needed at or stolen	10-94	Drag racing at
		10-96	Mental subject
		10-99	Records indicate wanted

Accuracy is of prime importance in radio work. Names should be spelled out in any instance where a file check is required or it is otherwise important that the correct spelling be known. Names should be spelled with a word-code by the officer transmitting. The following word code is good:

WORD CODE

A	Adam	I	Ida	R	Robert
B	Boy	J	John	S	Sam
C	Charles	K	King	T	Tom
D	David	L	Lincoln	U	Union
E	Edward	M	Mary	V	Victor
F	Frank	N	Nora	W	William
G	George	O	Ocean	X	X-ray
H	Henry	P	Paul	Y	Young
		Q	Queen	Z	Zebra

In using the word-code for spelling, transmit as follows:

"... JONES, J-JOHN, O-OCEAN, N-NORA, E-EDWARD, S-SAM." Do not say: "J AS IN JOHN" or "J LIKE IN JOHN" or similar wordy recitals.

In cases where numbers must be transmitted, such as license and serial numbers, the receiving officer should repeat each completed number on the air so that the sending officer can verify that it was correctly heard and understood.

B. HEADQUARTERS TRANSMISSIONS

A ranking officer should always be in command of headquarters radio. A dispatcher trained in radio procedures may be permitted to send out routine complaints or other items as received, but all important messages, including instructions to make arrests, alarms of major crimes and similar things should be screened by the ranking officer to insure that proper instructions are issued, that important instructions are not overlooked and that problems of identification, force to be used, road blocks and similar matters requiring police skill and experience are correctly handled. It should be the ranking officer's duty to also coordinate closely the work of the radio dispatcher and any complaint desk or officer, if complaint duties are not handled by the radio dispatcher.

C. FIELD TRANSMISSIONS

In order to keep transmission brief, officers should eliminate the use of unnecessary expressions or formal courtesies, such as "Roger," "Wilco," "Over and out," "Do you want to," "Will you please," "Yes, sir," "Thank you," and so on. Transmissions must be brief, businesslike and impersonal.

D. LISTENERS

It must always be remembered that police frequencies may be overheard by anyone on a large number of radio receivers purchasable almost anywhere. Consequently, matters of a confidential nature should not be put over the air except in extreme emergencies.

E. AUTHORITY

Standing instructions should exist in all departments having radio as to the authority of the headquarters dispatcher to make assignments of mobile units and officers and procedures for instances where mobile units have current assignments when they are called by the dispatcher to take a new assignment, or to take some police action of higher priority.

Generally speaking, the dispatcher should have final and complete authority as to assignments and all should understand that he is working closely with and expressing the instructions of the ranking officer in charge of communications.

The dispatcher should log all assignments as made and the exact time, for immediate reference and for a permanent record.

F. RADIO LOGS

Federal Communications Commission rules require that a radio log be maintained at each base (fixed) station from which transmissions are made (Federal Communications Commission Rules and Regulations, Section 89.175). Maintaining a log is also in accordance with proper police practice and procedure. Logs maintained by police agencies should include all transmissions and messages received and the exact time of each. Abbreviations may be used to reduce the work involved. These logs should also contain notations of exact time station identifying call letters were broadcast, and the full signature of the operator, showing time at beginning and end of his period of responsibility or tour of duty.

Mobile unit operators should not be required to keep radio logs. It is dangerous, since they will often be driving while receiving or transmitting.

V. POLICE TELETYPE NETWORKS

Chapter 533, Laws of 1931, established a basic system of coordinated teletypewriter communications, "for the purpose of prompt collection and distribution of information throughout the State of New York as the police problems of the state may require" (Exec. L. Sec. 217).

The Superintendent of State Police is responsible for the system's installation, operation and maintenance. The system is available for use by any department or division of the government of New York State, or by any municipal, county, town, village, railroad or other special police department lawfully maintained by any New York corporation (Exec. L. Sec. 219).

The original "basic system" has been expanded over the years since it was established. The current system is operated in conjunction with computers which do both data recording and message routing. Its modern and current name is "Computer Oriented Police information System," and it is commonly referred to by police officers as "COPS."

The COPS teletype network connects with and is part of the Nationwide Law Enforcement Teletype System (known to police as "LETS" or "N-LETS"). LETS covers the 48 continental states (not Alaska or Hawaii).

COPS is also directly connected to the National Crime Information Center ("NCIC") operated by the FBI in Washington, DC, and the NCIC computers. These computers store crime data from throughout the United States.

A. DESCRIPTION OF "COPS"

The Computer Oriented Police-information System of New York is a teletype network divided into districts, under the control of New York State Police Headquarters. Each district is generally co-extensive with the territory assigned to the various State Police stations. State and Troop Headquarters are "control points."

"Control points" control the teletypewriter circuits in the geographical area assigned them. The individual circuits have varying numbers of teletype machines and stations. All circuits terminate in the computer located at State Police Headquarters in Albany. The teletypewriter stations are located in municipal police departments, sheriff's offices, and other law enforcement agencies, including, of course, New York State Police installations.

All teletypewriter machines on the COPS system are equipped with "selective coding equipment" which permits each teletype machine to receive only those messages addressed to it.

Messages to police departments and other law enforcement agencies not on the COPS network are sent to the station nearest or most accessible to the department to which directed, to be forwarded by telephone or personal delivery. No special instructions in messages are required to secure this service. However, it will only be done in case of messages sent direct to or for the attention of a particular department. An "All Points Bulletin" ("APB") will be sent only to stations on the COPS network. If it is desired that one or more police agencies not on COPS receive an alarm, an individual direction to such agency(ies) is necessary.

B. COMPUTER CONTROL

The entire COPS network is under the control of its computer in Albany. All messages are transmitted by the computer exactly as received from the sending machines. It is thus essential that every person preparing teletype messages for sending via a COPS teletypewriter shall make certain that only correct messages are delivered to communications personnel for sending.

1. Through selective coding and automatic switching by the computer, the various teletype machines receive only messages addressed to them, except that "control points" receive also all messages on the "circuits" which they control.
2. The computer is designed to hold up and store teletype traffic for any station when the station is out of service due to routine maintenance, mechanical or electronic trouble, change of paper, etc. It will then send the traffic when the station returns to service.

C. OPERATING RULES AND PROCEDURES

Operating rules and detailed procedures for sending messages on the basic system are set out in the COPS Operating Manual. Copies may be obtained from the New York State Police. Operating rules and procedures must be strictly adhered to. Unless there is exact adherence to proper message construction and to proper codes, the computer will not accept or will misdirect messages.

1. Officers must be familiar with and comply with the following basic Regulations:
    a. Message traffic shall be brief and in the form prescribed.
    b. No message may be sent without proper authorization.
    c. All message traffic must be official business.
    d. Only the messages of duly authorized member agencies shall be transmitted.
    e. Member stations shall transmit official messages without charge for State Police personnel and for members of police departments without teletypewriter service.
    f. Requests of military authorities for use of system to report the arrest of deserters or other military personnel shall be honored.
    g. All messages are confidential and shall not be divulged to unauthorized persons.
    h. The official time of the system is Eastern Standard except that Daylight Saving Time shall be used whenever it is officially in effect.

D. TELETYPE MESSAGES REQUIRED BY LAW

When any peace officer or police agency in New York receives a complaint that a felony has been committed and if the perpetrator thereof has not been apprehended within five hours after such complaint was received, such police agency must cause information of such felony to be dispatched over the police communications system. Police agencies not connected with basic system must transmit such information to the nearest or most convenient teletypewriter station, from where it will be immediately dispatched in conformity with the regulations governing the system (Exec. L. Sec. 221).

1. The paramount consideration in respect to the messages sent in compliance with this law is that they shall accurately inform all police agencies that criminals are abroad and could be in any one of their jurisdictions.
2. Any classification of teletype which conforms to COPS regulations will comply with this law.

E. PERSONS WANTED

Section 173 of the Criminal Procedure Law provides that when a warrant has been issued in New York for the arrest of a person for a crime or offense, any officer having received a communication in the official course of business of the existence of such warrant may arrest such person, although the officer does not have the warrant in his possession at the time of arrest, if the arrest would otherwise have been proper if the officer had the warrant in his possession. The officer must advise the person arrested of the crime or offense charged and of the fact that a warrant has been issued.

Any officer originating any communication in the official course of business involving the commission of a misdemeanor or lesser offense must include therein the fact that a warrant of arrest has or has not been issued and further indicate, when appropriate, that the warrant has been endorsed for "nighttime" and Sunday execution."

Messages on persons wanted from police agencies in states other than New York are covered by Section 843 of the Criminal Procedure Law, which permits arrest without a warrant upon reasonable information that the defendant stands charged in the courts of another state with a crime punishable by death or imprisonment for a term exceeding one year. The official teletype message will constitute "reasonable information."

1. Messages on persons wanted from Canada or any foreign country must be handled in accordance with Federal law. Defendants can only be extradited by Canada or other foreign countries through the government of the United States, in accordance with Federal statute, treaties and conventions. Section 3184 of Title 18, United States Code, provides that any justice or judge of the United States, any United States Commissioners authorized by a US District Court or any New York judge of a court of record of general jurisdiction may, on complaint made under oath, issue a warrant of arrest for a person charged with a crime in the jurisdiction of any foreign government, if the crime is one provided for by treaty or convention between the United States and that foreign government. The teletype message may be used as the basis for complaint by New York officers in such cases.

F. WARRANT AND EXTRADITION

All messages on persons wanted (whether File 5, or other classifications) must state whether a warrant has been issued or facts justifying arrest without a warrant. If no warrant has been issued and one is required, the message must state "CHECKING ON WARRANT."

1. If a message is directed outside New York State, it must also state whether the requesting authority will extradite (e.g., "WARRANT ISSUED, WILL EXTRADITE," or "WAREX") and, if this fact has not been determined, must state "CHECKING ON EXTRADITION."
2. No message concerning a person wanted will be relayed outside New York State unless it has a statement as to warrant and extradition.
3. An "ADDED INFORMATION" message should be directed to the same points as the original message as soon as the facts have been ascertained as to warrant and extradition if the original message stated "CHECKING ON WARRANT" or "CHECKING ON WARRANT AND EXTRADITION" or "WARRANT ISSUED, CHECKING ON EXTRADITION."
4. Wording such as "HOLD FOR INVESTIGATION," "DETAIN FOR THIS DEPARTMENT," etc., cannot be used in any messages on persons wanted, and messages containing such phrases will not be forwarded.

Messages on persons wanted should include all available information required to accurately identify the persons to be taken into custody, including the exact time of the crime or incident, when known, in order to protect arresting officers.

1. When the fingerprint classification (abbreviated "FPC") of a wanted person is known, it must be included in the person wanted message.
2. Such messages shall also include any information known that wanted persons are armed with a dangerous weapon or are otherwise dangerous or have suicidal tendencies.

G. RETENTION OF TELETYPE MESSAGE COPIES

The printed message or "printout" which teletype machines produce (both inquiries of and answers from the computer or other agencies) is a necessary link in establishing "probable cause" warranting the arrest of an individual and should be preserved with the case file. It is not critical whether the document preserved is the original or the copy, but the original is best. The printout should go directly into the file of the agency taking arrest action, to be preserved for any necessary future use.

If a police agency having no teletypewriter terminal of its own has an officer who stops a suspicious car and the officer communicates with a police agency which has a terminal, and is told moments later that he has a "hit," the terminal employee who answers the officer's inquiry should note in writing on the printout sheet how, when and to whom he furnished the information. He should initial his notation, and then forward the printout to the inquiring officer's agency for retention in that agency's case file. This establishes a chain of evidence for the official police communication.

There is no set time as to how long a message printout should be retained. It should be retained as long as there is any chance the defendant will raise a question on the probable cause for his arrest. Some persons arrested and prosecuted in state courts, after arrest on a printout, may receive long sentences and be confined in a penitentiary for several years. Subsequently they may decide to raise the question of arrest in Federal Court on an appeal of some kind. Permanent retention of the printout would seem to be the most desirable rule in any case where an actual arrest is made based on the message.

H. CASES INVOLVING PROPERTY

In any case involving property in which the complainant's only or primary interest is recovery of the property, a message must not be sent unless a warrant has been issued. This rule is for the protection of arresting officers.

I. STOLEN CARS

Whenever a stolen car is reported by a message on the basic system, and is recovered, it should not be released to any person unless and until a full cancellation of the message reporting it stolen has been sent by the department which originated the stolen message and has been received by the department which recovered the car.

J. EMERGENCY MESSAGES

Emergency messages may include only matters requiring immediate transmission and attention, such as hit-and-run, armed robbery, temporary whereabouts of wanted persons, or other urgent matters.

K. CRIMINAL RECORD REQUESTS

New York State Identification and Intelligence System (NYSIIS). - Requests directed to NYSIIS for record information will be sent to and handled by NYSHS, day or night, seven days a week.

1. NYSIIS does its utmost to handle teletypewriter messages requesting information on an immediate basis. It is an imposition to request and in most cases, an impossibility for them to check and reply to a long list of names on a teletype request. Except in a rare case of extreme emergency, lengthy lists of names to be checked should be sent by mail or otherwise and not over the "COPS" system.

L. FIREARMS RECORDS

New York State Police Headquarters (Pistol Permit Section) maintains records of all pistol licenses issued in New York. It also keeps a lost or stolen weapons file, licensed pistol registration file and records of weapons purchased and sold by gun dealers (except gun dealers' records on purchases and sales in New York City). These files will be searched on request. Messages should be directed to "SP ALBANY, ATTN: PISTOL PERMIT SECTION." Requests to check New York City files on gun dealers' purchases and sales should be directed to the New York City Police Department.

M. DEFINITIONS

A full list of definitions applicable to all phases of operation of the basic system is published in the COPS Manual; however, the following teletype terms should be understood by all officers:

ACKNOWLEDGMENT - act by which an operator or machine signifies that a message has been received.

ADDED INFORMATION - message sent to supplement an original message and referred thereto.

APB (ALL POINTS BULLETIN) - a general alarm, to all terminals.

AUTHORITY - person responsible for the origination of a message.

BROADCAST - the transmission of a message on all circuits.

CANCELLATION - a message sent to cancel an original alarm.

CDC (CALL DIRECTING CODE) - directs message to its proper destination.

CORRECTION - a message sent to amend a previous message.

DIRECT MESSAGE - a message addressed to a specific agency or receiver.

EMERGENCY CANCELLATION - a message sent to cancel, without delay, previous message.

FINGERPRINT CLASSIFICATION - a listing of the kinds of fingerprint patterns, ridge counts and tracings and missing fingers in a subject's fingerprints, using a code notation for each of the ten fingers.

JUNK - any message or part thereof which is unintelligible by reason of mechanical or electrical difficulties.

MESSAGE NUMBER - numerals in the upper left-hand corner of a teletypewriter communication to distinguish it from other communications having the same point of origin.

MESSAGE TIME - the figures placed on a message after the sender's name, to indicate the time the typing was completed. Time based on the conventional time designator of ante meridian (AM) and post meridian (PM) (noon and midnight designated as 12-00 N and 12-00 MID, respectively). Eastern Standard Time used except when Daylight Saving Time is in effect.

PART CANCELLATION - a message sent by the originating station to cancel some portion of an original and/or previous message, using a new message number and the same file classification as the original.

REFERENCE - data by which an original message is identified, i.e., the message and file numbers, place and date of origin, message direction and subject.

REPLY - a message that answers a previous teletype message; must refer to the original and be designated by the word "REPLY."

SENDER - surname of operator who originally transmits a message.

N. AUTHORIZED ABBREVIATIONS

The following abbreviations may be used in teletype messages:

AA	Control Point, Troop "A," Batavia
ADDED INFO	Added information
AKA	Also known as
AM	Ante Meridian - (Between Midnight and Noon)
APB	All Points Bulletin
ASSIGN	Assignment
ASST	Assistant
ATL	Attempt to locate
ATTN	Attention
AUTH	Message sent on authority of
BB	Control Point, Troop "B," Malone
BCI	Bureau of Criminal Investigation
BLD	Build
BLK	Black
BRN	Brown
CC	Control Point, Troop "C," Sidney
C (in description)	Chinese
CANCEL	Cancellation
CAPT	Captain
CCT	Circuit
CHIEF INSPR	Chief Inspector
CODE SIG	Code Signal
COL	Colonel
COMP	Complexion
CORRECT	Correction
CP	Chief of Police
CPL	Corporal
CT/SGT	Chief Technical Sergeant
DD	Control Point, Troop "D," Oneida
DATA	We request owner's name, address, make of car, motor number, etc., on the following registration
DCT	Direct
DEP	Deputy
DK	Dark
DMV	Department of Motor Vehicles, Albany, NY
DOA	Dead on arrival
DOB	Date of birth
EE	Control Point, Troop "E," Canandaigua

ETA	Estimated time of arrival
F	Female
FF	Control Point, Troop "F," Middletown
FILE	File classification number
F/SGT	First Sergeant
FOA	For other authorities
FPC	Fingerprint classification
GG	Control Point, Troop "G," Loudonville
HQ	Division Headquarters, Albany
I	Indian
INV	Investigator
INSPR	Inspector
J	Japanese
KK	Control Point, Troop "K," Hawthorne
LETS	Nationwide Law Enforcement Teletype System
LIC	License number
LIEUT	Lieutenant
M	Male
MAJ	Major
MED	Medium
MESA	Referring to your message
MEX	Mexican
MID	Midnight
MOT	Motor
NCIC	National Crime Information Center
NFC	Negative file check
NYSIIS	New York State Identification and Intelligence System
NMN	No middle name
NYS	New York State
O (in description)	Other (meaning any other racial abbreviation not listed herein)
OFF	Officer
OPR	Operator
PART CANCEL	Partial cancellation
PD	Municipal Police Department
PD NYC	Police Department, City of New York
PM	Post Meridian (Between Noon and Midnight)
PTL	Patrolman
QQ	Control Point, Division Headquarters, Albany
REF	Please refer to our message
REG	Registration number
ROIR	Reply only if record
RP	Message repeated by
SER	Serial
SGT	Sergeant
SO	Sheriff
SP	State Police
SR INV	Senior Investigator
S/SGT	Staff Sergeant
SUPT	Superintendent
TT	Control Point, Troop "T," Elsmere
TOT	Turned over to
TPR	Trooper
T/SGT	Technical Sergeant
TWX	Teletypewriter Exchange System

UNK	Unknown
VIN	Vehicle Identification Number
VOID	Cancel our message
W	White
WAREX	Warrant issued will extradite
Z/SGT	Zone Sergeant

The permissible abbreviations for states of the United States, and for foreign countries, Canadian Provinces and Mexican states are set out In the COPS manual, phone book and postal directory.

VI. PREPARING TELETYPE MESSAGES

All messages for transmission over the basic system must be in the prescribed form and as brief as possible without losing clarity. Conformance with instructions for message construction set out in the COPS Manual is not only essential for use on the basic system of New York State but also permits the message to be correctly carried to other states in the continental United States over the Nationwide Law Enforcement Teletype System (LETS) and to the National Crime Information Center (NCIC) computers at the FBI in Washington, DC.

COPS Manuals may be found at all stations on the basic system, including local police stations as well as State Police stations and may be procured from the New York State Police at Albany.

A. MESSAGE FORM

Messages which do not conform (in construction or content) to the requirements set out in the COPS Manual will not be sent but will be returned to the point of origin for correction. Conformity is necessary so that every department in the state may operate with a minimum of delay and to give maximum protection to the individual officer who acts on the basis of information received in a teletype message over the basic system.

B. MESSAGE EXAMPLE

All messages on the basic system must have a heading, a body, an authority and a sender, in the form indicated by the following example:

EXAMPLE:
Line 1 ... NYAZ
Line 2 ... 6214 FILE 12 PD NYC APR 4-10 REPLY
Line 3 ... TO PD JAMESTOWN NY CODE 77
Line 4 ...
Line 5 ... MESA 381 FILE APR 3-10 APB UNK W M
Line 6 ... SUSPECT HARRY ROE WAS AT QUEENS COUNTY ADDRESS FROM 8-30 AM TO 12-00 MID APR 2-10 ACCORDING TO RELIABLE WITNESSESNO FURTHER INVESTIGATION BEING CONDUCTED. WRITTEN REPORT FOLLOWS.
2nd line below
body ..... AUTH LT MURPHY BROWN 6-17 PM
3rd line below
body NY03030

1. File 1 Messages (Stolen Motor Vehicles, Trailers or Motorcycles) and File 16 Messages (Lost and Stolen License Plates) are the only exceptions to the preceding rule as to form of teletype messages. They must be prepared in a special format, as shown later in this ongoing section.

2. All departments have been assigned NCIC code numbers, whether or not they have teletype facilities on the basic system are assigned two-letter call directing codes ("CDC's"). Both NCIC codes and CDC's are listed in the COPS Manual.
3. The individual lines of the sample message were prepared in accordance with the following rules:
   a. Line 1 contains a message's "call directing codes" (or "CDC's"). These are the means by which the computer determines the destination of the message. The police officer preparing the message must decide on its destination and use. It is the responsibility of the teletype operator to translate these into the proper CDC's (and "Function Codes," if any - the Function Codes give instructions as to computer activity in respect to the message). CDC's and Function Codes are all set out in the COPS Manual.
      (1) The first two letters in the example, on Line 1, are the CDC for the agency originating the message (i.e,. NY for New York City Police Department). The next two letters are the CDC for the department to which the message is destined (i.e. AZ for Jamestown Police Department). The correct CDC must always be ascertained from the COPS Manual
      (2) The CDC "SP" will send the message to all New York State Police teletype stations. The CDC "PD" will send it to all police agencies and sheriff's offices in New York. If a message is to go out of New York to an out-of-state law enforcement agency, the CDC for out-of-state is "IS" and must be followed by the CDC for the out-of-state destination.
      (3) If a message has an inquiry of or information for the New York State Identification and Intelligence System (NYSIIS), the proper CDC for NYSIIS is "QC."
   b. Lines 2 and 3 constitute the "heading" of the message. They show the identity of the message and its origin and destinations, spelled out in words and abbreviations. In the example, the message is the 6,214th message sent by the Police Department, New York City. It is a "File 12" (message concerning homicide). Line 3 (the second line of the heading) shows the message's destination and the code signal for special handling desired ("Code 77").
      (1) Every message must be designated by a number (in the example, "6214"). For every teletype station on the basic system, message numbering always begins with "1" for the first message sent after midnight of December 31 annually and messages are thereafter numbered consecutively throughout the year, straight through the last message sent on the following December 31st.
   c. Line 4 is always left blank
   d. Line 5 is always the reference line, if a reference is required and shows to what prior message, if any, the message relates.
   e. Line 6 and following are the body of the message. The body always begins on line 6 unless there is no reference, when it begins on line 5.
   f. The authority, sender and time sent are the next to last line of every message (in the example, this line is marked "2nd line below body" to show its placement when teletyped). The "authority" is the identity and rank of the officer who authorized the message, "Lt. Murphy" in the

example. "Brown" in the example is the teletype operator who sent the message.

    g. The last line of the message is the "NCIC Code" of the sending agency. Frequently a sending agency is not one with a station on the basic system and thus has no CDC. The NCIC code will be its identifier. In the example this is "NY 03030," marked "3rd. line below body" to show its placement when typed on the teletype machine.

C. FILE 1 AND FILE 16 MESSAGES

File 1 (Stolen Motor Vehicles, Trailers, and Motorcycles) and File 16 (Lost or Stolen License Plates) messages have a special format of their own. All the data on the stolen or lost item which the message sets out are automatically entered in the memory banks of the computer the instant the teletype message is received by it when the proper function code is included with the call directing codes (CDC's). Examples of a proper File 1 and a proper File 16 original message are as follows:

EXAMPLE, File 1:
Line 1 ... KORESPPDQLQJNX
Line 2 ... 235 FILE 1 SP CLAVERACK NY MAY 1-10
Line 3 ... TO APB
Line 4 ...
Line 5 ... 4A7528.NY.10..
Line 6 ... 09ME44217CO.
Line 7 ... 09.MERC.COU.2T. GRN/LGR
Line 8 ... 050170
Line 9 ... NY11001
Line 10 .. K0235.
Line 11 .. STOLEN GHENT NY 9 TO 11 PM-OWNER CHARLES A. DOE-
    1 MAIN-CLAVERACK NY 2nd line below
body ..... AUTH SGT ROE GREEN 11-50 PM
3rd line below body ..... NY 11001

EXPLANATION

1. The above message concerns a 2009 Mercury Cougar, color top green over light green body, hardtop, two-door, 2010 New York license plates 4A7528, owned by Charles A. Doe, 1 Main Street, Claverack, NY, and stolen at Ghent, NY, sometime between 9:00 and 11:00 PM on May 1, 2010. The individual lines of the example were prepared under the following rules:

    a. Line 1 contains the "CDC's" and "KO" is the CDC for the State Police at Claverack. In addition, this line has the function code "RE," a direction to the computer to include the data in the message in the computer memory bank. Function code "RE" is the same for all File 1 messages. "SP" is the CDC for all State Police installations with teletype. "PD" is the CDC for all police and sheriffs' offices with teletype installations. "QL" is the CDC for the New York State Motor Vehicle Department at Albany; "QJ" is the CDC for New York State Police Communications Headquarters, Albany, and "NX" is the CDC for the National Auto Theft Bureau (NATB) in New York City.

    b. Line 2 is the same as any other message and carries the message number, the "file, originating agency and date sent."

c. Line 3 is the same as any other message, showing the distribution desired - in the example, APB (the abbreviation for "all points bulletin" to all teletype installations on the basic system).
d. Line 4 is left blank as in other messages.
e. Line 5 gives the license plate data. These are always set out in this order: plate number, issuing state and year, followed by two periods for a private plate or an appropriate abbreviation from the COPS Manual for any other kind of plate (e.g., "DL" for dealers' plates, "OB" for passenger bus plates, "TK" for truck plates, etc.). Only private passenger automobile plates are represented solely by two periods, as in the example.
f. Line 6 gives the stolen vehicle's identification number its "VIN."
g. Line 7 sets out the description of the vehicle, using the codes set out in the COPS Manual for motor vehicles, always in the following order: year, make, model, style, color. In the example, these are: "09," "Merc" for Mercury, "COU" for Cougar model, "2T" for two-door hardtop style, and GRN/LGR for green top, light green body. Periods must be used in line 7 just as shown in the example (see paragraph on "Punctuation" later in this section).
h. Line 8 is the date of occurrence of the incident . The date must be set out with numerals for month, day and year. If the month or day is a single numeral it is preceded by 0. February third would thus be entered 0203, followed by the year or "020304" for February 3, 2004. October 20, 2004, would be "102004."
i. Line 9 carries the NCIC code of the originating police agency (SP Claverack is "NY 11001").
j. Line 10 is always the CDC of the originating agency and the message number (KO is the CDC for SP Claverack and the message number is 235).
k. Line 11 carries any pertinent information desired as to the theft, such as owner, time of theft, place of theft. Such data are restricted to a total of 42 characters and nothing past the 42 characters will be entered into the computer, although anything past 42 characters will be transmitted to all receiving an actual copy of the message. This is similar to the "body" of other teletype messages. Any readily recognizable abbreviations pertinent and suitable may be used in the 42 characters, contrary to the general rules that only authorized abbreviations may be used in other messages.
    (1) To include material information in 42 characters requires some thought and economy of phrasing but is not difficult. For example, the characters "ARMED V M" indicate an armed white male, the characters "STOLEN 32 CAL COLT REV GLV COMPT" indicate a .32 caliber Colt revolver which was in the glove compartment was stolen.
l. Second line below the body is the same as other messages, showing the authority for the message and the sender.
m. Third line below the body is also the same as in other messages, carrying the NCIC Code for the originating agency (same as Line 9 of File 1's).

EXAMPLE, File 16:

Line 1 ... KORGQLQJ
Line 2 ... 236 FILE 16 SP CLAVERACK NY MAY 1-10
Line 3 ... TO APB
Line 4 ...
Line 5 ... .2A2314.NY.10..1.
Line 6 ... 050110
Line 7 ... NY11001.
Line 8 ... K0236
Line 9 ... STOLEN GHENT
2nd line below
body ..... AUTH SGT ROE GREEN 11-52 PM
3rd line below body NY11001

EXPLANATION

1. The above message concerns the loss of a single license plate at 7:00 p.m. in Ghent, NY. The license plate is numbered "2A2314" and is a 2010 New York Plate, The individual lines of the message conform to rules as follows:

    a. Line 1 contains the CDC of the originating agency ("KO" for SP, Claverack) and the function code for the computer of "RG" which directs the computer to store the data in its memory bank and is the same for all File 16's. "QL" and "QJ" are the CDC's for the New York State Department of Motor Vehicles and the Communications Headquarters of the State Police, both at Albany.
    b. Line 2 is the same as both prior message examples.
    c. Line 3 is the same as both prior message examples, i.e. shows the destination of the message.
    d. Line 4 is blank, same as prior message example.
    e. Line 5 is same as in a File 1 message, showing the license plate in order of plate number, state of issue and year of issue. The periods indicated in the example must be used in all messages. The example shows one lost or stolen plate. If both plates had been lost or stolen, Line 5 would be: "2A2314.NY.10..2.".
    f. Line 6 shows date lost or stolen, same as Line 8 of a File 1 message.
    g. Line 7 shows the NCIC Code of the originating agency, same as Line 9 of a File 1 message.
    h. Line 8 shows the CDC of the originating agency and its message number, same as Line 10 of a File 1 message.
    i. Line 9 carries any pertinent information desired on the lost or stolen plates, usually in briefest form, as not over 11 characters will be included in the computer memory bank.
    j. Second line below body is authority and sender, same as any other message.
    k. Third line below body is NCIC Code for originating agency, same as any other message, and is same as in Line 7 of the example.

D. PUNCTUATION

In sending messages, the usual punctuation marks cannot be used. Instead of commas, colons, semi-colons and periods, a dash must be used, except in File 1 message lines 5, 6, 7, 8, 9 and 10 and File 16 message lines 5, 6, 7 and 8. The reason for use of periods in File 1 and File 16 messages is that the data they contain on the indicated lines must be fed into the computer in specific segments and the segments must be separated and indicated by periods. If a necessary character is missing from any one of the segments, a period must be put in its place in the message.

NUMBERS IN MESSAGES

All numbers used in teletype messages must be in numerals (e.g., 1, 2, 10, etc.) and not spelled out (e.g. "one," "two," "ten," etc.) except that decimals and fractions must be spelled out in words (e.g. "one-half," "ten and sixteen hundredths," etc., instead of "1/2," "10 16/100," etc.

F. ADDED INFORMATION, CORRECTION, REPLY, CANCELLATION

Every message except an original message must show in Line 2, as in the first message example herein, whether it is an "Added Information," "Correction," "Reply" or a "Cancellation." The proper designation, of course, is determined by the purpose or nature of the message.

G. CODE SIGNALS

A Code Signal is a number which, when included on Line 3 of a message ("CODE 77" in the first example prior), directs certain specific handling of the message by addressees. More than one code signal may be used in a message. Approved code signals and their meanings may be found in the COPS Manual.

H. FIFTH LINE, OTHER THAN ORIGINAL MESSAGES

The fifth line of all messages other than original messages is the reference line. The reference line shall show: (1) whether the message relates to a prior message from the sending station ("REF," or "VOID" on cancellations), or from another station ("MESA"); (2) the message number of the original message; (3) the date of the original message; (4) whether the original message was sent direct ("DCT") or to all points ("APB"); and (5) the subject of the original message, including the name of persons first listed on the fifth line of the original message (if any such listing in the original).

1. The license plate number of any stolen motor vehicle, motorcycle, trailer or lost or stolen plate must be on line five of any message relating to stolen vehicles or lost or stolen plates ("File 1" or "File 16" messages).

I. BODY OF MESSAGE

The body of every message should be as brief as possible. All messages are required to be clear and accurate. Telegraph style must be used in messages, leaving out all connecting words and other words not essential to clarity.

CONTENT

1. The first word in the body of every original message should where possible, indicate the purpose of the message, e.g., "STOLEN," "WANTED," "BURGLARY," "RECOVERED," etc. This rule does not apply to File 1 or File 16 messages.
2. The crime involved must be specified by name in all original messages relating to crimes. The pertinent section of the Penal Law, Criminal Procedure Law, etc., may be added for clarity where deemed necessary.
3. Where the bare name of the crime is not sufficiently descriptive, a brief notation of what the crime involved may be added, e.g., "CRIMINALLY NEGLIGENT HOMICIDE-HUNTING."
4. Messages concerning persons wanted or missing should list the persons' full names or brief descriptions, if names are unknown (e.g., "unknown white male," "unknown colored female"), and the license plate number of any vehicle in their possession, on the fifth line of the message.
5. Stolen motor vehicle, trailer or motorcycle ("File 1") messages must carry the license plate number as the first item on line five in all such messages.

6. The license number shall be shown on the fifth line of all messages dealing with vehicles used in or connected with a crime.
7. The plate number of lost or stolen license plates must be shown as the first item on the fifth line of all messages dealing with such plates ("File 16" messages).

The time and place of the crime must always be set out in an original message. They should be set out in the first part of the message.

Information in the body of a message shall be set out in the following sequence, when applicable:

SEQUENCE

1. Name of subject (unless listed above the body of the message on the fifth line of an original message or in the reference line of any other message).
2. Name and brief facts of crime.
3. Time and place of crime.
4. Warrant data, whether will extradite.
5. Description of persons, with items of description set out in the following order:
   Racial description (White, Colored, American
   Indian, Chinese, etc.);
   Sex, age, height, weight, color hair and eyes;
   Complexion, build;
   Clothing, marks and scars, peculiarities;
   Addresses, occupation, relatives.
   EXAMPLE:
   "W-F-28-5-5-120 LIGHT BRN HAIR-BRN EYES-FAIR
   COMP-MED BLD-BLUE PLAID KERCHIEF ON HEAD-BLK
   TOPCOAT-DK GREEN DRESS-BLK LOW HEEL SHOES-BLK
   BAG OVER SHOULDER-NO MARKS OR SCARS-UNDER
   MENTAL STRAIN-RESIDES 1 MAIN STREET-COHOES
   NY-UNEMPLOYED-MOTHER MRS JOHN R. DOE-SAME
   ADDRESS"
6. Description of Motor Vehicles, with items of description set out in the following order: License plate number, motor number and/or vehicle serial or identification number, year, make, model, color, distinguishing marks.
7. Description of Property, with items of description set out in the following order: Name, make, model, serial number, color, material, size, peculiarities and markings.
   EXAMPLES:
   TYPEWRITER-ROYAL PORTABLE-SER 1J4813996-GREEN PLASTIC
   FRAME-CHEMICAL SYMBOLS ON KEYBOARD-NO CASE
   WRISTWATCH-WALTHAM-SPRITE-SER UNK-WHITE GOLD-SMALL
   BAGUETTE DIAMONDS EACH SIDE-BRAIDED NARROW YELLOW GOLD
   WRIST BAND-ENGRAVED ON BACK CASE-TO JANE WITH LOVE

J. AUTHORITY FOR MESSAGES

Every message must show the rank and surname of the police member authorizing and responsible for the message (and his department if different from the department sending the message). "Authority" is shown by typing at left margin, on the second line below the body of the message, the abbreviation "AUTH" followed by the rank and name of authorizing officer.

K. FILE CLASSIFICATION CHART

The following File Classification Chart is required to be posted at every teletypewriter location associated with the basic system. This chart must be rigidly adhered to and the proper File Classification Number placed on every message. The File Classification Number assigned an original message must be used on all subsequent messages pertaining to and sent in connection with the same case. The File Classification number is used for message filing.

FILE CLASSIFICATION CHART

FILE	CLASSIFICATION
1	STOLEN MOTOR VEHICLES AND MOTORCYCLES
2	MOTOR VEHICLES - INFORMATION REQUESTS
3	EMERGENCY REPORTS TO DIVISION HEADQUARTERS
4	HIT AND RUN DRIVER
5	PERSONS - WANTED OR ESCAPED
6	PERSONS - MISSING
7	BURGLARY
8	ROBBERY AND HOLD UP
9	PROPERTY - LOST OR MISSING
10	PROPERTY - STOLEN (LARCENY)
11	ASSAULT
12	HOMICIDE
13	GENERAL POLICE INFORMATION
14	ORDERS AND ADMINISTRATIVE MESSAGES
15	REQUESTS FOR INFORMATION (MISC.)
16	LOST OR STOLEN LICENSE PLATES
20	CRIMINAL INVESTIGATIONS (BCI ONLY)
24	LEGAL BULLETINS AND OPINIONS
25	MISCELLANEOUS MESSAGES
26	TROUBLE REPORTS
27	WEATHER BUREAU FALLOUT DATA
28	ROAD CONDITIONS AND WEATHER REPORTS
44	TEST MESSAGES

DESCRIPTION

FILE 1: Use for all messages reporting stolen motor vehicles, trailers or motorcycles. In some agencies associated with the basic system, outside New York, stolen car messages are filed by license number and in others by motor, serial or identification number. It is thus necessary that all cancellations of File 1 messages list not only the license number but also the motor, serial or identification number, exactly as set out in the original message. The license plate number of the stolen vehicle must always be the first item on line five of any File 1 message except cancellations.

FILE 2: Use only for messages involving requests for motor vehicle, trailer, motorcycle or drivers' license information either from outside New York or from the New York State Department of Motor Vehicles. Whenever possible, File 2 messages must include the subject's full name, including middle name or initial and his address and date of birth.

1. Where a message is sent to the New York State Department of Motor Vehicles concerning only a check of a name, the message should be directed to one of

three sections of that Department, depending on the first letter of the subject's last name, as follows:

"TO DMV SEC 1" (for A through G)
"TO DMV SEC 2" (for H through O)
"TO DMV SEC 3" (for P through Z)

2. Whenever a license plate number check is desired, the direction should be merely "TO DMV."
3. Department of Motor Vehicles conviction records are maintained on electronic data processing equipment and it takes several days to furnish complete information, as the data tapes are not updated every day, but at stated intervals. Accurate and prompt service can only be provided if the Department is given accurate and complete information. The subject's name, date of birth, sex and license identification number must be furnished exactly as they appear on the person's operator's or chauffeur's license.
4. The following information should be considered as a guide to requesting information from the New York State Department of Motor Vehicles files to avoid unnecessary work and delayed communications:
    a. Where only the previous record for Driving While Intoxicated or while Ability is Impaired is required, do not request complete record of all convictions.
    b. Where only data on previous suspension or revocation of license are wanted, do not request complete record of all convictions.
    c. Where only convictions in past 18 months are wanted, so specify.
    d. In requesting check on nonresidents, specify that the subject is a nonresident, and pinpointing information desired. DMV maintains a file specifically showing speeding convictions and all vehicle and traffic misdemeanors involving nonresidents arrested in New York.
5. The electronic data processing includes only moving violations, vehicle and traffic misdemeanors and suspension and revocation data. Equipment violations, overload violations and non-moving violations (other than misdemeanors) are not included.
6. Where a complete accident and conviction record (known as a "safety record") is desired on a driver, the message should be sent promptly after the driver's arrest since the limitations of the electronic data processing will delay the reply. The request should specify "COMPUTER ABSTRACT REQUIRED."

Photostats from Department of Motor Vehicles: When photostats of drivers' licenses or any records are desired from the Department of Motor Vehicles, they should be requested directly of the Department by mail and no teletype message should be sent requesting photostats.

FILE 3: This classification is only used by the Few York State Police.

FILE 4: This classification is solely for hit-and-run (leaving the scene of accident) motor vehicle or motorcycle violations. Original messages must always include as much information as possible pertinent to the wanted motor vehicle and driver. File 4 classification applies whether the hit-and-run involves property damage, personal injury or both.

FILE 5: Use for messages concerning crimes other than assaults, burglaries, homicides and robberies (which are File 11, File 7, File 12 and File 8 respectively). File 5 should also be used for messages requesting arrest or announcing that persons are wanted and subject to arrest, including escapees from prisons, jails and mental institutions. File 5 sconcerning escapees from mental institutions should be restricted to New York only, unless the authorities of the institution specifically desire dissemination outside New York. All File 5 original messages on persons wanted must begin the body of the message with "WANTED," followed by the name of the crime or other item justifying the arrest.

FILE 6: Do not use for persons wanted for a crime. Use only in cases of persons missing over 24 hours, except no waiting period is required in case of young children, females 18 years of age and under, mentally incompetent persons or persons known to have been operating a motor vehicle. All File 6 messages must include the time or approximate time the subject left home and must indicate that either the sending authorities or the family or parents will promptly assume the duty of returning children, youths and mentally incompetent persons when located. If the missing person was known to be using a motor vehicle, the license plate number should be included in the message.

FILE 7: Use specifically for burglary. Do not include any larceny without burglary. File 7 original messages must state the type of building burglarized, methods of entry, and complete description of property taken and persons wanted.

FILE 8: Use for all robbery. Messages must adequately describe property taken and persons wanted.

FILE 9: Use for all messages relating to property which has been lost or is missing, except motor vehicle license plates (which are classified in File 16). Stolen property cannot be the subject of a File 9 message, nor any property which has been the subject of a crime. Original messages must adequately describe the property involved.
FILE 10: Use for all messages dealing with stolen property or property which has been the subject of any larceny. This includes aircraft and boats (but not motor vehicles, trailers, motorcycles or vehicle license plates, as these are File 1 and File 16, respectively). Property involved must be adequately described. Long lists of unidentifiable property have little value and should not be sent.

FILE 11: Use only for assault cases. (Motor vehicle hit-and-run cases are not included in File 11 but are classified in File 4).

FILE 12: All messages concerning homicides must be classified in File 12, including all criminal negligence homicides, whether vehicle or other.

FILE 13: Messages are to be classified in File 13 when they do not relate to a specific crime or arrest request in other file classifications and are of interest to police generally or in a special area. They may be sent direct to one or more stations or as all points bulletin as the facts indicate. File 13 messages would include reports of confidence games, notice that specific persons have been apprehended who may be wanted by other departments and their modus operandi (specifying distinctive or unusual features thereof). File 13's would also include notice that specific property has been recovered (including adequate description) and general police warnings. In all instances where a person is arrested for a serious crime, his name, aliases, description and fingerprint analysis or classification should be sent as an all points bulletin under File 13 for the information of all departments on the basic system.

FILE 14: This classification is only used by the New York State Police.

FILE 15: Use on messages requesting information from special files, arrest or criminal records, firearms records, dog licenses, ear tags, birth, marriage and death records, aircraft license data, lost, missing or overdue aircraft and other types of information.

FILE 16: Use only for messages dealing with motor vehicle or motorcycle license plates, whether lost or stolen. List plate numbers at beginning of 5th message line. The plate number must always be the first item on the fifth line of any File 16 message.

FILE 20: This classification is only used by the New York State Police.

FILE 24: Use on all messages concerning notice of new laws, legal opinions, legal bulletins and inquiries concerning laws or legal opinions. It is largely used by the New York State Police but may be used by any agency.

FILE 25: Use for all messages not dealing with crime and which do not fall within any file classification previously set out. It would include messages concerning notification of relatives of persons who have been killed. No messages may be sent under a File 25 classification in criminal cases.

FILE 26: Any report of trouble on the basic system or with a teletypewriter installation should be File Classification 26.

FILE 27: This classification is used solely for official fallout data.

FILE 28: This is used for road condition and weather reports.

FILE 44: Used for test messages.

L. DATA AVAILABLE ON PERSONS OR PROPERTY

The COPS computer is located at Communications Headquarters, New York State Police, Albany. On receipt of properly coded messages, it stores in its memory banks for later search all File 1 and File 16 message data on stolen motor vehicles, trailers, motorcycles and lost or stolen license plates. It also stores data as to vehicles used in commission of a crime and as to lost or stolen vehicle parts (by identification or serial number). Data on vehicles are stored by both license plate number and vehicle identification number ("VIN").

In addition, Communications Headquarters, State Police, Albany, maintains manual record files on stolen property and guns and on lost property. These will be automatically checked on receipt of messages concerning recovered property or guns.

The National Crime Information Center (NCIC) at Washington, DC, stores in its computers information on stolen vehicles and license plates, stolen or missing property and guns and on persons wanted for felonies or missing. Data on property is stored in the NCIC computers for individual items valued at $500 or more, or on loot from a single "job" worth $2,000.00 or more.

The New York State Identification and Intelligence System (NYSIIS) maintains files on persons wanted or missing covering New York. NYSIIS may be checked directly for wanted or missing persons data, by teletype message, or otherwise, such as direct telephone inquiry.

M. COMPARISON OF NCIC, NYSIIS, COPS DATA

The NCIC computer in Washington, DC, stores data received from the continental United States, including, of course, data from New York. Its "wanted" data cover the whole country. The same is true of its stolen car, stolen property or other banks of data. NYSIIS files cover only "wanted" or "missing" from New York state.

The COPS computer at Communications Headquarters, State Police, Albany, also stores only New York data. This includes New York vehicles or plates stolen anywhere and any vehicles or plates stolen in New York.

N. ENTERING DATA AND MAKING INQUIRIES

The COPS computer file on lost or stolen license plates and vehicle identification numbers and license plates is made up of data from File 1 and File 16 messages which automatically go into the computer when the proper function code is stated in Line 1 of the message. If the message's data meet the criteria required for entry into the NCIC computer in Washington, DC, the message is also automatically switched to the NCIC computer by the COPS computer.

Wanted data on persons should be forwarded to NYSIIS in accordance with the instructions pertaining thereto, as well as by appropriately coded message to NCIC, Washington, DC.

In checking on whether a "want" is outstanding for an individual, an inquiry should be sent to the NCIC Computer in Washington, DC. If a negative reply is received, inquiry will then be made automatically, by the State Police, by *"hot line"* telephone to NYSIIS at Albany, and the inquiring agency will be automatically informed of the result of the NYSIIS inquiry.

The COPS computer and the basic system are directly connected with the NCIC computers in Washington, DC. This *"interface"* makes all the information stored in the NCIC computers automatically available to those making inquiries on the basic system. Inquiries to NCIC and COPS can be made from any teletype machine on the basic system. If a *"no record"* reply is received by an inquirer, from the COPS computer in Albany, on a license plate or *"VIN"* inquiry, the inquiry is automatically routed to the NCIC computers in Washington. A reply will be sent from NCIC within approximately two minutes.

O. MESSAGE RECORD SHEET

Each teletypewriter control point must list and periodically check status of all teletype messages originating in its area which are subject to cancellation. A form similar to the one shown should be used by other stations. Messages should not be entered on the form until they are ready for filing on the fourth day after their receipt.

1. Each teletype installation is expected to use the form to list in numerical order all messages originating at the installation. Messages which are subject to future cancellation should be checked at least once each month, to keep all files clear of inactive messages.
2. In Column 2, *"origin,"* designate for each message the agency originating the message.
3. Sample form:

27

HASKINS POLICE DEPARTMENT
TELETYPE MESSAGE NUMBER AND
CANCELLATION RECORD

MSG. #	ORIGIN	FILE	DATE	SUMMARY	CANCEL MSG. #
1	Haskins	4	4-15-08	Hit-Run A/A	
2	"	5	4-15-08	John Jones, Petit Larc. 36	
3	"	11	4-16-08	Assault Case	
4	Lake Como	6	4-16-08	Leo Moran, Missing	

P. CANCELLATIONS AND CORRECTIONS

A cancellation is advice that a prior message is no longer valid and that no further action is to be taken in respect to the prior message. A correction amends a previous message. Stations are responsible for promptly sending all necessary full or part cancellations and all corrections. Failure to cancel or correct a message or part of a message may result in serious harm when police action is taken on the basis of a message which should have previously been cancelled or corrected and was not. The responsibility for any such occurrence will be placed squarely on the offending department and its responsible personnel.